HOW TO READ THE BIBLE FOR ALL ITS WORTH

Gordon D. Fee & Douglas Stuart

HOW TO READ THE BIBLE FOR ALL ITS WORTH

Second Edition

A GUIDE TO UNDERSTANDING THE BIBLE

ZondervanPublishingHouse
Academic and Professional Books
Grand Rapids, Michigan

A Division of HarperCollins*Publishers*

How to Read the Bible for All Its Worth
Copyright © 1981, 1993 by Gordon D. Fee and Douglas Stuart

Requests for information should be addressed to:
Zondervan Publishing House
Academic and Professional Books
Grand Rapids, Michigan 49530

Library of Congress Cataloging-in-Publication Data
Fee, Gordon D.
    How to read the Bible for all its worth : a guide to understanding the Bible /
Gordon D. Fee and Douglas Stuart. — 2nd ed.
        p.   cm.
    Includes bibliographical references and indexes.
    ISBN 0-310-38491-5
    1. Bible—Study and teaching. I. Stuart, Douglas K. II. Title.
BS600.2.F43   1993   92-40881
220.6'1—dc20   CIP

Cover design: Zondervan Publishing House
Cover illustration: Patrick Kelly

Printed in the United States of America

93 94 95 96 97 / DH / 9 8 7 6 5 4 3 2 1

*For our parents
Donald and Grace Fee
and
Streeter and Merle Stuart
from whom we learned
our love for the Word*

Contents

Abbreviations of Translations

GNB	The Good News Bible (formerly Today's English Version), 1976
JB	The Jerusalem Bible, 1966
KJV	The King James Version (also, the Authorized Version), 1611
LB	The Living Bible, 1971
NAB	The New American Bible, 1970
NASB	The New American Standard Bible, 1960
NEB	The New English Bible, 1961
NIV	The New International Version, 1973
NRSV	The New Revised Standard Version, 1991
RSV	The Revised Standard Version, 1952

Preface

In one of our lighter moments we toyed with the idea of calling this book *Not Just Another Book on How to Understand the Bible.* Wisdom prevailed, and the "title" lost out. But such a title would in fact describe the kind of urgency that caused this book to be written.

How-to-understand-the-Bible books abound. Some are good; others are not so good. Few are written by biblical scholars. Some of these books approach the subject from the variety of methods one can use in studying Scripture; others try to be basic primers in hermeneutics (the science of interpretation) for the layperson. These latter usually give a long section of general rules (rules that apply to all biblical texts) and another section of specific rules (rules that govern special types of problems: prophecy, typology, figures of speech, etc.).

Of the "basic primer" type books we recommend especially *Knowing Scripture,* by R. C. Sproul (InterVarsity). For a heavier and less readable, but very helpful, dose of the same one should see A. Berkeley Mickelson's *Interpreting the Bible* (Eerdmans). The closest thing to the kind of book we have written is *Better Bible Study,* by Berkeley and Alvera Mickelson (Regal).

But this is "not just another book"—we hope. The uniqueness of what we have tried to do has several facets:

1. As one may note from a glance at the table of contents, the basic concern of this book is with the understanding of the different types of the literature (the *genres*) that make up the Bible. Although we do speak to other issues, this generic approach has controlled all that has been done. We affirm that there is a real difference between a psalm, on the one hand, and an epistle on the other. Our concern is to help the reader to read and study the Psalms as poems, and the

Epistles as letters. We hope to show that these differences are vital and should affect both the way one reads them and how one is to understand their message for today.

2. Even though throughout the book we have repeatedly given guidelines for *studying* each genre of Scripture, we are equally concerned with the intelligent *reading* of Scripture—since that is what most of us do the most. Anyone who has tried, for example, to read through Leviticus, Jeremiah, or Proverbs, as over against 1 Samuel or Acts, knows full well that there are many differences. One can get bogged down in Leviticus, and who has not felt the frustration of completing the reading of Isaiah or Jeremiah and then wondering what the "plot" was? In contrast, 1 Samuel and the Acts are especially readable. We hope to help the reader appreciate these differences so that he or she can read intelligently and profitably the nonnarrative parts of the Bible.

3. This book was written by two seminary professors, those sometimes dry and stodgy people that other books are written to get around. It has often been said that one does not have to have a seminary education in order to understand the Bible. That is true, and we believe it with all our hearts. But we are also concerned about the (sometimes) hidden agenda that suggests that a seminary education or seminary professors are thereby a *hindrance* to understanding the Bible. We are so bold as to think that even the "experts" may have something to say.

Furthermore, these two seminary professors also happen to be believers, who think we should *obey* the biblical texts, not merely read or study them. It is precisely that concern that led us to become scholars in the first place. We had a great desire to understand as carefully and as fully as possible what it is that we are to know about God and his will in the twentieth century.

These two seminary professors also regularly preach and teach the Word in a variety of church settings. Thus we are regularly called upon not simply to be scholars but to wrestle with how the Bible applies, and that leads to our fourth item.

4. The great urgency that gave birth to this book is hermeneutics; we wrote especially to help believers wrestle with the questions of application. Many of the urgent problems in the church today are basically struggles with bridging the hermeneutical gap—with moving from the "then and there" of the original text to the "here and now" of our own life settings. But this also means bridging the

gap between the scholar and layperson. The concern of the scholar is primarily with what the text *meant;* the concern of the layperson is usually with what it *means.* The believing scholar insists that we must have both. Reading the Bible with an eye *only* to its meaning for us can lead to a great deal of nonsense as well as to every imaginable kind of error—because it lacks controls. Fortunately, most believers are blessed with at least a measure of that most important of all hermeneutical skills—common sense.

On the other hand, nothing can be so dry and lifeless for the church as making biblical study purely an academic exercise in historical investigation. Even though the Word was originally given in a concrete historical context, its uniqueness is that that historically given and conditioned Word is ever a living Word.

Our concern, therefore, must be with both dimensions. The believing scholar insists that the biblical texts first of all *mean what they meant.* That is, we believe that God's Word for us today is first of all precisely what his Word was to them. Thus we have two tasks: First, to find out what the text originally meant; this task is called *exegesis.* Second, we must learn to hear that same meaning in the variety of new or different contexts of our own day; we call this second task *hermeneutics.* In its classical usage, the term "hermeneutics" covers both tasks, but in this book we consistently use it only in this narrower sense. To do both tasks well should be the goal of Bible study.

Thus in chapters 3 through 13, which deal in turn with ten different kinds of literary genres, we have given attention to both needs. Since exegesis is always the first task, we have spent much of our time emphasizing the uniqueness of each of the genres. What is a biblical psalm? What are their different kinds? What is the nature of Hebrew poetry? How does all this affect our understanding? But we are also concerned with how the various Psalms function as Word of God. What is God trying to say? What are we to learn, or how are we to obey? Here we have avoided giving rules. What we have offered are guidelines, suggestions, helps.

We recognize that the first task—exegesis—is often considered to be a matter for the expert. At times that is true. But one does not have to be an expert to learn to do the basic tasks of exegesis well. The secret lies in learning to ask the right questions of the text. We hope, therefore, to guide the reader in learning to ask the right questions of each biblical genre. There will be times when one will finally want to consult the experts as well. We shall also give some practical guidelines in this matter.

Each author is responsible for those chapters that fall within his area of specialty. Thus, Professor Fee wrote chapters 1–4, 6–8, and 13, and Professor Stuart wrote chapters 5 and 9–12. Although each author had considerable input into the other's chapters, and although we consider the book to be a truly joint effort, the careful reader will also observe that each author has his own style and manner of presentation. Special thanks go to some friends and family who have read several of the chapters and offered helpful advice: Frank DeRemer, Bill Jackson, Judy Peace, and Maudine, Cherith, Craig, and Brian Fee. Special thanks also to our secretaries, Carrie Powell and Holly Greening, for typing both rough drafts and final copy.

In the words of the child that moved Augustine to read a passage from Romans at his conversion experience, we say, "*Tolle, lege,* Take up and read." The Bible is God's eternal Word. Read it, understand it, obey it.

Permission has been granted by Baker Book House, Grand Rapids, Michigan, to use material in chapters 3, 4, and 6, that appeared earlier in different form as "Hermeneutics and Common Sense: An Exploratory Essay on the Hermeneutics of the Epistles," in *Inerrancy and Common Sense* (ed. J. R. Michaels and R. R. Nicole, 1980), pp. 161–86; and "Hermeneutics and Historical Precedent—A Major Problem in Pentecostal Hermeneutics," in *Perspectives on the New Pentecostalism* (ed. R. P. Spittler, 1976), pp. 118–32.

1

Introduction: The Need to Interpret

Every so often we meet someone who says with great feeling, "You don't have to interpret the Bible; just read it and do what it says." Usually, such a remark reflects the layperson's protest against the "professional" scholar, pastor, teacher, or Sunday school teacher, who, by "interpreting," seems to be taking the Bible away from the common man or woman. It is their way of saying that the Bible is not an obscure book. "After all," it is argued, "any person with half a brain can read it and understand it. The problem with too many preachers and teachers is that they dig around so much they tend to muddy the waters. What was clear to us when we read it isn't so clear anymore."

There is a lot of truth in that protest. We agree that Christians should learn to read, believe, and obey the Bible. And we especially agree that the Bible should not be an obscure book if studied and read properly. In fact we are convinced that the single most serious problem people have with the Bible is not with a *lack* of understanding, but with the fact that they understand most things too well! The problem with such a text as "Do everything without complaining or arguing" (Phil. 2:14), for example, is not with understanding it, but with obeying it—putting it into practice.

We are also agreed that the preacher or teacher is all too often prone to dig first and look later, and thereby to cover up the plain meaning of the text, which often lies on the surface. Let it be said at the outset—and repeated throughout, that the aim of good interpretation is not uniqueness; one is not trying to discover what no one else has ever seen before.

Interpretation that aims at, or thrives on, uniqueness can usually be attributed to pride (an attempt to "out clever" the rest of the world), a false understanding of spirituality (wherein the Bible is full of deep truths waiting to be mined by the spiritually sensitive person with special insight), or vested interests (the need to support a theological bias, especially in dealing with texts that seem to go against that bias). Unique interpretations are usually wrong. This is not to say that the correct understanding of a text may not often *seem* unique to someone who hears it for the first time. But it is to say that uniqueness is *not* the aim of our task.

The aim of good interpretation is simple: to get at the "plain meaning of the text." And the most important ingredient one brings to that task is enlightened common sense. The test of good interpretation is that it makes good sense of the text. Correct interpretation, therefore, brings relief to the mind as well as a prick or prod to the heart.

But if the plain meaning is what interpretation is all about, then why interpret? Why not just read? Does not the plain meaning come simply from reading? In a sense, yes. But in a truer sense, such an argument is both naïve and unrealistic because of two factors: the nature of the reader and the nature of Scripture.

The Reader as an Interpreter

The first reason one needs to learn *how* to interpret is that, whether one likes it or not, every reader is at the same time an interpreter. That is, most of us assume as we read that we also understand what we read. We also tend to think that *our understanding* is the same thing as the Holy Spirit's or human author's *intent*. However, we invariably bring *to* the text all that we are, with all of our experiences, culture, and prior understandings of words and ideas. Sometimes what we bring to the text, unintentionally to be sure, leads us astray, or else causes us to read all kinds of foreign ideas into the text.

Thus, when a person in our culture hears the word "cross," centuries of Christian art and symbolism cause most people automatically to think of a Roman cross (†), although there is little likelihood that that was the shape of Jesus' cross, which was probably shaped like a "T." Most Protestants, and Catholics as well, when they read texts about the church at worship, automatically envision people sitting in a building with "pews" much like their own. When Paul says (in the KJV), "Make not provision for the flesh, to fulfil the lusts thereof" (Rom. 13:14), people in most English-speaking cultures are apt to think that "flesh" means the "body" and therefore that Paul is speaking of "bodily appetites."

But the word "flesh," as Paul uses it, seldom refers to the body—and in this text it almost certainly did not—but to a spiritual malady, a sickness of spiritual existence sometimes called "the sinful nature." Therefore, without intending to do so, the reader is interpreting as he or she reads, and unfortunately too often interprets incorrectly.

This leads us to note further that in any case the reader of an English Bible is already involved in interpretation. For translation is in itself a (necessary) form of interpretation. Your Bible, whatever translation you use, which is your *beginning* point, is in fact the *end result* of much scholarly work. Translators are regularly called upon to make choices regarding meanings and *their* choices are going to affect how *you* understand.

Good translators, therefore, take the problem of our language differences into consideration. But it is not an easy task. In Romans 13:14, for example, shall we translate "flesh" (as in KJV, RSV, NRSV, NASB, etc.) because this is the word Paul used, and then leave it to an interpreter to tell us that "flesh" here does not mean "body"? Or shall we "help" the reader and translate "sinful nature" (as in the NIV, GNB, etc.) because this is what Paul's word really *means?* We will take up this matter in greater detail in the next chapter. For now it is sufficient to point out how the *fact* of translation in itself has already involved one in the task of interpretation.

The need to interpret is also to be found by noting what goes on around us all the time. A simple look at the contemporary church, for example, makes it abundantly clear that not all "plain meanings" are equally plain to all. It is of more than passing interest that most of those in today's church who argue that women should keep silent in church on the basis of 1 Corinthians 14:34–35 at the same time deny the validity of speaking in tongues and prophecy, the very context in which the "silence" passage occurs. And those who affirm that women, as well as men, should pray and prophesy on the basis of 1 Corinthians 11:2–16 often deny that they should necessarily do so with their heads covered. For some, the Bible "plainly teaches" believers' baptism by immersion; others believe they can make a biblical case for infant baptism. Both "eternal security" and the possibility of "losing one's salvation" are preached in the church, but never by the same person! Yet both are affirmed as the plain meaning of biblical texts. Even the two authors of this book have some disagreements as to what certain texts "plainly" mean. Yet all of us are reading the same Bible and we all are trying to be obedient to what the text "plainly" means.

Besides these recognizable differences among "Bible-believing Christians," there are also all kinds of strange things afloat. One can usually recognize the cults, for example, because they have an authority in addition to the Bible. But not all of them do; and in every case they bend the truth by the way they select texts from the Bible itself. Every imaginable heresy or practice, from the Arianism (denying Christ's deity) of the Jehovah's Witnesses and The Way, to baptizing for the dead among Mormons, to snake handling among Appalachian sects, claims to be "supported" by a text.

Even among more theologically orthodox people, however, many strange ideas manage to gain acceptance in various quarters. For example, one of the current rages among American Protestants, especially charismatics, is the so-called wealth and health gospel. The "good news" is that God's will for you is financial and material prosperity! One of the advocates of this "gospel" begins his book by arguing for the "plain sense" of Scripture and claiming that he puts the Word of God first and foremost throughout his study. He says that it is not what we *think* it says but what it *actually* says that counts. The "plain meaning" is what he is after. But one begins to wonder what the "plain meaning" really is when financial prosperity is argued as the will of God from such a text as 3 John 2, "Beloved, I wish above all things that thou mayest prosper and be in health, even as thy soul prospereth" (KJV)—a text that in fact has nothing at all to do with financial prosperity. Another example takes the plain meaning of the story of the rich young man (Mark 10:17–22) as precisely the opposite of "what it actually says," and attributes the "interpretation" to the Holy Spirit. One may rightly question whether the plain meaning is being sought at all; perhaps the plain meaning is simply what such a writer wants the text to mean in order to support his pet ideas.

Given all this diversity, both within and without the church, and all the differences even among scholars, who supposedly know "the rules," it is no wonder that some argue for no interpretation, just reading. But as we have seen, that is a false option. The antidote to *bad* interpretation is not *no* interpretation, but *good* interpretation, based on common-sense guidelines.

The authors of this book labor under no illusions that by reading and following our guidelines everyone will finally agree on the "plain meaning," *our* meaning! What we do hope to achieve is to heighten the reader's sensitivity to specific problems inherent in each genre, to known *why* different options exist and how to make common-sense judgments, and especially to be able to discern between good and not-so-good interpretations—and to know what makes them one or the other.

The Nature of Scripture

A more significant reason for the need to interpret lies in the nature of Scripture itself. Historically the church has understood the nature of Scripture much the same as it has understood the person of Christ—the Bible is at the same time both human and divine. As Professor George Ladd once put it: "The Bible is the Word of God given in the words of [people] in history." It is this dual nature of the Bible that demands of us the task of interpretation.

Because the Bible is *God's Word,* it has *eternal relevance;* it speaks to all humankind, in every age and in every culture. Because it is God's Word, we must listen—and obey. But because God chose to speak his Word through *human words in history,* every book in the Bible also has *historical particularity;* each document is conditioned by the language, time, and culture in which it was originally written (and in some cases also by the oral history it had before it was written down). Interpretation of the Bible is demanded by the "tension" that exists between its *eternal relevance* and its *historical particularity*.

There are some, of course, who believe that the Bible is merely a human book, and that it contains only words of people in history. For these people the task of interpreting is limited to historical inquiry. Their interest, as with Cicero or Milton, is with the religious ideas of the Jews, Jesus, or the early church. The task for them, therefore, is purely a historical one. What did these words mean to the people who wrote them? What did they think about God? How did they understand themselves?

On the other hand, there are those who think of the Bible only in terms of its eternal relevance. Because it is God's Word, they tend to think of it only as a collection of propositions to be believed and imperatives to be obeyed—although invariably there is a great deal of picking and choosing among the propositions and imperatives. There are, for example, Christians who, on the basis of Deuteronomy 22:5 ("A woman must not wear men's clothing," NIV), argue literally that a woman should not wear slacks or shorts. But the same people seldom take literally the other imperatives in that list, which include building a parapet around the roof of one's house (v. 8), not planting two kinds of seeds in a vineyard (v. 9), and making tassels on the four corners of one's cloak (v. 12).

The Bible, however, is *not* a series of propositions and imperatives; it is not simply a collection of "Sayings from Chairman God," as though he looked down at us from heaven and said: "Hey you down there, learn these truths. Number 1, There is no God but One, and I am he. Number 2, I am the Creator of all things, including humankind"—and so on, all the way through proposition number 7,777 and imperative number 777.

These propositions of course are true; and they are found in the Bible (though not quite in that form). Indeed such a book might have made many things easier for us. But, fortunately, that is *not* how God chose to speak to us. Rather he chose to speak his eternal truths within the particular circumstances and events of human history. This also is what gives us hope. Precisely because God chose to speak in the context of real human history, we may take courage that these same words will speak again and again in our own "real" history, as they have throughout the history of the church.

The fact that the Bible has a human side is our encouragement; it is also our challenge, and is the reason that we need to interpret. Two things should be noted in this regard:

1. In speaking through real persons, in a variety of circumstances, over a 1500-year period, God's Word was expressed in the vocabulary and though patterns of those persons and conditioned by the culture of those times and circumstances. That is to say, God's Word to us was first of all his Word to them. If they were going to hear it, it could only have come through events and in

language *they* could have understood. Our problem is that we are so far removed from them in time, and sometimes in thought. This is the major reason one needs to learn to interpret the Bible. If God's Word about women wearing men's clothing or people having parapets around houses is to speak to us, we first need to know what it said to its original hearers—and why.

Thus the task of interpreting involves the student/reader at two levels. First, one has to hear the Word they heard; he or she must try to understand what was said to them back *then and there*. Second, one must learn to hear that same Word in the *here and now*. We will say more about these two tasks below.

2. One of the most important aspects of the human side of the Bible is that to communicate his Word to all human conditions, God chose to use almost every available kind of communication: narrative history, genealogies, chronicles, laws of all kinds, poetry of all kinds, proverbs, prophetic oracles, riddles, drama, biographical sketches, parables, letters, sermons, and apocalypses.

To interpret properly the "then and there" of the biblical texts, one must not only know some general rules that apply to all the words of the Bible, but one needs to learn the special rules that apply to each of these literary forms (genres). And the way God communicates his Word to us in the "here and now" will often differ from one form to another. For example, we need to know *how* a psalm, a form that was often addressed *to God,* functions as God's Word *to us,* and how psalms differ from the "laws," which were often addressed to people in cultural situations no longer in existence. *How* do such "laws" speak to us, and how do they differ from the moral "laws," which are always valid in all circumstances? Such are the questions the dual nature of the Bible forces upon us.

The First Task: Exegesis

The first task of the interpreter is called *exegesis*. Exegesis is the careful, systematic study of the Scripture to discover the original, intended meaning. This is basically a historical task. It is the attempt to hear the Word as the original recipients were to have heard it, to find out what was *the original intent of the words of the Bible*. This is the task that often calls for the help of the "expert," that person whose training has helped him or her to know well the language and circumstances of the texts in their original setting. But one does *not* have to be an expert to do good exegesis.

In fact, everyone is an exegete of sorts. The only real question is whether you will be a good one. How many times, for example, have you heard or said, "What Jesus *meant* by that was . . ." or "Back in those days, they used to . . ."? Those are exegetical expressions. Most often they are employed to explain the differences between "them" and "us"—why we do not build parapets around our houses, for example, or to give a reason for our using a text in a new or different way—why hand-shaking has often taken the place of the "holy kiss." Even when such ideas are not articulated, they are in fact practiced all the time in a kind of common sense way.

The problem with much of this, however, is (1) that such exegesis is often too selective, and (2) that often the sources consulted are not written by true "experts," that is, they are secondary sources that also often use other secondary sources, rather than the primary sources. A few words about each of these must be given:

1. Although everyone employs exegesis at times, and although quite often such exegesis is well done, it nonetheless tends to be employed *only* when there is an obvious problem between the biblical texts and modern culture. Whereas it must indeed be employed for such texts, we insist that it is *the first step in reading EVERY text.* At first, this will not be easy to do, but learning to think exegetically will pay rich dividends in understanding and will make even the reading, not to mention the studying, of the Bible a much more exciting experience. But note well: Learning to think exegetically is not the *only* task; it is simply the *first* task.

The real problem with "selective" exegesis is that one will often read one's own, completely foreign, ideas into a text and thereby make God's Word something other than what God really said. For example, one of the authors of this book recently received a letter from a well-known evangelical, who argued that the author should not appear in a conference with another well-known person, whose orthodoxy was somewhat suspect. The biblical reason given for avoiding the conference was 1 Thessalonians 5:22: "Abstain from all appearance of evil" (KJV). But had our brother learned to read the Bible exegetically, he would not have used the text in that way. For that is Paul's final word in a *paragraph* to the Thessalonians regarding charismatic utterances in the community. "Don't treat prophecies with contempt," Paul says. "Rather, test everything; and hold fast to the good, but avoid every evil form." The "avoidance of evil" has to do with "prophecies," which, when tested, are found not to be of the Spirit. To make this text mean something God did not intend is to abuse the text, not use it. To avoid making such mistakes one needs to learn to think exegetically, that is, to begin back then and there, and to do so with every text.

2. As we will soon note, one does not *begin* by consulting the "experts." But when it is necessary to do so, one should try to use the better sources. For example, in Mark 10:23 (Matt. 19:23; Luke 18:24), at the conclusion of the story of the rich your man, Jesus says, "How hard it is for the rich to enter the kingdom of God." He then adds: "It is easier for a camel to go through the eye of a needle than for a rich man to enter the kingdom." It is often said that there was a gate in Jerusalem known as the "Needle's Eye," which camels could go through only by kneeling, and with great difficulty. The point of this "interpretation" is that a camel could in fact go through the "Needle's Eye." The trouble with this "exegesis," however, is that it is simply not true. There never was such a gate in Jerusalem at any time in its history. The earliest known "evidence" for that idea is found in the eleventh century (!), in a commentary by a Greek churchman named Theophylact, who had the same difficulty with the text that we do. After all, it is *impossible* for a camel to go through the eye of a needle, and that was precisely Jesus' point. It is impossible for one who trusts in riches to enter the kingdom. It takes a miracle for a rich person to get saved, which is quite the point of what follows: "All things are possible with God."

Learning to Do Exegesis

How, then, do we learn to do good exegesis, and at the same time avoid the pitfalls along the way? The first part of most of the chapters in this book will explain how one goes about this task for each of the genres in particular. Here we simply want to overview what is involved in the exegesis of any text.

At its highest level, of course, exegesis requires knowledge of many things we do not necessarily expect the readers of this book to know: the biblical languages; the Jewish, Semitic, and Hellenistic backgrounds; how to determine the original text when the manuscripts have variant readings; the use of all kinds of primary sources and tools. But you can learn to do good exegesis even if you do not have access to all of these skills and tools. To do so, however, you must learn first what you can do with your own skills, and second you must learn to use the work of others.

The *key* to good exegesis, and therefore to a more intelligent reading of the Bible, is *to learn to read the text carefully and to ask the right questions of the text*. One of the best things one could do in this regard would be to read Mortimer J. Adler's *How to Read a Book* (1940, rev. ed. with Charles Van Doren, New York: Simon and Schuster, 1972). Our experience over many years in college and seminary teaching is that many people simply do not know how to read well. To read or study the Bible intelligently demands careful reading, and that includes learning to ask the right questions of the text.

There are two basic kinds of questions one should ask of every biblical passage: those that relate to *context* and those that relate to *content*. The questions of context are also of two kinds: *historical* and *literary*. Let us briefly note each of these.

The Historical Context

The historical context, which will differ from book to book, has to do with several things: the *time* and *culture* of the author and his readers, that is, the geographical, topographical, and political factors that are relevant to the author's setting; and the *occasion* of the book, letter, psalm, prophetic oracle, or other genre. All such matters are especially important for understanding.

It simply makes a difference in understanding to know the personal background of Amos, Hosea, or Isaiah, or that Haggai prophesied *after* the exile, or to know the messianic expectations of Israel when John the Baptist and Jesus appeared on the scene, or to understand the differences between the cities of Corinth and Philippi and how these affect the churches in each. One's reading of Jesus' parables is greatly enhanced by knowing something about the customs of Jesus' day. Surely it makes a difference in understanding to know that the "penny" (KJV), or denarius, offered to the workers in Matthew 20:1–16 was the equivalent of a full day's wage. Even matters of topography are important. One who was raised in the American West—or East for that matter—must be careful not to think of "the mountains that surround Jerusalem" (Ps. 125:2) in terms of his or her own experience of mountains!

To answer most of these kinds of questions, one will need some outside help. A good Bible dictionary, such as the four-volume *International Standard Bible Encyclopedia* (ed. G. W. Bromiley, Grand Rapids: Eerdmans, 1988) or the five-volume *Zondervan Pictorial Encyclopedia of the Bible* (ed. Merrill C. Tenney, Grand Rapids: Zondervan, 1975) or the one-volume *New Bible Dictionary* (ed. J. D. Douglas, Grand Rapids: Eerdmans, 1962), will generally supply the need here. If one wishes to pursue a matter further, the bibliographies at the end of each article will be a good place to start.

The more important question of historical context, however, has to do with the *occasion* and *purpose* of each biblical book and/or of its various parts. Here one wants to have an idea of what was going on in Israel or the church that called forth such a document, or what the situation of the author was that caused him to write. Again, this will vary from book to book, and it is much less crucial for Proverbs, for example, than for 1 Corinthians.

The answer to this question is usually to be found—when it can be found—within the book itself. But you need to learn to read with your eyes open for such matters. If you want to corroborate your own findings on these questions, you might consult your Bible dictionary again, or the introduction to a good commentary on the book, or look at *Eerdman's Handbook to the Bible* (ed. David Alexander and Pat Alexander, Grand Rapids: Eerdmans, 1973). But make your own observations first!

The Literary Context

This is what most people mean when they talk about reading something in its context. Indeed this is *the* crucial task in exegesis, and fortunately it is something one can do well without necessarily having to consult the "experts." Essentially *literary context* means that words only have meaning in sentences, and for the most part biblical sentences only have meaning in relation to preceding and succeeding sentences.

The most important contextual question you will ever ask, and it must be asked over and over of every sentence and every paragraph is, "What's the point?" We must try to trace the author's train of thought. What is the author saying and why does he or she say it right here? Having made that point, what is he or she saying next, and why?

This question will vary from genre to genre, but it is *always* the crucial question. The goal of exegesis, you remember, is to find out what the original author intended. To do this task well, it is imperative that one use a translation that recognizes poetry and paragraphs. One of the major causes of inadequate exegesis by readers of the King James Version, and to a lesser degree of the New American Standard, is that every verse has been printed as a paragraph. Such an arrangement tends to obscure the author's own logic. Above all else, therefore, one must learn to recognize units of thought, whether they be paragraphs (for prose) or lines and sections (for poetry). And, with the aid of an adequate translation, this is something the reader can do.

The Questions of Content

The second major category of questions one asks of any text has to do with the author's actual content. "Content" has to do with the meanings of words, the grammatical relationships in sentences, and the choice of the original text where the manuscripts have variant readings. It also includes a number of the items mentioned above under "historical context," for example, the meaning of denarius, or a Sabbath day's journey, or "high places," etc.

For the most part, these are the questions of meaning that one ordinarily asks of the biblical text. When Paul says in 2 Corinthians 5:16, "Even though we have known Christ according to the flesh, yet now we know Him thus no longer" (NASB), one should want to know, Who is "according to the flesh," Christ or the one knowing him? It makes a considerable difference in meaning to learn that "we" know Christ no longer "from a worldly point of view" is what Paul intends, not that we know Christ no longer "in His earthly life."

To answer these kinds of questions one will ordinarily need to seek outside help. Again, the quality of one's answers to such questions will usually depend on the quality of the sources one uses. This is the place where you will finally want to consult a good exegetical commentary. But please note that consulting a commentary, as essential as that will be at times, is the *last* thing one does.

The Tools

For the most part, then, you can do good exegesis with a minimum amount of outside help, provided that that help is of the highest quality. We have mentioned four such tools: a good Bible dictionary, a good Bible handbook, a good translation, and good commentaries. There are other kinds of tools, of course, especially for topical or thematic kinds of study. But for reading or studying the Bible book by book, these are the essential ones.

Because a good translation (or better, several good translations) is the absolutely basic tool for one who does not know the original languages, the next chapter is devoted to this matter. Learning to choose a good commentary is also important, but because that is the last thing one does, an appendix on commentaries concludes the book.

The Second Task: Hermeneutics

Although the word "hermeneutics" ordinarily covers the whole field of interpretation, including exegesis, it is also used in the narrower sense of seeking the contemporary relevance of ancient texts. In this book we will use it exclusively in this way, to ask the questions about the Bible's meaning in the "here and now."

It is this matter of the here and now, after all, that brings us to the Bible in the first place. So why not start here? Why worry about exegesis? Surely the same Spirit who inspired the writing of the Bible can equally inspire one's reading of it. In a sense this is true, and we do not by this book intend to take from anyone the joy of devotional reading of the Bible and the sense of direct communication involved in such reading. But devotional reading is not the only kind one should do. One must also read for learning and understanding. In short, one must also learn *to study* the Bible, which in turn must inform one's devotional reading. And that brings us to our insistence that proper "hermeneutics" begins with solid "exegesis."

The reason one must *not begin* with the here and now is that *the only proper control for hermeneutics is to be found in the original intent of the biblical text*. As noted earlier in this chapter, this is the "plain meaning" one is after. Otherwise biblical texts can be made to mean whatever they mean to any given reader. But such hermeneutics becomes pure subjectivity, and who then is to say that one person's interpretation is right, and another's is wrong. Anything goes.

In contrast to such subjectivity, we insist that the original meaning of the text—as much as it is in our power to discern it—is the objective point of control. We are convinced that the Mormons' baptizing for the dead on the basis of 1 Corinthians 15:29, or the Jehovah's Witnesses' rejection of the deity of Christ, or the snake handlers' use of Mark 16:18, or the "prosperity evangelists'" advocating the American dream as a Christian right on the basis of 3 John 2 are all improper interpretation. In each case the error is in their hermeneutics, precisely because their hermeneutics is not controlled by good exegesis. They have started with the here and now and have read into the texts meanings that were not originally there. And what is to keep one from killing one's daughter because of a foolish vow, as did Jephthah (Judg. 11:29–40), or to argue, as one preacher is reported to have done, that women should never wear their hair up in a top knot ("bun") because the Bible says "topknot go down" ("Let him who is on the house*top not go down*," Mark 13:15)?

It will be argued, of course, that common sense will keep one from such foolishness. Unfortunately common sense is not so common. We want to know what the Bible means *for us*—legitimately so. But we cannot make it mean anything that pleases us, and then give the Holy Spirit "credit" for it. The Holy Spirit cannot be called in to contradict himself, and he is the one who inspired the original intent. Therefore, his help for us will be in the discovering of that original intent, and in guiding us as we try faithfully to apply that meaning to our own situations.

The questions of hermeneutics are not at all easy, which is probably why so few books are written on this aspect of our subject. Nor will all agree on how one goes about this task. But this is the crucial area, and believers need to learn to talk to one another about these questions—and to listen. On this one thing, however, there must surely be agreement. A *text cannot mean what it never meant*. Or to put that in a positive way, the true meaning of the biblical text for us is what God originally intended it to mean when it was first spoken. This is the starting point. How we work it out from that point is what this book is basically all about.

Someone will surely ask, "But is it not possible for a text to have an additional (or fuller, or deeper) meaning, beyond its original intent? After all, this happens in the New Testament itself in the way it sometimes uses the Old Testament." In the case of prophecy, we would not close the door to such a possibility, and would argue that, with careful controls, a second, or fuller, meaning is possible. But how does one justify it at other points? Our problem is a simple one. Who speaks for God? Roman Catholicism has less of a problem here; the magisterium, the authority vested in the official teaching of the church, determines for all the fuller sense of the text. Protestants, however, have no magisterium, and we should be properly concerned whenever anyone says he or she has God's deeper meaning to a text—especially so, if the text never meant what it is now made to mean. Of such things are all the cults born, and innumerable lesser heresies.

It is difficult to give rules for hermeneutics. What we offer throughout the following chapters, therefore, are guidelines. You may not agree with our guidelines. We do hope that your disagreements will be with Christian charity, and perhaps our guidelines will serve to stimulate your own thinking on these matters.

2

The Basic Tool:
A Good Translation

The sixty-six books of the Protestant Bible were originally written
in three different languages: Hebrew (most of the Old Testament),
Aramaic (a sister language to Hebrew used in half of Daniel and
two passages in Ezra), and Greek (all of the New Testament). We
assume that most of the readers of this book do not know these
languages. That means, therefore, that for you the basic tool for
reading and studying the Bible is a good English translation, or, as
will be argued in this chapter, *several* good English translations.

As we noted in the last chapter, the very fact that you are
reading God's Word in translation means that you are already
involved in interpretation—and this is so whether one likes it or
not. But to read in translation is not a bad thing; it is simply
inevitable. What this does mean, however, is that in a certain sense,
the person who reads the Bible only in English is at the mercy of the
translator(s), and translators have often had to make choices as to
what in fact the original Hebrew or Greek was really intending to
say.

The trouble with using only *one* translation, be it ever so good,
is that one is thereby committed to the exegetical choices of that
translation as the Word of God. The translation you are using may
be correct, of course; but it also may be wrong.

Let's take, for example, the following four translations of
1 Corinthians 7:36:

> KJV: "If a man think that he behaveth himself uncomely
>   toward his virgin. . . ."

28

NASB: "If a man think that he is acting unbecomingly toward his virgin daughter. . . ."

NIV: "If anyone thinks he is acting improperly toward the virgin he is engaged to. . . ."

NEB: "If a man has a partner in celebacy and feels that he is not behaving properly towards her. . . ."

The KJV is very literal, but not very helpful, since it leaves the term "virgin" and the relationship between the "man" and "his virgin" ambiguous. Of one thing, however, one may be absolutely certain: Paul did not *intend* to be ambiguous. He intended one of the other three options, and the Corinthians, who had raised the problem in their letter, knew which one—indeed they knew nothing of the other two.

It should be noted here that *none* of these other three is a *bad* translation, since any of them is a legitimate option as to Paul's intent. However, only one of them can be the *correct* translation. The problem is, which one? For a number of reasons, the NIV reflects the best exegetical option here. However, if you regularly read only the NASB (which has the least likely option here) then you are committed to an *interpretation* of the text that may not be the right one. And this kind of thing can be illustrated a thousand times over. So, what to do?

First, it is probably a good practice to use mainly one translation, provided it really is a good one. This will aid in memorization, as well as give you consistency. Also, if you are using one of the better translations, it will have notes in the margin at many of the places where there are difficulties. However, for the *study* of the Bible, you should use *several* well-chosen translations. The best thing to do is to use translations that *one knows in advance will tend to differ*. This will highlight where many of the difficult exegetical problems lie. To resolve these problems you will usually want to have recourse to your commentary.

But which translation should you use, and which of the several should you study from? No one can necessarily speak for someone else on this matter. But your choice should *not* be simply because "I like it," or "This one is so readable." We want you to like your translation, and if it is a really good one, it will be readable. However, to make an intelligent choice, you need to know some things both about the science of translation itself as well as about some of the various English translations.

The Science of Translation

There are two kinds of choices that a translator must make: textual and linguistic. The first kind has to do with the actual wording of the original text. The second has to do with one's theory of translation.

The Question of Text

The translator's first concern is to be sure that the Hebrew or Greek text he or she is using is as close as possible to the original wording as it left the author's hands (or the hands of the scribe taking it down by dictation). Is this what the psalmist actually wrote? Are these the very words of Mark or Paul? Indeed, why should anyone think otherwise?

Although the details of the problem of text in the Old and New Testaments differ, the basic concerns are the same: (1) no original copies (manuscripts) exist; (2) what does exist are thousands of copies (including copies of very early translations), produced by hand, and copied by hand repeatedly over a period of about fourteen hundred years; (3) although the vast majority of manuscripts, which for both testaments come from the later medieval period, are very much alike, these later manuscripts differ significantly from the earlier copies and translations. In fact, there are over five thousand Greek manuscripts of part or all of the New Testament, as well as thousands in Latin, and no two of them anywhere in existence are exactly alike.

The problem, therefore, is to sift through all the available material, compare the places where the manuscripts differ (these are called "variants"), and determine which of the variants represent errors and which one most likely represents the original text. Although this may seem like an imposing task—and in some ways it is—the translator does not despair, because he or she also knows something about textual criticism, the science that attempts to discover the original texts of ancient documents.

It is not our purpose here to give the reader a primer in textual criticism. This you may find in convenient form in the articles by Bruce Waltke (Old Testament) and Gordon Fee (New Testament) in *Biblical Criticism: Historical, Literary and Textual* (Grand Rapids: Zondervan, 1978). Our purpose here is to give some basic information about textual criticism so that you will know why translators must do it and so that you can make better sense of the marginal notes in your translation that say, "Other ancient authorities add. . . ." or "Some manuscripts do not have. . . ."

For the purposes of this chapter, there are three things you should be aware of:

1. *Textual criticism is a science that works with careful controls.* There are two kinds of evidence that the translator considers in making textual choices: external evidence (the character and quality of the manuscripts) and the internal evidence (the kinds of mistakes made by copyists). Scholars sometimes differ as to how much weight they give either of these strands of evidence, but all are agreed that the combination of strong external and strong internal evidence together makes the vast majority of choices somewhat routine. But for the remainder, where these two lines of evidence seem to collide, the choices are more difficult.

The *external evidence* has to do with the quality and age of the manuscripts that support a given variant. For the Old Testament this usually amounts to a choice between the Hebrew manuscripts, nearly all of which are medieval copies, and manuscripts of the Greek translations (the Septuagint [LXX]), which are much earlier. Scholarship has demonstrated that the Hebrew manuscripts by and large reflect a very ancient text; nonetheless, it often needs correcting from the Septuagint. Sometimes neither the Hebrew nor Greek yields a tolerable sense, at which times conjectures are necessary.

For the New Testament, the better external evidence was preserved in Egypt. When that early evidence is also supported by equally early evidence from other sectors of the Roman Empire, such evidence is usually seen to be conclusive.

The *internal evidence* has to do with the copyists and authors. When translators are faced with a choice between two or more variants, they usually can detect which readings are the mistakes because scribal habits and tendencies have been carefully analyzed by scholars and are now well known. Usually the variant that best explains how all the others came about is the one we presume to be the original text. It is also important for the translator to know a given biblical author's style and vocabulary, because these, too, play a role in making textual choices.

As already noted, for the vast majority of variants found among the manuscripts, the best (or good) external evidence combines with the best internal evidence to give us an extraordinarily high degree of certainty about the original text. This may be illustrated thousands of times over simply by comparing the KJV (which was based on poor, late manuscripts) with a contemporary translation like the NRSV or NIV. We will note three variants as illustrations of the work of textual criticism:

1 Samuel 8:16

KJV: "your goodliest young men and your asses"

NIV: "the best of your cattle and donkeys"

The text of the NIV ("your cattle") comes from the Septuagint, the usually reliable Greek translation of the Old Testament made in Egypt around 250–150 B.C. The KJV follows the medieval Hebrew text, reading "young men," a rather unlikely term to be used in parallel to "donkeys." The origin of the miscopy in the Hebrew text, which the KJV followed, is easy to understand. The word for "your young men" in Hebrew was written *bhrykm,* while "your cattle" was *bqrykm.* The incorrect copying of a single letter by a scribe resulted in a change of meaning. The Septuagint was translated some time before the miscopy was made, so it preserved the original "your cattle." The accidental change to "your young men" was made later, affecting medieval Hebrew manuscripts, but too late to affect the premedieval Septuagint.

Mark 1:2

KJV: "As it is written in the prophets. . . ."

NIV: "It is written in Isaiah the prophet. . . ."

The text of the NIV is found in all the best early Greek manuscripts. It is also the only text found in all early translations (Latin, Coptic, and Syriac) and is the only text known among all the church fathers, except one, before the ninth century. It is easy to see what happened in the later Greek manuscripts. Since the citation that follows is a combination of Malachi 3:1 and Isaiah 40:3, a later copyist "corrected" Mark's original text to make it more precise.

1 *Corinthians* 11:29

KJV: "he that eateth and drinketh unworthily"

NIV: "anyone who eats and drinks"

The word "unworthily" is not found in any of the earliest and best Greek manuscripts. Its presence in the Latin translations and later Greek manuscripts can easily be explained as an addition brought in from verse 27, where *all* known manuscripts have "unworthily." There is no good way to explain how it might have been dropped out of verse 29 in all the early manuscripts had it been there originally.

It should be noted here that for the most part translators work from Greek and Hebrew texts edited by careful, rigorous scholarship. For the New Testament this means that the "best text" has already been determined by scholars who are experts in this field. But it also means, for both testaments, that the translators themselves have access to an "apparatus" (textual information in footnotes) that includes the significant variants with their manuscript support.

2. *Although textual criticism is a science, it is not an exact science, because it deals with too many human variables.* Occasionally, especially when the translation is the work of a committee, the translators will themselves be divided as to which variant represents the original text and which is (are) the scribal error(s). Usually at such times the majority choice will be found in the actual translation, while the minority choice will be in the margin.

The reason for the uncertainty is either that the best manuscript evidence conflicts with the best explanation of the corruption or that the manuscript evidence is evenly divided and either variant can explain how the other came to be. We can illustrate this from 1 Corinthians 13:3:

NIV text: "surrender my body to the flames"

NIV margin: "surrender my body that I may boast"

In Greek the difference is only one letter: *kauthēsōmai/kauchēsōmai*. Both variants have good early support, and both have some inherent difficulties in interpretation (1 Corinthians was written well before Christians were martyred by burning; yet it is difficult to find an appropriate meaning for "that I may boast"). Here is one of those places where a good commentary will probably be necessary in order for you to make up your own mind.

The preceding example is a good place for us also to refer you back to the last chapter. You will note that the choice of the correct text is one of the *content* questions. A good exegete must know, if it is possible to know, which of these words is what Paul actually wrote. On the other hand, it should be also noted that Paul's *point* here finally is little affected by that choice. In either case, he means that if one gives the body over to some extreme sacrifice, or the like, but lacks love, it is all for nothing.

This, then, is what it means to say that translators must make textual choices, and it also explains one of the reasons why translations will sometimes differ—and also why translators are themselves interpreters. Before we go on to the second reason why translations differ, we need to make a note here about the King James Version.

3. The KJV is not only the most widely used translation in the world, it is also a classic expression of the English language. Indeed, it coined phrases that will be forever embedded in our language. However, for the New Testament, the only Greek text available to the 1611 translators was based on late manuscripts, which had accumulated the mistakes of over a thousand years of copying. Few of these mistakes—and we must note that there are many of them—make any difference to us doctrinally, but they often *do* make a difference in the meaning of certain specific texts.

This is why for study *you should use almost any modern translation rather than the KJV.* How to choose between modern translations takes us to the next kinds of choices translators have to make.

The Questions of Language

The next two kinds of choices—verbal and grammatical—bring us to the actual science of translation. The problem has to do with the transferring of words and ideas from one language to another. To understand what various theories underlie our modern translations, you will need to become acquainted with the following technical terms:

Original language: The language that one is translating *from;* in our case, Hebrew, Aramaic, or Greek.

Receptor language: The language that one is translating *into;* in our case, English.

Historical distance: This has to do with the differences that exist between the original language and the receptor language, both in matters of words, grammar, and idioms, as well as in matters of culture and history.

Theory of translation: This has to do with the degree to which one is willing to go in order to bridge the gap between the two languages. For example, should *lamp* be translated "flashlight" or "torch" in cultures where these serve the purpose a lamp once did? Or should one translate it "lamp" and let the reader bridge the gap for himself or herself? Should *holy kiss* be translated "the handshake of Christian love" in cultures where public kissing is offensive?

Notice how these three terms apply to the following basic theories of translation:

Literal: The attempt to translate by keeping as close as possible to the exact words and phrasing in the original language, yet still make sense in the receptor language. A literal translation will keep the historical distance intact at all points.

Free: The attempt to translate the *ideas* from one language to another, with less concern about using the exact words of the original. A free translation, sometimes also called a paraphrase, tries to eliminate as much of the historical distance as possible.

Dynamic equivalent: The attempt to translate words, idioms, and grammatical constructions of the original language into precise equivalents in the receptor language. Such a translation keeps historical distance on all historical and most factual matters, but "updates" matters of language, grammar, and style.

Translators are not always consistent, but one of these theories will govern the translators' basic approach to their task. At times the literal or free translations can be excessive, so much so that Clarence Jordan in his Cottonpatch Version can translate Paul's letter to Rome as to Washington (!), while Robert Young, in a literal translation published in 1862, can transform 1 Corinthians 5:1 into this impossible English (?): "Whoredom is actually heard of among you, and such whoredom as is not even named among the nations—as that one hath the wife of the father [!]"

The several translations of the whole Bible that are currently easily accessible might be placed on a historical-distance scale in the somewhat arbitrary way, as shown on the next page.

Literal			Dynamic equivalence		Free	
KJV	RSV	NRSV	NIV	GNB	PHILLIPS	LB
NASB			NAB	JB		
			NEB			

The best translational theory is dynamic equivalence. A literal translation is often helpful as a *second* source; it will give you confidence as to what the Greek or Hebrew actually looked like. A free translation also can be helpful—to stimulate your thinking about the possible meaning of a text. But the basic translation for reading and studying should be something like the NIV.

The problem with a literal translation is that it keeps distance at the wrong places—in language and grammar. Thus the translator often renders the Greek or Hebrew into English that is otherwise never written or spoken that way. It is like translating *maison blanc* from French to English as "house white." For example, no native English-speaking person would *ever* have said "coals of fire" (KJV, Rom. 12:20). That is a literal rendering of the Greek construction, but what it *means* in English is "burning coals" (NIV) or "live coals" (NEB).

A second problem with a literal translation is that it often makes the English ambiguous, where the Greek or Hebrew was quite clear to the original recipients. For example, in 2 Corinthians 5:16 the Greek phrase *kata sarka* can be translated literally "'(to know) according to the flesh" (as in the NASB). But this is not an ordinary way of speaking in English. Furthermore the phrase is ambiguous. Is it the person who is *being known* who is "according to the flesh," which seems to be implied in the NASB, and which in this case would mean something like "by their outward appearance"? Or is the person who *is "knowing"* doing so "according to the flesh," which would mean "from a worldly point of view"? In this case the Greek is clear, and the NIV correctly translates: "So from now on [since we have been raised to a new life, v. 15] we regard no one from a worldly point of view."

The problem with a free translation, on the other hand, especially for study purposes, is that the translator updates the original author too much. Furthermore, such a "translation" all too often comes close to being a commentary. A free translation is *always* done by a single translator, and unless the translator is also a skilled exegete who knows the various problems in *all* of the biblical passages, there is a danger that the reader will be misled. This is especially true of the popular, but unfortunately not altogether accurate, *Living Bible*. We can live with such translations as "flashlights" (Ps. 119:105), or "handshakes" (1 Peter 5:14), or "pancakes" (Gen. 18:6), but to translate the Greek word *charismata* ("spiritual gifts") as "special abilities" in 1 Corinthians 12–14 is to take too much liberty. The Living Bible translation of 1 Corinthians 11:10, "as a sign that she is under man's authority," is especially misleading since the original implies that *she* is the one who has the authority. In 1 Peter 5:13, the biblical author deliberately used the cryptic designation *Babylon* for Rome; it is surely better to have that explained somewhere than to translate it "Rome" and destroy Peter's purposefully cryptic usage. As readable as the *Living Bible* is, it simply has too many inaccuracies and rewritings for it to be one's only—or even primary—Bible.

The New Revised Standard Version (NRSV) is much more accurate than the Living Bible and is not a free translation, but it has taken certain liberties with the text in order to be gender neutral when speaking about people. This results in sometimes abnormal English that is "politically correct" but not very idiomatic. Thus in John 3:4 the NRSV has the awkward sentence "Can one enter a second time into the mother's womb and be born?" compared with the more normal original RSV: "Can one enter a second time into the mother's womb and be born?" compared with the more normal original RSV: "Can he enter a second time into his mother's womb and be born?" Likewise, for Psalm 1, whereas the RSV helpfully preserves the intended contrast between the lone righteous person ("Blessed is the man who . . . ," v. 1) and the many who are wicked ("The wicked are not so . . . ," v. 4), this contrast is eliminated by the NRSV's pluralizing of the entire psalm ("Happy are those who . . . ," etc.) in an effort to avoid the gender distinctions that can occur with singular pronouns.

The way various translations handle the problem of "historical distance" can best be noted by illustrating several of the kinds of problems involved.

    1. *Weights, measures, money.* This is a particularly difficult area.

Does one transliterate the Greek and Hebrew terms ("ephah," "homer," etc.), or try to find their English equivalents? If one chooses to go with equivalents in weights and measures, does one use the standard "pounds" and "feet," or does one look to the future and translate "liters" and "meters"? Inflation can make mockery of monetary equivalents in a few years. The problem is further complicated by the fact that measures or money are often used to suggest contrasts or startling results, as in Matthew 18:24–28 or Isaiah 5:10. To transliterate in these cases will likely cause an English reader to miss the point of the passage.

The KJV, followed closely by the RSV and NRSV, was inconsistent in these matters. For the most part they transliterated, so that we got "baths" "ephahs," "homers," "shekels," and "talents." Yet the Hebrew 'ammah was translated "cubit," the zereth a "span," and the Greek mna (mina) became the British pound, while the denarius became a mere penny. For Americans all of these have the effect of being meaningless or misleading.

The NASB uses "cubit" and "span," but otherwise consistently transliterates and then puts an English equivalent in the margin (expect for John 2:6, where the transliteration is in the margin!). This is also the way the NIV chose to go, except for "cubits," which are turned into feet, and all the marginal notes are given both in English standards and in metric equivalents. Unfortunately they give no note at all in Matthew 20:2, where the fact that the denarius was a regular day's wage is important to the parable; moreover, in Mark 14:5 they abandon this principle altogether by translating the three hundred denarii into the equivalent, "more than a year's wage."

The Living Bible, as may be expected, turns everything into equivalents, but often they are not precise, and the turning of denarii into dollar amounts of the 1960s is a precarious procedure at best.

We would argue that either equivalents or transliterations with marginal notes would be good procedure with most weights and measurements. However, the use of equivalents is surely to be preferred in the passages like Isaiah 5:10 and Matthew 18:24–28. Note how much more meaningful the GNB renders these verses than does the NASB:

Isaiah 5:10

NASB   "For ten acres of vineyard will yield only one bath of
         wine. And a homer of seed will yield but an ephah of
         grain."

GNB: "The grapevines growing on five acres of land will
         yield only five gallons of wine. Ten bushels of seed will
         produce only one bushel of grain."

Matthew 18:24, 28

NASB: "There was brought to him one who owed him ten
         thousand talents. . . . But that slave went out and
         found one of his fellow slaves who owed him a
         hundred denarii."

GNB: "One of them was brought in who owed him millions
         of dollars. . . . Then the man went out and met one of
         his fellow servants who owed him a few dollars."

2. *Euphemisms.* Almost all languages have euphemisms for
matters of sex and toilet. A translator has one of three choices in
such matters: (1) translate literally, but perhaps leave an English-
speaking reader bewildered or guessing, (2) translate the *literal
equivalent,* but perhaps offend or shock the reader, or (3) translate
with an *equivalent euphemism.*

Option 3 is probably the best, if there is an appropriate
euphemism. Otherwise it is better to go with option 2, especially
for matters that generally no longer require euphemisms in English.
Thus to have Rachel say, "I'm having my period" (Gen. 31:35 NIV;
cf. GNB) is to be preferred to the literal "the manner of women is
upon me" (NASB, cf. KJV, RSV). For the same idiom in Genesis 18:11
the GNB is consistent ("Sarah had stopped having her monthly
periods"), while the NIV is much freer ("Sarah was past the age of
childbearing"). Similarly, "He forced her, and lay with her" (2 Sam.
13:14 KJV) becomes simply "He raped her" in the NIV and GNB.

There can be dangers in this, however, especially when
translators themselves miss the meaning of the idiom, as can be seen
in the NIV, GNB, and LB translation of 1 Corinthians 7:1: "It is good
for a man not to marry." The idiom "to touch a woman" in every
other case in antiquity means to have sexual intercourse with a
woman, and never means anything close to "marry." Here the NAB,
which has found an equivalent euphemism, is much to be preferred:
"A man is better off having no relations with a woman."

3. *Vocabulary.* When most people think of translation, this is

the area they usually have in mind. It seems like such a simple task: find the English word that means the same as the Hebrew or Greek word. But finding precisely the right word—that is what makes translation so difficult. Part of the difficulty is not only in the choosing of an appropriate English word, but also to choose a word that will not already be filled with connotations that are foreign to the original language.

The problem is further complicated by the fact that some Hebrew or Greek words have ranges of meaning different from anything in English. In addition some words can have several shades of meaning, as well as two or more considerably different meanings. And a deliberate play on words is usually impossible to translate from one language to another.

We have already noted how various translations have chosen to interpret "virgin" in 1 Corinthians 7:36. In chapter 1 we also noted the difficulty in rendering Paul's use of the word *sarx* ("flesh"). In most cases, almost anything is better than the literal "flesh." The NIV hands this word especially well: "sinful nature" when Paul is contrasting "flesh" and "spirit," but "human nature" in Romans 1:3 where it refers to Jesus' Davidic descent, "from a worldly point of view" in 2 Corinthians 5:16 noted above (cf. 1 Cor. 1:26 "by human standards"), and "body" when it means that (as in Col. 1:22).

This kind of thing can be illustrated many times over and is one of the reasons why a translation by dynamic equivalent is much to be preferred to a literal translation.

4. *Grammar and Syntax.* Even though most Indo-European languages have a great many similarities, each language has its own preferred structures as to how words and ideas are related to each other in sentences. It is at these points especially where translation by dynamic equivalent is to be preferred. A literal translation tends to abuse or override the ordinary structures of the receptor language by directly transferring into it the syntax and grammar of the original language. Such direct transfers are usually *possible* in the receptor language, but they are seldom *preferable*. From hundreds of examples, we choose two as illustrations, one from Greek and one from Hebrew.

a. One of the characteristics of Greek is its fondness for what are known as genitive constructions. The genitive is the ordinary case of possession, as in "my book." Such a true possessive can also, but only very awkwardly, be rendered "the book of me." However other "possessives" in English, such as "God's grace," do not so much mean, for example, that God owns the grace as that he gives it, or that it comes from him. Such "nontrue" possessives can always be translated into English as "the grace *of* God."

The Greek language has a great profusion of these latter kinds of genitives, which are used, for example, as descriptive adjectives, to express source, to connote special relationships between two nouns, etc. A literal translation almost invariably transfers these into English with an *"of"* phrase, but frequently with strange results, such as the "coals of fire" noted above, or "the word of his power" (Heb. 1:3 KJV). Both of these are clearly adjectival or descriptive genitives, which in the NIV are more accurately rendered "burning coals" and "his powerful word." Similarly the NASB's "steadfastness of hope" (1 Thess. 1:3) and "joy of the Holy Spirit" (1:6) are translated in the NIV "endurance inspired by hope" and "joy given by the Holy Spirit." These are not only to be preferred; they are in fact more accurate, because they give a genuine English equivalent rather than a literal, Greek way of expressing things, which in English would be nearly meaningless.

Interestingly enough, in one of the few places where the KJV (followed by the RSV, but not the NASB) offered something of an equivalent (1 Cor. 3:9), the translators missed the meaning of the genitive altogether. Apparently they were led astray by the word *fellow-workers* and thus translated, "For we are labourers together with God: ye are God's husbandry, ye are God's building." But in Paul's sentence each occurrence of *God* is clearly a *possessive* genitive, with an emphasis on both *we* (Paul and Apollos) and *you* (the church as God's field and building) as belonging to him. This is correctly translated in the NIV as, "For we are God's fellow workers; you are God's field, God's building." Paul's point is made even more clearly in the NAB: "We are God's co-workers, while you are his cultivation, his building."

b. Thousands of times in the Old Testament the KJV translators woodenly followed the Hebrew word order in a way that does not produce normal, idiomatic English. Did you ever notice, for example, how many verses (or sentences) in the KJV begin with the word *and*? Read Genesis 1, and note that with the single exception of verse 1, every verse of the chapter begins with *and*, a total of thirty times. Now compare the NIV. It reduces the number of occurrences of *and* to eleven, while at the same time improving the flow of the language so that it sounds more natural to the ear.

The NIV translators produced an improved translation by taking seriously the fact that the vast majority of prose sentences in Old Testament Hebrew begin with one of the two Hebrew forms for the word *and*. The word for *and* appears even when there is absolutely nothing preceding to which the sentence logically connects. In fact, six books of the Old Testament (Joshua, Judges, 1 Samuel, Ezra, Ruth and Esther) begin in Hebrew with the word *and*, though they obviously do not follow anything. Accordingly, it is now recognized by Hebrew grammarians that *and* at the beginning of a sentence is virtually the equivalent of the use of capitalization at the beginning of English sentences. This does not mean that the Hebrew *and* should *never* be translated by the English *and*, it simply means that "and" is only *sometimes,* and certainly not a majority of the time, the best translation in English. The simple English sentence beginning with a capital letter will do nicely in most cases.

Another example is the KJV's "and it came to pass." This is not used in normal English speech anymore, and it was rare even in the seventeenth century when the KJV was undertaken. Because this Hebrew narrative verb form was followed literally and woodenly, the resulting translation was "and it came to pass," which thereafter occupied a prominent position in Old Testament style but nowhere else in English speech. We once heard a sermon on the concept that all things are temporary and shall eventually pass away (cf. 1 Cor. 13:8–10) based on the frequency of the clause "and it came to pass," which the preacher misunderstood to mean: "And it came *in order to* pass away." In fact, the NIV translators rightly do not translate the Hebrew clause as such. Judiciously rendering Hebrew into English requires an equivalent *meaning,* not an equivalent word or clause pattern.

On Choosing a Translation

We have been trying to help you choose a translation. We shall conclude with a few summary remarks about several translations.

First, it should be noted that we have not tried to be exhaustive. There are still other translations of the whole Bible that we have not included in our discussion, not to mention over seventy-five others of the New Testament alone that have appeared in the twentieth century. Several of those latter are excellent, and well worth using (e.g., Weymouth, 1903; Helen Montgomery, 1924; Williams 1937). Among these also are several free translations, two of which are much to be preferred to the *Living Bible* because of their higher degree of accuracy (Phillips, 1947; F. F. Bruce [epistles of Paul only], 1965).

Among the whole Bible translations not discussed are some that are theologically biased, such as the Jehovah's Witnesses' *New World Translation* (1961). This is an extremely literal translation, filled with the heretical doctrines of this cult. Others of these translations are eccentric, such as that by George Lamsa (1940), who believed that a Syriac translation from around A.D. 400 held the keys to everything. One should probably also include here the *Amplified Bible*, which has had a run of popularity far beyond its worth. It is far better to use several translations, note where they differ, and then check out those differences in another source, than to be led to believe that a word can mean one of several things in any given sentence, with the reader left to choose whatever best strikes his or her fancy.

Which translation, then, should you read? We would venture to suggest that the NIV is as good a translation as you will get. The GNB and NAB are also especially good. One would do well to have two or all three of these. The NIV is a committee translation by the best scholarship in the evangelical tradition; the NAB is a committee translation by the best scholarship in the American Catholic tradition. The GNB is an outstanding translation by a single scholar, Robert G. Bratcher, who regularly consulted with others, and whose expertise in linguistics has brought the concept of dynamic equivalence to translation in a thoroughgoing way.

Along with one or more of these, you would also do well to use one or more of the following: the NASB, the RSV, or the NRSV. These are attempts to update the KJV. The translators used better original texts and thereby eliminated most of the nonoriginal matter in the KJV. At the same time they tried to adhere as closely as possible to the *language* of the KJV and yet still modernize it some. The RSV and NRSV are by far the better translations; the NASB is much more like the KJV and therefore far more literal—to the point of being wooden.

Along with one or more of these, we recommend you also

consult either the NEB or JB—or both. Both of these are committee translations. The NEB is the product of the best of British scholarship, and is therefore filled with British idioms not always familiar to American readers. The JB is an English translation from the French *Bible de Jerusalem*. Both of these translations tend to be freer at times than the others described here as dynamic equivalent. But both of them have some outstanding features and are well worth using in conjunction with the others.

In the following chapters we will follow the NIV, unless otherwise noted. If you were regularly to read this translation, and then consult at least one from three other categories (RSV/NRSV/NASB; GNB/NAB; NEB/JB), you would be giving yourself the best possible start to an intelligent reading and study of the Bible.

3

The Epistles:
Learning to Think Contextually

We start our discussion of the various biblical genres by looking at the New Testament Epistles. One of our reasons for starting here is that they appear to be so easy to interpret. After all, who needs special help to understand that "all have sinned" (Rom. 3:23), that "the wages of sin is death" (Rom. 6:23), and that "by grace you have been saved, through faith" (Eph. 2:8), or the imperatives "live by the Spirit" (Gal. 5:16) and "live a life of love" (Eph. 5:2)?

On the other hand, the "ease" of interpreting the Epistles can be quite deceptive. This is especially so at the level of hermeneutics. One might try leading a group of Christians through 1 Corinthians, for example, and see how many are the difficulties. "How is Paul's opinion (7:25) to be taken as God's Word?" some will ask, especially when they personally dislike some of the implications of that opinion. And the questions continue. How does the excommunication of the brother in chapter 5 related to the contemporary church, especially when he can simply go down the street to another church? What is the point of chapters 12–14, if one is in a local church where charismatic gifts are not accepted as valid for the twentieth century? How do we get around the clear implication in 11:2–16 that women should wear a head covering when praying and prophesying—or the clear implication that they are to pray and prophesy in the community gathered to worship?

It becomes clear that the Epistles are *not* as easy to interpret as is often thought. Thus, because of their importance to the Christian faith and because so many of the important hermeneutical issues are raised here, we are going to let them serve as models for the exegetical and hermeneutical question we want to raise throughout the book.

The Nature of the Epistles

Before we look specifically at 1 Corinthians as a model for exegeting the Epistles, some general words are in order about all the Epistles (all the New Testament except the four Gospels, Acts, and the Revelation).

First, it is necessary to note that the Epistles themselves are not a homogeneous lot. Many years ago Adolf Deissmann, on the basis of the vast papyrus discoveries, made a distinction between letters and epistles. The former, the "real letters," as he called them, were nonliterary, that is, they were not written for the public and posterity, but were intended only for the person or persons to whom they were addressed. In contrast to the letter, the epistle was an artistic literary form or a species of literature that was intended for the public. Deissmann himself considered all the Pauline Epistles as well as 2 and 3 John to be "real letters." Although some other scholars have cautioned that one should not reduce all the letters of the New Testament to one or other of these categories—in some instances it seems to be a question of more or less—the distinction is nevertheless a valid one. Romans and Philemon differ from one another not only in content but also to the degree that one is far more personal than the other. And in contrast to any of Paul's letters, 2 Peter and 1 John are far more like epistles.

The validity of this distinction may be seen by noting the *form* of ancient letters. Just as there is a standard form to our letters (date, salutation, body, closing, and signature), so there was for theirs. Thousands of ancient letters have been found, and most of them have a form exactly like those in the New Testament (cf. the letter of the council in Acts 15:23–29). The form consists of six parts:

1. name of the writer (e.g., Paul)
2. name of the recipient (e.g., to the church of God in Corinth)
3. greeting (e.g., Grace and peace to you from God our Father . . .)

4. prayer wish or thanksgiving (e.g., I always thank God for you . . .)
5. body
6. final greeting and farewell (e.g., The grace of the Lord Jesus Christ be with you . . .)

The one variable element in this form is number 4, which in most of the ancient letters takes the form of a prayer wish (almost exactly like 3 John 2), or else is missing altogether (as in Galatians, 1 Timothy, Titus), although at times one finds a thanksgiving and prayer (as often in Paul's letters). In three of the New Testament Epistles this thanksgiving turns into a doxology (2 Corinthians, Ephesians, 1 Peter; cf. Rev. 1:5–6).

It will be noted that the New Testament Epistles that lack either formal elements 1–3 or 6 are those that fail to be true letters, although they are partially epistolary in form. Hebrews, for example, which has been described as three parts tract and one part letter, was indeed sent to a specific group of people, as 10:32–34 and 13:1–25 make clear. Note especially the letter form of 13:22–25. Yet chapters 1–10 are little like a letter and are in fact an eloquent homily in which the argument as to Christ's total superiority to all that has preceded is interspersed with urgent words of exhortation that the readers hold fast their faith in Christ (2:1–4; 3:7–19; 5:11–6:20; 10:19–25). Indeed, the author himself calls it his "word of exhortation" (13:22).

First John is similar in some ways, except that it has *none* of the formal elements of a letter. Nonetheless, it was clearly written for a specific group of people (see e.g., 2:7, 12–14, 19, 26) and looks very much like the body of a letter with all the formal elements shorn off. The point is, it is not simply a theological treatise for the church at large.

James and 2 Peter both are addressed as letters, but both lack the familiar final greeting and farewell; both also lack specific addressees, as well as any personal notations by the writers. These are the closest things in the New Testament "epistles," that is, tracts for the whole church, although 2 Peter seems to have been called forth by some who were denying the Second Coming (3:1–7). James, on the other hand, so completely lacks an overall argument that it looks more like a collection of sermon notes on a variety of ethical topics than a letter.

Despite this variety of kinds, however, there is one thing that all of the Epistles have in common, and this is *the* crucial thing to note in reading and interpreting them: they are all what are technically called *occasional documents* (i.e., arising out of and intended for a specific occasion), and they are from the *first century*. Although inspired by the Holy Spirit and thus belonging to all time, they were first written out of the context of the author to the context of the original recipients. It is precisely these factors—that they are occasional and that they belong to the first century—that make their interpretation difficult at times.

Above all else, their *occasional* nature must be taken seriously. This means that they were occasioned, or called forth, by some special circumstance, either from the reader's side or the author's. Almost all of the New Testament letters were occasioned from the reader's side (Philemon and perhaps James and Romans are exceptions). Usually the occasion was some kind of behavior that needed correcting, or a doctrinal error that needed setting right, or a misunderstanding that needed further light.

Most of our problems in interpreting the Epistles are due to this fact of their being occasional. We have the answers, but we do not always know what the questions or problems were, or even if there was a problem. It is much like listening to one end of a telephone conversation and trying to figure out who is on the other end and what that unseen party is saying. Yet in many cases it is especially important for us to try to hear "the other end," so that we know what our passage is an answer to.

One further point here. The occasional nature of the Epistles also means that they are *not* first of all theological treatises; they are not compendia of Paul's or Peter's theology. There is theology implied, but it is always "task theology," theology being written for or brought to bear on the task at hand. This is true even of Romans, which is a fuller and more systematic statement of Paul's theology than one finds elsewhere. But it is only *some* of his theology, in this case it is theology born out of his own special task as apostle to the Gentiles. It is his special struggle for Gentile rights to God's grace and how this is related to the whole problem of "Law" that causes the discussion to take the special form it does in Romans and that causes *justification* to be used there as the primary metaphor for salvation. After all, the word *justify,* which predominates in Romans

(15 times) and Galatians (8), occurs only two other times in all of Paul's other letters (1 Cor. 6:11; Titus 3:7).

Thus one will go to the Epistles again and again for Christian theology; they are loaded with it. But one must always keep in mind that they were not primarily written to expound Christian theology. It is always theology at the service of a particular need. We will note the implications of this for hermeneutics in our next chapter.

Given these important preliminaries, how then does one go about the exegesis, or an informed exegetical reading, of the Epistles? From here on, we will proceed with a case study of 1 Corinthians. We know that not every epistle will be like this one, but nearly all the questions one needs to ask of any epistle are raised here.

The Historical Context

The first thing one must try to do with any of the Epistles is to form a tentative but informed reconstruction of the situation that the author is speaking to. What was going on in Corinth that caused Paul to write 1 Corinthians? How did he come to learn of their situation? What kind of relationship and former contacts has he had with them? What attitudes do they and he reflect in this letter? These are the kinds of questions you want answers to. So what do you do?

First, you need to consult your Bible dictionary or the introduction to your commentary to find out as much as possible about Corinth and its people. Among other important things you should note that by ancient standards it was a relatively young city, only ninety-four years old when Paul first visited it. Yet because of its strategic location for commerce, it was cosmopolitan, wealthy, a patron of the arts, religious (at least twenty-six temples and shrines), and well known for its sensuality. With a little reading and imagination one can see that it was a bit of New York, Los Angeles, and Las Vegas, all wrapped up in one place. Therefore, it will hardly be a letter to the community church in Rural Corners, U.S.A. All of this will need to be kept in mind as you read to note how it will affect your understanding on nearly every page.

Second, and now especially for study purposes, you need to develop the habit of reading the whole letter through in one sitting. You will need to block out an hour or less to do this, but *nothing* can ever substitute for this exercise. It is the way one reads every other letter. A letter in the Bible should be no different. There are some things you should be looking for as you read, but you are not now trying to grasp the meaning of every word or sentence. It is the big view that counts first.

We cannot stress enough the importance of reading and rereading. Once you have divided the letter into its logical parts or sections, you will want to begin the study of every section precisely the same way. Read and reread; and keep your eyes open!

As you read the whole letter through, it would be helpful to jot down a few, *very brief,* notes with references. This is for the sake of those who have a hard time making mental notes. What things should you note as you read for the big picture? Remember, the purpose here is first of all to reconstruct the problem. Thus we suggest four kinds of notes:

1. what you notice about the recipients themselves; e.g., whether Jew or Greek, wealthy or slave, their problems, attitudes, etc.;
2. Paul's attitudes;
3. any specific things mentioned as to the specific occasion of the letter;
4. the letter's natural, logical divisions.

If all of this is too much at one sitting and causes you to lose the value of reading it through, then read first, and afterwards go back quickly through the letter with a skim reading to pick up these items. Here are the kinds of things you might have noticed, grouped according to the four suggested categories:

1. The Corinthian believers are chiefly Gentile, although there are also some Jews (see 6:9–11; 8:10; 12:2, 13); they obviously love wisdom and knowledge (1:18–2:5; 4:10; 8:1–13; hence the irony in 6:5); they are proud and arrogant (4:18; 5:2, 6) even to the point of judging Paul (4:1–5; 9:1–18); yet they have a large number of internal problems.

2. Paul's attitude toward all of this fluctuates between rebuke (4:8–21; 5:2; 6:1–8), appeal (4:14–17; 16:10–11), and exhortation (6:18–20; 16:12–14).

3. Concerning the occasion of the letter, you might have noted that in 1:10–12 Paul says he has been *informed* by people from Chloe's household; 5:1 also refers to reported information. In 7:1

he says, "Now for the matters you wrote about," which means he has also received a letter from the church. Did you also notice the repetition of "now about" in 7:25; 8:1; 12:1; 16:1; and 16:12? Probably these are all items from their letter that he is taking up one at a time. One further thing: Did you notice the "arrival" of Stephanas, Fortunatus, and Achaicus in 16:17? Since Stephanas is to be "submitted to" (v. 16), it is certain that these men (or Stephanas, at least) are leaders in the church. Probably they brought the letter to Paul as a kind of official delegation.

If you did not catch all of these things, do not give up. We have gone over this material a lot of times, and it is all familiar turf. The important thing is to learn to read with your eyes open to picking up these kinds of clues.

4. We come now to the important matter of having a working outline of the letter. This is especially important for 1 Corinthians because it is easier to study or read this letter in convenient "packages." not all of Paul's letters are made up of so many separate items, but such a working outline is nonetheless always useful.

The place to begin is with the obvious major divisions. In this case 7:1 is the big clue. Since here Paul first mentions their letter to him, and since in 1:10–12 and 5:1 he mentions items reported to him, we may initially assume that the matters in chapters 1–6 are all responses to what has been reported to him. Introductory phrases and subject matter are the clues to all other divisions in the letter. There are four in the first six chapters:

> the problem of division in the church (1:10–4:21);
> the problem of the incestuous man (5:1–13);
> the problem of lawsuits (6:1–11);
> the problem of fornication (6:12–20).

We have already noted the clues to dividing most of chapters 7–16—on the basis of the introductory formula "now about." The items not introduced by that formula are three, 11:2–16; 11:17–34, and 15:1–58. Probably the items in chapter 11 (at least 11:17–34) were also reported to him but are included here because everything from chapters 8 to 14 deals with worship in some way or another. It is difficult to know whether chapter 15 is a response to the report or to the letter. The phrase "how can some of your say" in verse 12 does not help that much because Paul could be quoting either a report or their letter. In any case the rest of the letter can easily be outlined.

about behavior within marriage (7:1–24);
about virgins (7:25–40);
about food sacrificed to idols (8:1–11:1);
the covering of women's heads in church (11:2–16);
the problem of abuse at the Lord's Table (11:17–34);
about spiritual gifts (12–14);
the bodily resurrection of believers (15:1–58);
about the collection (16:1–11);
about the return of Apollos (16:12);
concluding exhortations and greetings (16:13–24).

It may be that by following the divisions in the NIV you failed to note the division at 7:25, or that you divided chapters 1–4, 8–10, and 12–14 into smaller groupings. But do you also see that these latter three are complete units? For example, note how thoroughly chapter 13 belongs to the whole argument of 12 to 14 by the mention of specific spiritual gifts in verse 1–2 and 8.

Before we go on, two things should be noted carefully. (1) The only other place in Paul's letters where he takes up a succession of independent items like this is 1 Thessalonians 4–5. For the most part, the other letters basically form one long argument—although sometimes the argument has several clear parts to it. (2) This is only a tentative outline. We know what occasioned the letter only at the surface—a report and a letter. But what we really want to know is *the precise nature of each of the problems in Corinth* that called forth each specific response from Paul. For our purposes here, therefore, we will spend the rest of our time zeroing in on only one item, the problem of division in chapters 1–4.

The Historical Context of 1 Corinthians 1–4

As you approach each of the smaller sections of the letter, you need to repeat much of what we have just done. If we were giving you an assignment for each lesson, it would go like this: (1) Read 1 Corinthians 1–4 through at least two times (preferably in two different translations). Again, you are reading to get the big picture, to get a "feel" for the whole argument. After you have read it through the second time (or even the third or fourth if you want to read it in each of your translations), go back and (2) list in a notebook everything you can that tells you something about the recipients and their problem. Try to be thorough here and list everything, even if after a closer look you want to go back and scratch some items off as not entirely relevant. (3) Then make another list of key words and repeated phrases that indicate the subject matter of Paul's answer.

One of the reasons for choosing this section as a model is not only that it is so crucial to much of 1 Corinthians, but also, frankly, because it is a difficult one. If you have read the whole section with care with an eye for the problem, you may have noted, or even were frustrated by, the fact that although Paul begins by specifically spelling out the problem (1:10–12), the beginning of his answer (1:18–3:4) does not seem to speak to the problem at all. In fact, one might initially think 1:18–3:4 to be a digression except that Paul does not argue as a man off on a tangent and that in the conclusion in 3:18–23 "wisdom" and "foolishness" (key ideas in 1:18–3:4) are joined with "boasting about men" and references to Paul, Apollos, and Cephas. The crucial matter for discovering the problem, then, is to see how all this might fit together.

The place to begin is by making note of what Paul specifically says. In 1:10–12 he says they are divided in the name of their leaders (cf. 3:4–9; 3:21–22; 4:6). But did you also notice that the division is not merely a matter of differences of opinion among them? They are in fact quarreling (1:12; 3:3) and "taking pride in one man *over against* another" (4:6; cf. 3:21).

All of this seems clear enough. But a careful reading with an eye for the problem should cause two other things to surface.

1. There appears to be some "bad blood" between the church and Paul himself. This becomes especially clear in 4:1–5 and 4:18–21. With that in mind, one might legitimately see the quarreling and division to be not simply a matter of some of them *preferring* Apollos to Paul, but of their actually being opposed to Paul.

2. One of the key words in this section is *wisdom* or *wise* (26 times in chapters 1–3, and only 18 more times in all of Paul's letters). And it is clear that this is more often a pejorative term than a favorable one. God is out to set aside the wisdom of this world (1:18–22, 27–28; 3:18–20). He has done so by the cross (1:18–25), by his choice of the Corinthian believers (1:26–31), and by

the weakness of Paul's preaching (2:1-5). Christ, through the cross, has "become for us wisdom from God" (1:30), and *this* wisdom is revealed *by* the Spirit to those who *have* the Spirit (2:10-16). The use of *wisdom* in this way in Paul's argument makes it almost certain that this, too, is a part of the problem of division. But how? At the least, we can guess that they are carrying on their division over leaders and their opposition to Paul in the name of wisdom.

Anything we say beyond that will lie in the area of speculation, or educated guessing. Since the term *wisdom* is a semitechnical one for philosophy as well, and since itinerant philosophers of all kinds abounded in the Greek world of Paul's time, we suggest that the Corinthian believers were beginning to think of their new Christian faith as a new "divine wisdom," which in turn caused them to evaluate their leaders in merely human terms as they might any of the itinerant philosophers. But note, as helpful as this "guess" might be, it goes beyond what can be said on the basis of the text itself.

From Paul's answer three important things can be said for sure: (1) On the basis of 3:5-23 it is clear that they have seriously misunderstood the nature and function of leadership in the church. (2) Similarly, on the basis of 1:18-3:4 they seem to have misunderstood the basic nature of the Gospel. (3) On the basis of 4:1-21 they also are wrong in their judgments on Paul and need to reevaluate their relationship to him. You will notice that with this we have now begun to move to an analysis of Paul's answer.

The Literary Context

The next step in studying the Epistles is to learn to trace Paul's argument as an answer to the problem tentatively set out above. You will recall from chapter 1 that this, too, is something you can do without initial dependence on the scholars.

If we were to give you an assignment for this part of the "lesson," it would go like this: Trace the argument of 1 Corinthians 1:10-4:21, paragraph by paragraph, and in a sentence or two explain the point of each paragraph for the argument as a whole—or explain how it functions as a part of Paul's answer to the problem of division.

We simply cannot stress enough the importance of your learning to THINK PARAGRAPHS, and not just as natural units of thought, but as the absolutely necessary key to understanding the argument in the various epistles. You will recall that the one question you need to learn to ask over and again is, *What's the point?* Therefore, you want to be able to do *two* things: (1) In a compact way state the *content* of each paragraph. *What* does Paul say in this paragraph? (2) In another sentence or two try to explain *why* you think Paul says this right at this point. How does this content contribute to the argument?

Since we cannot here do this for all of 1 Corinthians 1–4, let us go into some detail with the three crucial paragraphs in the second part of Paul's answer: 3:5–16. Up to this point Paul, under inspiration of the Spirit, has responded to their inadequate understanding of the Gospel by pointing out that the heart of the Gospel—a crucified Messiah—stands in contradiction to human wisdom (1:18–25), as does God's choice of those who make up the new people of God (1:26–31)—as though Paul had said to them, "So you think the gospel is a new kind of wisdom, do you? How can that be so? Who in the name of wisdom would have chosen *you* to become the new people of God?" Paul's own preaching also serves as an illustration of the divine contradiction (2:1–5). Now all of this is indeed wisdom, Paul assures them in 1:6–16, but it is wisdom revealed by the Spirit to God's new people—those who have the Spirit. Since the Corinthians *do* have the Spirit, he continues now by way of transition, they should stop acting like those who do *not* (3:1–4). That they are still acting "like mere men" is evidenced by their quarreling over Paul and Apollos.

How, then, do the next three paragraphs function in this argument? For 3:5–9, the *content* deals with the nature and function of the leaders over whom they are quarreling. Paul emphasizes that they are merely servants, not lords, as the Corinthian slogans seem to be making them. In verses 6–9, by means of an analogy from agriculture, he makes two points about their servant status, both of which are crucial to the Corinthian misunderstanding: (1) Both Paul and Apollos are one in a common cause, even though their tasks differ and each will receive his own "pay." (2) Everything and everyone belongs to God—the church, the servants, the growth.

Notice how crucial to the problem these two points are. They are dividing the church on the basis of its leaders. But these leaders are not *lords* to whom one belongs. They are servants, who, even though they have differing ministries, are one in the same cause. And these servants belong to God, just as the Corinthians themselves do.

Another text that has often been wrongly interpreted because of the failure to think paragraphs is 3:10–15. Note two things: (1) At the end of verse 9 Paul shifts the metaphor from agriculture to architecture, which will be the metaphor used throughout this paragraph. (2) The particulars in both metaphors are the same (Paul plants/lays the foundation; Apollos waters/builds on the foundation; the Corinthian church is the field/building; God owns the field/building). However, the *point* of each paragraph differs. The point of 3:10–15 is clearly expressed in verse 10, "But each one should be careful how he or she builds." And it is clear from Paul's elaboration of the metaphor that one can build well or poorly, with differing final results. Note that what is being built throughout is the church; there is not even a hint that Paul is referring to how each individual Christian builds his or her life on Christ, which in fact is totally irrelevant to the argument. What Paul does here is to turn the argument slightly to warn those who lead the church that they must do so with great care, because a day of testing is coming. Building the church with human wisdom or eloquent speech that circumvents the Cross is building with wood, hay, and stubble.

The text that follows, 3:16–17, has also frequently been misapplied, partly because it is well known that a little later (6:19) Paul calls the Christian's body "the temple of the Holy Spirit." Thus the present verses, too, have been individualized to refer to one's abuse of the body or neglect one's spiritual life. Elsewhere, however, Paul uses the temple metaphor in a collective sense to refer to the church as God's temple (2 Cor. 6:16; Eph. 2:19–22). That is surely his intention here, which the NIV tries to bring out by translating "you yourselves are God's temple."

What, then, is Paul's point in this context? The Corinthian church was to be *God's* temple in Corinth—over against all the other temples in the city. To put that in our words, they were God's option in Corinth, his alternative to the Corinthian lifestyle. What made them God's temple was the presence of the Spirit in their midst. But by their divisions they were destroying God's temple. Those responsible for it, Paul says, will themselves be destroyed by God, because the church in Corinth was precious (i.e., sacred) to him.

Paul's inspired argument has now come full term. He began by exposing their inadequate understanding of the Gospel, a Gospel that is not only *not* based on human wisdom but in every way stands as the contradiction to it. Then he turns to expose their inadequate understanding of leadership in the church, and at the same time warns both the leaders and the church itself of God's judgment on those who promote division. In 3:18–23 he brings these two themes together in a concluding statement. Human wisdom is folly; therefore, "no more boasting about men!"

Notice as we summarize this analysis: (1) the exegesis is self-contained; that is, we have not had to go outside the text once to understand the point, (2) there is nothing in the text that does not fit into the argument, and (3) all of this makes perfectly good sense of everything. This, then, is what exegesis is all about. This was God's Word *to them*. You may have further questions about specific points of content, for which you can consult your commentary. *But all of what we have done here, you can do.* It may take practice—in some cases even some hard work of thinking; but you can do it, and the rewards are great.

One More Time

Before we conclude this chapter, let us go through the process of exegesis one more time for practice, and this time in a somewhat easier passage outside of 1 Corinthians, but a passage that also deals with disunity in the church.

Read Philippians 1:27–2:13 several times. Note that Paul's argument to here has gone something like this. *The occasion* is that Paul is in prison (1:13, 17) and the Philippian church has sent a gift through a member named Epaphroditus (4:14–18). Apparently Epaphroditus became sick and the church heard of it and was saddened (2:26); but God spared him, so now Paul is sending him back (2:25–30) with this letter in order to (1) tell them how things are with him (1:12–26), (2) thank them for their gift (4:10, 14–19), and (3) exhort them on a couple of matters: to live in harmony (1:27–2:17; 4:2–3), and to avoid the Judaizing heresy (3:1–4:1).

Paul has just completed the section telling them how he is getting along in his imprisonment. This new section is a part of the exhortation. Notice, for example, how he is no longer talking about himself as in verses 12–26. Did you notice this clear shift from I/me/my to you/your in verse 27?

What then is the point of each paragraph in this section?

The first paragraph, 1:27–30, begins the exhortation. The point seems to be what we read in verse 27, they should "stand firm in one Spirit." This is an exhortation to unity, especially because they are facing opposition. (Note: If we decide that v. 27 is really the point of the paragraph, then we have to ask, "What's the point of vv. 28–30 and the emphasis on opposition and suffering?" Notice how he tried to answer this.)

How does 2:1–4 relate to unity? First, he repeats the exhortation (vv. 1–2, which now makes us sure we were right about the first paragraph). But the point now is that humility is the proper attitude for the believers to have unity.

Now you try it with 2:5–11. What is the point? Why this appeal to the humiliation and exaltation of Christ? Your answer does not have to be in our words, but surely should include the following: Jesus in his incarnation and death is the supreme example of the humility Paul wants them to have. (You will notice that when you ask the questions *this* way, the *point* of the paragraph is *not* to teach us something new about Christ. He is appealing to these great truths about Christ to get the Philippians to *be like* him, not simply to *know about* him.)

Go on to 2:12–13. Now what is the point? This is clearly the conclusion. Notice the word *therefore*. Given Christ's example, they are now to obey Paul. In what? Surely in having unity, which also requires humility.

Finally, you might note from the way Paul here deals with the problem of disunity, that the similar problem in Corinth was surely of a much more serious and complex nature. This should further help to confirm our reconstruction of the problem there.

The Problem Passages

We have purposely led you through two passages where we are convinced you could have done most of this kind of exegesis on your own, given that you have learned to think paragraphs and to ask the right historical and contextual questions. But we are well aware that there are all those other texts, the kinds of texts we are repeatedly asked about—the meaning of "because of the angels" in

1 Corinthians 11:10, or "baptism for the dead" in 1 Corinthians 15:29, or Christ's preaching to the "spirits in prison" in 1 Peter 3:18, or "the man of lawlessness" in 2 Thessalonians 2:3. In short, how do we go about finding the meaning of the problem passages?

Here are some guidelines:

1. In many cases the reason the texts are so difficult for us is that, frankly, they were not written to us. That is, the original author and his readers are on a similar wavelength that allows the inspired author to *assume* a great deal on the part of his readers. Thus, for example, when Paul tells the Thessalonians that they are to recall that he "used to tell [them] these things," and therefore "you know what is holding him back" (2 Thess. 2:5–6), we may need to learn to be content with our *lack* of knowledge. What he had told them orally they could now fit into what he was saying by letter. Our lack of the oral communication makes the written one especially difficult. But we take it as a truism: what God wants us to know he has communicated to us; what he has not told us may still hold our interest, but our uncertainty at these points should make us hesitant about being dogmatic.

2. Nonetheless, as we have suggested before, even if one cannot have full certainty about some of the details, very often the *point* of the whole passage is still within one's grasp. Whatever it was the Corinthians were doing in "baptizing for the dead," we do know *why* Paul referred to this practice of theirs. Their own action was a kind of "proof from experience" that they were not consistent in rejecting a future resurrection of believers.

3. Despite some uncertainty as to some of the precise details, one needs to learn to ask what can be said *for certain* about a text and what is possible but not certain. Look at 1 Corinthians 15:29 again as an example. What can be said for certain? Some of the Corinthians really were being "baptized for the dead," whether we like to admit that or not. Moreover, Paul neither condemns nor condones their practice; he simply refers to it—for a totally different reason from the actual practice itself. But we do not know and probably never will know *who* was doing it, *for whom* they were doing it, and *why* they were doing it. The details and the meaning of the practice, therefore, are probably forever lost to us.

4. On such passages one needs to consult a good commentary. As we point out in the appendix, it is the handling of just such a passage that separates the good commentaries from all the others.

The good ones will list and at least briefly discuss the various options that have been suggested as solutions, with reasons for and against. You may not always go along with the individual commentator's choices, but you do need to be informed about the variety of options, and good commentaries will do that for you.

Finally, we suggest that even scholars do not have all the answers. You can more or less count on it that where there are four to fourteen viable options as to what a text meant, even the scholars are guessing! Texts like 1 Corinthians 15:29 (on which there are at least forty different guesses) should serve to give us proper humility.

What we have done in this chapter, however, is only *half* the task. It is the *essential* first half, but now we want to go on to ask how these various texts apply to us. We have learned to hear God's Word to them. What about his Word to us? That is the concern of the next chapter.

4

The Epistles: The Hermeneutical Questions

We come now to what we referred to previously as hermeneutical questions. What do these texts mean to *us*? This is the crux of everything, and compared with this task, exegesis is relatively easy. At least in exegesis, even if there are disagreements at particular points, most people are agreed upon the parameters of meaning; there are limitations of possibilities set by the historical and literary contexts. Paul, for example, cannot have meant something that he and his readers had never heard of; his meaning at least has to have been a first-century possibility.

However, no such consensus of parameters seems to exist for hermeneutics (learning to hear the meaning in the contexts of our own day). *All* people "do" hermeneutics, even if they know nothing about exegesis. It is no wonder that there are so many differences among Christians; what is the more amazing is that there are not far more differences than actually exist. The reason for this is that there *is* in fact a common ground of hermeneutics among us, even if we have not always articulated it.

What we want to do in this chapter is first of all to delineate the common hermeneutics of most believers, show its strengths and weaknesses, and then discuss and offer guidelines for several areas where this common hermeneutics seems inadequate. The big issue among Christians committed to Scripture as God's Word has to do with the problems of cultural relativity, what is cultural and therefore belongs to the first century alone and what transcends culture and is thus a Word for all seasons. That problem will therefore receive a considerable amount of attention.

Our Common Hermeneutics

Even if you are among those who may have asked, "Herman who?" when confronted with the word *hermeneutics,* you are in fact involved in hermeneutics all the time. What is it that all of us do as we read the Epistles? Very simply, we bring our enlightened common sense to the text and apply what we can to our own situation. What does not seem to apply is simply left in the first century.

None of us, for example, has ever felt called by the Holy Spirit to take a pilgrimage to Troas in order to carry Paul's cloak from Carpus's house to his Roman prison (2 Tim. 4:13), even though the passage is clearly a command to do that. Yet from that same letter most Christians believe that God tells them in times of stress that they are to "endure hardship . . . like a good soldier of Jesus Christ" (2:3). None of us would ever think to question what has been done with either of these passages—although many of us may have moments of struggle in graciously obeying the latter.

Let it be emphasized here that most of the matters in the Epistles fit very nicely into this common-sense hermeneutics. For most texts it is not a matter of whether one *should* or not; it is more a matter of "stirring one another up by way of reminder" (2 Peter 1:15, KJV).

Our problems—and differences—are generated by those texts that lie somewhere in between these two, where some of us think we should obey exactly what is stated and others of us are not so sure. Our hermeneutical difficulties here are several, but they are all related to one thing—our lack of consistency. This is the great flaw in our common hermeneutics. Without necessarily intending to, we bring our theological heritage, our ecclesiastical traditions, our cultural norms, or our existential concerns to the Epistles as we read them. And this results in all kinds of selectivity or "getting around" certain texts.

It is interesting to note, for example, that everybody in American evangelicalism or fundamentalism would agree with our common stance on 2 Timothy 2:3 and 4:13. However, the cultural milieu of most of the same Christians causes them to argue against obedience to 1 Timothy 5:23: "Stop drinking water only, and use a little wine because of your stomach and your frequent illnesses." That had only to do with Timothy, not with us, we are told, because water was unsafe to drink back then. Or else, it is even argued that *wine* really meant "grape juice"—although one wonders how that could have happened when Welch's processing and refrigeration were not available! But why is this personal word limited to Timothy while the exhortation to continue in the Word (2 Tim. 3:14–16), which is also an imperative addressed only to Timothy, becomes an imperative for all people at all times? Mind you, one might well be right in bypassing 1 Timothy 5:23 as not having present personal application, but on what hermeneutical grounds?

Or take the problems that many traditional churchgoers had with the "Jesus people" in the late 1960s and early 1970s. Long hair on boys had already become the symbol of a new era in the hippie culture of the 1960s. For Christians to wear that symbol, especially in light of 1 Corinthians 11:14, "Does not nature itself teach you that for a man to wear long hair is degrading to him" (RSV), seemed like an open defiance of God himself. Yet most of those who quoted that text against the youth culture allowed for Christian women to cut their hair short (despite v. 15), did not insist on women's heads being covered in worship, and never considered that "nature" came about by a very *un*natural means—a haircut.

These two examples simply illustrate how culture dictates what is common sense for any one of us. But other things also dictate common sense—ecclesiastical traditions, for example. How is it that in many evangelical churches women are forbidden to speak in church on the basis of 1 Corinthians 14:34–35, yet in many of the same churches everything else in chapter 14 is argued *against* as not belonging to the twentieth century? How is it that verses 34–35 belong to all times and cultures, while verses 1–5, or 26–33, and 39–40, which give regulations for prophesying and speaking in tongues, belong only to the first-century church?

Notice further how easy it is for twentieth-century Christians to read their own tradition of church order into 1 Timothy and Titus. Yet very few churches have the plural leadership that seems clearly to be in view there (1 Tim. 5:17; Titus 1:5; Timothy was *not* the pastor; he was a temporary delegate of Paul's to set things in order and to correct abuses). And still fewer churches actually "enroll widows" under the guidelines of 1 Timothy 5:3–15.

And have you noticed how our prior theological commitments cause many of us to read that commitment into some texts while we read around others? It comes as a total surprise to some Christians when they find out that other Christians find support for infant baptism in such texts as 1 Corinthians 1:16; 7:14 or Colossians 2:11–12, or that others find evidence for a two-stage Second Coming in 2 Thessalonians 2:1, or that still others find evidence for sanctification as a second work of grace in Titus 3:5. For many in the Arminian tradition, who emphasize the believer's free will and responsibility, texts like Romans 8:30; 9:18–24; Galatians 1:15; and Ephesians 1:4–5 are something of an embarrassment. Likewise many Calvinists have their own ways of getting around 1 Corinthians 10:1–13; 2 Peter 2:20–22; and Hebrews 6:4–6. Indeed our experience as teachers is that students from these traditions seldom ask what these texts mean; they want to know "how to answer" these texts!

After the last few paragraphs, we have probably lost a lot of friends, but we are trying to illustrate how thoroughgoing the problem is, and how Christians need to talk to one another in this crucial area. What kinds of guidelines, then, are needed in order to establish more consistent hermeneutics for the Epistles?

The Basic Rule

You will recall from chapter 1 that we set out as a basic rule the premise that *a text cannot mean what it never could have meant to its author or his or her readers*. This is why exegesis must always come first. It is especially important that we repeat this premise here, for this at least establishes some parameters of meaning. This rule does not always help one find out what a text *means*, but it does help to set limits as to what it *cannot* mean.

For example, the most frequent justification for disregarding the imperatives about seeking spiritual gifts in 1 Corinthians 14 is a particular interpretation of 1 Corinthians 13:10, which states that "when the perfect comes, the imperfect will pass away" (RSV). We are told that the perfect *has* come, in the form of the New Testament, and therefore the imperfect (prophecy and tongues) have ceased to function in the church. *But this is one thing the text cannot mean* because good exegesis totally disallows it. There is no possible way Paul could have meant that—after all, his readers did not know there was going to be a New Testament, and the Holy Spirit would not have allowed Paul to write something totally incomprehensible to them.

The Second Rule

The second basic rule is actually a different way of expressing our common hermeneutics. It says: *Whenever we share comparable particulars (i.e., similar specific life situations) with the first-century setting, God's Word to us is the same as his Word to them.* It is this rule that causes most of the theological texts and the community-directed ethical imperatives in the Epistles to give modern-day Christians a sense of immediacy with the first century. It is still true that "all have sinned" and that "by grace we are saved through faith." Clothing ourselves with "compassion, kindness, humility, gentleness and patience" (Col. 3:12) is still God's Word to those who are believers.

The two longer texts we exegeted in the preceding chapter seem to be of this kind. Once we have done our exegesis and have discovered God's Word to them, we have immediately brought ourselves under that same Word. We still have local churches, which still have leaders who need to hear the Word and take care how they build the church. It appears that the church has too often been built with wood, hay, and stubble, rather than with gold, silver, and precious stones, and such work when tried by fire has been found wanting. We would argue that 1 Corinthians 3:16–17 is still God's address to us as to our responsibilities to the local church. It must be a place where God's Spirit is known to dwell, and which therefore stands as God's alternative to the sin and alienation of worldly society.

The great caution here is that we do our exegesis well, so that we have confidence that our situations and particulars are genuinely comparable to theirs. This is why the careful reconstruction of their problem is so important. For example, it is significant for our hermeneutics to note that the lawsuit in 1 Corinthians 6:1–11 was between two Christian brothers before a pagan judge out in the open marketplace in Corinth. We would argue that the point of the text does not change if the judge happens to be a Christian or because the trial takes place in a courthouse. The wrong is for two brothers to go to law outside the church, as verses 6–11 make perfectly clear. On the other hand, one might rightly ask whether this would still apply to a Christian suing a corporation in modern America, for in this case not all the particulars would remain the same—although one's decision should surely take Paul's appeal to the nonretaliation ethic of Jesus (v. 7) into account.

All of what has been said thus far seems easy enough. But the question as to how a text such as 1 Corinthians 6:1–11 might apply *beyond* its specific particulars is but one of the several kinds of questions that needs to be discussed. The rest of this chapter addresses four such problems.

The Problem of Extended Application

The first problem is the one just mentioned. When there are comparable particulars and comparable contexts in today's church, is it legitimate to extend the application of the text to other contexts, or to make a text apply to a context totally foreign to its first-century setting?

For example, it might be argued that even though 1 Corinthians 3:16–17 addresses the local church, it also presents the principle that what God has set aside for himself by the indwelling of his Spirit is sacred and whoever destroys that will come under God's awful judgment. May not this principle now be applied to the individual Christian to teach that God will judge the person who abuses his or her body? Similarly, 1 Corinthians 3:10–15 is addressing those with building responsibilities in the church, and warns of the loss they will suffer who build poorly. Since the text speaks of judgment and salvation "as by fire," is it legitimate to use this text to illustrate the security of the believer?

If these are deemed legitimate applications, then we would seem to have good reason to be concerned. For inherent in such application is the bypassing of exegesis altogether. After all, to apply 1 Corinthians 3:16–17 to the individual believer is precisely what many in the church have erroneously done for centuries. Why do exegesis at all? Why not simply begin with the here and now and fall heir to centuries of error?

We would argue, therefore, that when there are comparable situations and comparable particulars, God's Word *to us* in such texts must always be limited to its original intent. Furthermore, it should be noted that the extended application is usually seen to be legitimate because it is true, that is, it is clearly spelled out in other passages where that is the *intent* of the passage. If that be the case, then one should ask whether what one learns only by extended application can truly be the Word of God.

A more difficult case is presented by a text such as 2 Corinthians 6:14, "Do not be yoked together with unbelievers." Traditionally this text has been interpreted as forbidding marriage between a Christian and non-Christian. However, the metaphor of a *yoke* is rarely used in antiquity to refer to marriage, and there is nothing whatever in the context that remotely allows marriage to be in view here.

Our problem is that we cannot be certain as to *what* the original text is forbidding. Most likely it has something to do with idolatry, perhaps as a further prohibition of attendance at the idol feasts (cf. 1 Cor. 10:14–22). Can we not, therefore, legitimately "extend" the principle of this text, since we cannot be sure of its original meaning? Probably so, but again, only because it is indeed a biblical principle that can be sustained apart from this single text.

The Problem of Particulars That Are Not Comparable

The problem here has to do with two kinds of texts in the Epistles: those that speak to first-century issues that for the most part are without any twentieth-century counterparts, and those texts that speak to problems that *could* possibly happen also in the twentieth century but are highly unlikely to do so. What does one do with such texts, and how do they address us? Or do they?

An example of the first kind of text is to be found in 1 Corinthians 8–10, where Paul speaks to three kinds of issues: (1) Christians who are arguing for the privilege of continuing to join their pagan neighbors at their feasts in the idol temples (see 8:10; 10:14–22), (2) the Corinthians' calling into question Paul's apostolic authority (see 9:1–23), (3) food sacrificed to idols that was sold in the open market (10:23–11:1).

Sound exegesis of these passages indicates that Paul answers these problems as follows: (1) They are absolutely forbidden to attend the idol feasts because of the stumbling-block principle (8:7–13), because such eating is incompatible with life in Christ as it is experienced at his table (10:16–17), and because it means to participate in the demonic (10:19–22). (2) Paul defends his right to financial support as an apostle, even though he has given it up; he also defends his actions (9:19–23) in matters of indifference. (3) Idol food sold in the marketplace may be purchased and eaten; and it may also be freely eaten in someone else's home. In the latter context it may also be refused if it might create a problem for someone else. One may eat anything to the glory of God; but one should not do something that deliberately offends.

Our problem is that this kind of idolatry is simply unknown in Western cultures, so that problems (1) and (3) simply do not exist. Moreover, we no longer have apostles in Paul's sense of those who have actually encountered the Risen Lord (9:1; cf. 15:8) and who have founded and have authority over new churches (9:1–2; cf. 2 Cor. 10:16).

The second kind of text may be illustrated by the incestuous man in 1 Corinthians 5:1–11, or by people getting drunk at a meal in conjunction with the Lord's Table (1 Cor. 11:17–22), or by people wanting to force circumcision on noncircumcised Christians (Gal. 5:2). These things could happen but are highly improbable in our culture.

The question is, how do the answers to these nontwentieth-century problems speak to twentieth-century Christians? We suggest that proper hermeneutics here must take two steps.

First, we must do our exegesis with particular care so that we hear what God's Word to them really was. In most cases a clear *principle* has been articulated, which usually will transcend the historical particularity to which it was being applied.

Second, and here is the important point, the "principle" does not now become timeless to be applied at random or whim to any and every kind of situation. We would argue that it must be applied to *genuinely comparable situations*.

To illustrate both of these points: First, Paul forbids participation in the temple meals on the basis of the stumbling-block principle. But note that this does *not* refer to something that merely offends another believer. The stumbling-block principle refers to something one believer feels he can do in good conscience, and which, by his action or persuasion, he induces another believer to do, who cannot do so in good conscience. After all, the brother or sister is "destroyed" by *emulating* another's action; he or she is not merely *offended* by it. The principle would seem to apply, therefore, only to truly comparable situations.

Second, Paul finally absolutely forbids participation in the temple meals because it means to participate in the demonic. Christians have often been confused as to what constitutes demonic activity. Nonetheless this seems to be a normative prohibition for Christians against all forms of spiritism, witchcraft, astrology, etc.

Again, we may not have apostles, and most Protestants do not think of their ministers as standing in the apostolic succession. But the principle that "those who preach the gospel should receive their living from the gospel" (1 Cor. 9:14) certainly seems applicable to contemporary ministries, since it is corroborated elsewhere in Scripture (e.g., 1 Tim. 5:17–18).

The problem of eating marketplace idol food (1 Cor. 10:23–11:1) presents an especially difficult dimension of this hermeneutical problem. Such food was a matter of indifference—both to God and to Paul. But it was *not* so to others. The same was true of food and drink and the observance of days in Romans 14, and various similar matters in Colossians 2:16–23.

The problem for us is, how does one distinguish matters of indifference from matters that count, a problem that is especially intensified because these things change from culture to culture and from one Christian group to another, just as they appear to have done in the first century. In twentieth-century America alone the list of such matters has included clothing (length of dresses, ties, women's slacks), cosmetics, jewelry, entertainment and recreation (movies, TV, cards, dancing, mixed swimming), athletics, food, and drink. As with those who judged Paul's freedom on the matter of idol food, so it always is that those who think abstinence from any one of these constitutes holiness before God do *not* think of them as matters of indifference.

What, then, makes something a matter of indifference? We suggest the following as guidelines:

1. What the Epistles specifically indicate as matters of indifference may still be regarded as such: food, drink, observance of days, etc.

2. Matters of indifference are not inherently moral, but are cultural—even if it stems from *religious* culture. Matters that tend to differ from culture to culture, therefore, even among genuine

believers, may usually be considered to be matters of indifference (wine and nonwine cultures, e.g.).

3. The sin lists in the Epistles (e.g., Rom. 1:29–30; 1 Cor. 5:11; 6:9–10; 2 Tim. 3:2–4) never include the first-century equivalents of the items we have listed above. Moreover, such equivalents are never included among the various lists of Christian imperatives (e.g, Rom. 12; Eph. 5; Col. 3; etc.).

We know that not all will agree with our assessment. However, according to Romans 14, people on both sides of any of these matters are neither to judge nor disparage one another. The free person is not to flaunt his or her freedom; the person for whom such matters are a deep personal conviction is not to condemn someone else.

The Problem of Cultural Relativity

This is the area where most present-day difficulties—and differences—lie. It is the place where the problem of God's *eternal Word* having been given in *historical particularity* comes most sharply into focus. The problem has the following steps: (1) The Epistles are occasional documents of the first century, conditioned by the language and culture of the first century, which spoke to specific situations in the first-century church. (2) Many of the specific situations in the Epistles are so completely conditioned by their first-century setting that all recognize that they have little or no personal application as a Word for today, except perhaps in the most distant sense of one's deriving some principle from them (e.g., bringing Paul's cloak from Carpus's house in Troas). (3) Other texts are also thoroughly conditioned by their first-century settings, but the Word to them may be translated into new, but comparable settings. (4) It is not possible, therefore, that still others of the texts, although they appear to have comparable particulars, are also conditioned by their first-century setting and need to be translated into new settings or simply left in the first century?

Nearly all Christians, at least to a limited degree, do translate Bible texts into new settings. Without articulating it in precisely this way, this is why twentieth-century evangelicals leave "a little wine for thy stomach's sake" in the first century, do not insist on head-coverings or long hair for women today, and do not practice the "holy kiss." Many of the same evangelicals, however, wince when a woman's teaching in the church (when men are present) is also defended on these grounds, and they become downright indignant when homosexuality is defended on the same grounds.

Frequently there have been some who have tried to reject the idea of cultural relativity altogether, which has led them more or less to argue for a wholesale adoption of first-century culture as the divine norm. But such a rejection is usually only moderately successful. They may keep their daughters home, deny them an education, and have the farther arrange for their marriage, but they usually allow them to learn to read and go out in public without a veil. The point is that it is extremely difficult to be consistent here, precisely because there is no such thing as a divinely ordained culture; cultures are in fact different, not only from the first to the twentieth century, but in every conceivable way in the twentieth century itself.

Rather than rejection, we suggest that the recognition of a degree of cultural relativity is a valid hermeneutical procedure and is an inevitable corollary of the occasional nature of the Epistles. But we also believe that to be valid, one's hermeneutics must operate within recognizable guidelines.

We would suggest the following guidelines, therefore, for distinguishing between items that are culturally relative, on the one hand, and those that transcend their original setting, on the other hand, and have normativeness for all Christians of all times. We do not contend for these guidelines as "once for all given to the saints," but they do reflect our current thinking, and we would encourage further discussion and interaction (Many of these have been worked out in conjunction with our former colleague, David M. Scholer).

1. One should first distinguish between the central core of the message of the Bible and what is dependent upon or peripheral to it. This is not to argue for a canon within the canon (i.e., to elevate certain parts of the New Testament as normative for other parts); it is to safeguard the Gospel from being turned into law through culture or religious custom, on the one hand, and to keep the Gospel itself from changing to reflect every conceivable cultural expression, on the other hand.

Thus the fallenness of all mankind, redemption from that fallenness as God's gracious activity through Christ's death and resurrection, the consummation of that redemptive work by the return of Christ, etc., are clearly part of that central core. But the holy kiss, women's head coverings, and charismatic ministries and gifts seem to be more peripheral.

2. Similarly, one should be prepared to distinguish between what the New Testament itself sees as inherently moral and what is not. Those items that are inherently moral are therefore absolute and abide for every culture; those that are not inherently moral are therefore cultural expressions and may change from culture to culture.

Paul's sin lists, for example, never contain cultural items. Some of the sins may indeed be more prevalent in one culture than another, but there are never situations in which they may be considered Christian attitudes or actions. Thus adultery, idolatry, drunkenness, homosexual activity, thievery, greed etc. (1 Cor. 6:9–10) are *always* wrong. This does not mean that Christians have not from time to time been guilty of any of these. But they are not viable moral choices. Paul, by inspiration of the Spirit, says, "And that is what some of you *were*. But you were washed, . . ."

On the other hand, footwashing, exchanging the holy kiss, eating marketplace idol food, women having a head covering when praying or prophesying, Paul's personal preference for celibacy, or a woman's teaching in the church are not *inherently* moral matters. They become so only by their use or abuse in given contexts, when such use or abuse involves disobedience or lack of love.

3. One must make special note of items where the New Testament itself has a uniform and consistent witness and where it reflects differences. The following are examples of matters on which the New Testament bears uniform witness: love as the Christian's basic ethical response, a nonretaliation personal ethic, the wrongness of strife, hatred, murder, stealing, practicing homosexuality, drunkenness, and sexual immorality of all kinds.

On the other hand, the New Testament does not appear to be uniform on such matters as women's ministries in the church (see Rom. 16:1–2, where Phoebe is a "deacon" in Cenchrea; Rom. 16:7, where Junia—*not* Junias, which is an unknown masculine name—is named among the apostles; Rom. 16:3, where Priscilla is Paul's fellow worker—the same word used of Apollos in 1 Cor. 3:9; Phil. 4:2–3; and 1 Cor. 11:5 over against 1 Tim. 2:12 [and 1 Cor. 14:34–35, which is suspect textually]), the political evaluation of Rome (see Rom. 13:1–5 and 1 Peter 2:13–14 over against Rev. 13–18), the retention of one's wealth (Luke 12:33;

18:22 over against 1 Tim. 6:17–19), or eating food offered to idols (1 Cor. 10:23–29 over against Acts 15:29; Rev. 2:14, 20). By the way, if any of these suggestions caused an emotional reaction on your part, you might ask yourself why.

Sound exegesis may cause us to see greater uniformity than appears to be the case now. For example, in the matter of food offered to idols, one can make a good exegetical case for the Greek word in Acts and Revelation to refer to going to the temples to eat such food. In this case the attitude would be consistent with Paul's in 1 Corinthians 10:14–22. However, precisely because these other matters appear to be more cultural than moral, one should not be disturbed by a lack of uniformity. Likewise, one should not pursue exegesis only as a means of finding uniformity, even at the cost of common sense or the plain meaning of the text.

4. It is important to be able to distinguish within the New Testament itself between principle and specific application. It is possible for a New Testament writer to support a relative application by an absolute principle and in so doing not make the application absolute. Thus in 1 Corinthians 11:2–16, for example, Paul appeals to the divine order of creation (v. 3) and establishes the principle that one should do nothing to distract from the glory of God (especially by breaking convention) when the community is at worship (vv. 7, 10). The specific application, however, seems to be relative, since Paul repeatedly appeals to "custom" or "nature" (vv. 6, 13–14, 16).

This leads us to suggest that one may legitimately ask at such specific applications, "Would this have been an issue for us had we never encountered it in the New Testament documents?" In Western cultures the failure to cover a woman's head (especially her hair) with a full-length veil would probably create no difficulties at all. In fact, if she were literally to obey the text in most American churches, she would thereby almost certainly abuse the "spirit" of the text. But with a little thinking one can imagine some kinds of dress—both male and female—that would be so out of place as to create the same kind of disruption of worship.

5. It might also be important, as much as one is able to do this with care, to determine the cultural options open to any New Testament writer. The degree to which a New Testament writer agrees with a cultural situation in which there is *only one option* increases the possibility of the cultural relativity of such a position.

Thus, for example, homosexuality was both affirmed and condemned by writers in antiquity, yet the New Testament takes a singular position against it. On the other hand, attitudes toward slavery as a system or toward the status and role of women were basically singular; no one denounced slavery as an evil, and women were held to be basically inferior to men. The New Testament writers also do not denounce slavery as an evil; on the other hand, they generally move well beyond the attitudes toward women held by their contemporaries. But in either case, to the degree to which they reflect the prevalent cultural attitudes in these matters they are thereby reflecting the only cultural option in the world around them.

6. One must keep alert to possible cultural differences between the first and twentieth centuries that are sometimes not immediately obvious. For example, to determine the role of women in the twentieth-century church, one should take into account that there were few educational opportunities for women in the first century, whereas such education is the expected norm in our society. This may affect our understanding of such texts as 1 Timothy 2:9–15. Likewise, a participatory democracy is a radically different thing from the government of which Paul speaks in Romans 13:1–7. It is expected in a participatory democracy that bad laws are to be changed and bad officials are to be ousted. That has to affect how one brings Romans 13 into twentieth-century America.

7. One must finally exercise Christian charity at this point. Christians need to recognize the difficulties, open the line of communication with one another, start by trying to define some principles, and finally have love for and a willingness to ask forgiveness from those with whom they differ.

Before we conclude this discussion, it may be helpful for us to see how these guidelines apply to two current issues: the ministry of women and homosexuality—especially since some who are arguing for women's ministries are using some of the same arguments to support homosexuality as a valid Christian alternative.

The question of women's role in the church as a teacher or proclaimer of the Word basically focuses on two texts: 1 Corinthians 14:34–35 and 1 Timothy 2:11–12. In both cases "silence" and "submission" are enjoined—although in neither case is the submission necessarily to her husband—and in 1 Timothy 2 she is not permitted to teach or to "have authority over" a man. Full compliance with this text in the twentieth century would seem to rule out not only a woman's preaching and teaching in the local church, but it also would seem to forbid her writing books on biblical subjects that men might read, teaching Bible or related subjects (including religious education) in Christian colleges or Bible institutes where men are in her classes, and teaching men in missionary situations. But those who argue against women teaching in the contemporary church seldom carry the interpretation this far. And almost always they make the matters about clothing in the preceding verse (1 Tim. 2:9) to be culturally relative.

On the other hand, that 1 Timothy 2:11–12 might be culturally relative can be supported first of all by exegesis of all three of the Pastoral Epistles. Certain women were troublesome in the church at Ephesus (1 Tim. 5:11–15; 2 Tim. 3:6–9) and they appear to have been a major part of the cause of the false teachers' making headway there. Since women are found teaching (Acts 18:26) and prophesying (Acts 21:8; 1 Cor. 11:5) elsewhere in the New Testament, it is altogether likely that 1 Timothy 2:11–12 speaks to a local problem. In any case, the guidelines above support the possibility that the prohibition in 1 Timothy 2:11–12 is culturally relative.

The question of homosexuality, however, is considerably different. In this case the guidelines stand against its being culturally relative. The whole Bible has a consistent witness against homosexual activity as being morally wrong.

In recent years some people have argued that the homosexuality that the New Testament speaks against is that in which people abuse others and that private monogamous homosexuality between consenting adults is a different matter. They argue that on exegetical grounds it cannot be proved that such homosexuality is forbidden. It is also argued that culturally these are twentieth-century options not available in the first century. Therefore, they would argue that some of our guidelines (e.g., 5, 6) open the possibility that the New Testament prohibitions against homosexuality are also culturally relative, and they would further argue that some of the guidelines are not true or are irrelevant.

The problem with this argument, however, is that it does not hold up exegetically or historically. The homosexuality Paul had in view in Romans 1:24–28 is clearly *not* of the "abusive" type; it is homosexuality of choice between men and women. Furthermore,

Paul's word *homosexual* in 1 Corinthians 6:9 literally means genital homosexuality between males. Since the Bible as a whole witnesses against homosexuality, and invariably includes it in moral contexts, and since it simply has not been proved that the options for homosexuality differ today from those of the first century, there seem to be no valid grounds for seeing it as a culturally relative matter.

The Problem of Task Theology

We noted in the last chapter that much of the theology in the Epistles is task oriented and therefore is not systematically presented. However, this must not be taken to mean that one cannot in fact systematically present the theology that is either expressed in or derived from statements in the Epistles. To the contrary, this is one of the mandatory tasks of the Bible student. He or she must always be forming—and "reforming"—a biblical theology on the basis of sound exegesis. And very often, we readily acknowledge, a given writer's theology is found in his presuppositions and implications as well as in his explicit statements.

All we want to do here is to raise some cautions as one goes about the task of theology, cautions that are the direct result of the occasional nature of the Epistles.

1. Because of their occasional nature, we must be content at times with some limitations to our theological understanding. For example, to get the Corinthians to see how absurd it was for them to have two brothers going to the pagan court for a judgment, Paul states that Christians will someday judge both the world and angels (1 Cor. 6:2–3). But beyond that the texts say nothing. Thus we may affirm as a part of Christian eschatology (our understanding of the final consummation) that Christians will in fact exercise judgments at the Eschaton. But we simply do not know what that means or how it is going to be worked out. *Beyond the affirmation itself, everything else is mere speculation.*

Similarly, in 1 Corinthians 10:16–17 Paul argues *from* the nature of the Corinthians' own participation in the Lord's Supper that they may not likewise participate in the meals at the idol temple. What Paul says about that participation seems indeed to go beyond the theology of the Supper found in most of evangelical Protestantism. Here is not mere remembrance, but actual participation in the Lord himself. From other New Testament texts we may further argue that the participation was by means of the Spirit and the benefits came by faith. But even here we are going outside the immediate texts to express Paul's understanding in a theological way, and many would not agree with our choice of outside texts. Our point is that we simply are *not* told what the precise nature of that participation is nor how the benefits come to the believer. We all *want* to know, but our knowledge is defective precisely because of the occasional nature of the statements. What is said beyond what the texts themselves reveal cannot have the same biblical or hermeneutical import as what can be said on the basis of solid exegesis. We are merely affirming, therefore, that in Scripture God has given us all we *need,* but not necessarily all that we *want.*

2. Sometimes our theological problems with the Epistles derive from the fact that we are asking *our* questions of texts that by their occasional nature are answering only *their* questions. When we ask them to speak directly to the question of abortion, or of remarriage, or of infant baptism, we want them to answer the questions of a later time. Sometimes they may do that, but often they will not, because the question had not been raised back then.

There is a clear example of this within the New Testament itself. On the question of divorce Paul says, "not I, but the Lord" (1 Cor. 7:10), meaning Jesus himself spoke to that question. But to the question raised in a Greek environment as to whether a believer should divorce a pagan partner, Jesus apparently had no occasion to speak. The problem simply lay outside his own Jewish culture. But Paul did have to speak to it, so he said "I, not the Lord" (v. 12). One of the problems, of course, is that we ourselves do not possess Paul's apostolic authority nor his inspiration. The only way we can therefore speak to such questions is on the basis of a whole biblical theology, that includes our understanding of creation, the Fall, redemption, and the final consummation. That is, we must attempt to bring a biblical worldview to the problem. But no proof texting, when there are no immediately relevant texts!

These, then, are some of our hermeneutical suggestions for reading and interpreting the Epistles. Our immediate aim is for greater precision and consistency; our greater aim is to call us all to greater obedience to what we do hear and understand.

5

The Old Testament Narratives: Their Proper Use

The Bible contains more of the type of literature called "narrative" than it does of any other literary type. For example, over 40 percent of the Old Testament is narrative. Since the Old Testament itself constitutes three-quarters of the bulk of the Bible, it is not surprising that the single most common type of literature in the entire Bible is narrative. The following Old Testament books are largely or entirely composed of narrative material: Genesis, Joshua, Judges, Ruth, 1 and 2 Samuel, 1 and 2 Kings, 1 and 2 Chronicles, Ezra, Nehemiah, Daniel, Jonah, and Haggai. Moreover, Exodus, Numbers, Jeremiah, Ezekiel, Isaiah, and Job also contain substantial narrative portions. In the New Testament, large portions of the four Gospels and almost all of the Acts are also narrative.

It is our presupposition that the Holy Spirit knew what he was doing when he inspired so much of the Bible in the form of narrative. We think it is obvious that this type of literature serves God's revelatory purpose well. How it serves his purposes and how we are to make good and proper use of it in our service to God is what this chapter is about.

The Nature of Narratives

What Narratives Are

Narratives are stories. Although from time to time we use the word *story* to describe them, we prefer the word *narrative* because *story* has come to mean something that is fictional, as in "bedtime story" or "a likely story." It also tends to mean a *single* story with a single set of characters and a single plot. The Bible, on the other hand, contains what we often hear called *God's story*—a story that is utterly true, crucially important, and often complex. It is a magnificent story, grander than the greatest epic, richer in plot and more significant in its characters and descriptions than any humanly composed story could ever be. So for those portions of this great divine story that have a story form, the term *narrative* is preferred in technical usage since it is a more objective, less prejudicial term.

Bible narratives tell us about things that happened—but not just any things. Their purpose is to show God at work in his creation and among his people. The narratives glorify him, help us to understand and appreciate him, and give us a picture of his providence and protection. At the same time, they also provide illustrations of many other lessons important to our lives.

All narratives have a plot and characters (whether divine, human, animal, vegetable, or whatever). The Old Testament narratives, however, have plots that are part of a special overall plot, and have a special cast of characters, the most special of whom is God himself.

Three Levels of Narratives

It will help you as you read and study Old Testament narratives to realize that the story is being told, in effect, on three levels. The *top level* is that of the whole universal plan of God worked out through his creation. Key aspects of the plot at this top level are the initial creation itself; the fall of humanity; the power and ubiquity of sin; the need for redemption; and Christ's incarnation and sacrifice. This top level is often referred to as the "story of redemption" or "redemptive history."

Key aspects of the *middle level* center on Israel: the call of Abraham; the establishment of an Abrahamic lineage through the patriarchs; the enslaving of Israel in Egypt; God's deliverance from bondage and the conquest of the promised land of Canaan; Israel's frequent sins and increasing disloyalty; God's patient protection and pleading with them; the ultimate destruction of northern Israel and then of Judah; and the restoration of the holy people after the Exile.

Then there is the *bottom level*. Here are found all the hundreds of *individual* narratives that make up the other two levels: the narrative of how Joseph's brothers sell him to Arab caravaneers heading for Egypt; the narrative of Gideon's doubting God and testing him via the fleece; the narrative of David's adultery with Bathsheba; et al.

Note this carefully: every individual Old Testament narrative (bottom level) is at least a part of the greater narrative of Israel's history in the world (the middle level), which in turn is a part of the ultimate narrative of God's creation and his redemption of it (the top level). This ultimate narrative goes beyond the Old Testament through the New Testament. You will not fully do justice to any individual narrative without recognizing its part within the other two. Sometimes a narrative is made up of a group of shorter, individual narratives. Such a narrative may be referred to as a "compound narrative." For all practical purposes, what we say about the three levels of narratives is not affected by the recognition that compound narratives exist throughout the Bible.

We hope that an awareness of this hierarchy of narratives will help you to be more Christian in your application of Old Testament narratives in your own life and in your service to others. When Jesus taught that the Scriptures ". . . bear witness to me" (John 5:27– 29), he was obviously not speaking about every short individual passage of the Old Testament. Those individual passages, including narratives, that are messianic or otherwise identified in the New Testament as typological of Christ (cf. 1 Cor. 10:4) are an important part of the Old Testament, but constitute only a small portion of its total revelation. However, Jesus spoke of the ultimate, top level of the narrative, in which his atonement was the central act, and the subjection of all creation to him was the climax of its plot. Thus he taught that the Scriptures in their entirety bear witness to him and focus toward his loving lordship.

What we have, then, are individual narratives (sometimes of a compound nature) within a major narrative within an ultimate narrative. Some of the compound narratives are composed of a large number of shorter individual narratives. This is typical of all stories that have subplots and therefore is not surprising. In the New Testament we have individual narratives (Luke-Acts), within the ultimate narrative of God's whole story as it is told in the Bible. The Old Testament is similar. For example, the large compound narrative that we call the "Joseph narrative" (Gen. 37–50) contains many shorter individual narratives about Joseph, such as the narrative of his first dreams (Gen. 37:5–11), the narrative of his rise and fall as a slave of Potiphar (Gen. 39), the narrative of his burial of Jacob in Canaan (Gen. 50:1–14), etc. Yet all are part of the great, entire Bible narrative.

There is nothing wrong with studying any individual narrative all by itself. Indeed, that is highly desirable. But for the fullest sense, you must finally see that individual narrative within its larger contexts.

What Narratives Are Not

1. Old Testament narratives are not just stories about people who lived in Old Testament times. They are first and foremost stories about what *God* did to and through those people. In contrast to human narratives, the Bible is composed especially of divine narratives. God is the hero of the story—if it is in the Bible. Characters, events, developments, plot and story climaxes all occur, but behind these, God is the supreme "protagonist" or leading decisive character in all narratives.

2. Old Testament narratives are not allegories or stories filled with hidden meanings. But there may be aspects of narratives that are not easy to understand. The ways that God works in history, the ways he influences human actions and implements his own will via human beings (sometimes contrary to people's own desire; cf. Gen. 50:20) are not always comprehensible to us. We are often not told precisely all that God did in a certain situation that caused it to happen the way the Old Testament reports it. And even when we *are* told what he did, we are not always told *how* or *why* he did it.

In other words, narratives do not answer all our questions about a given issue. They are limited in their focus, and give us only one part of the overall picture of what God is doing in history. We have to learn to be satisfied with that limited understanding, and restrain our curiosity at many points, or else we will end up trying to read between the lines so much that we end up reading *into* stories things that are not there, making allegories of what are in fact historical accounts. As is the case with parables (chap. 8), narratives can be abused in this manner.

Reading *into* stories is what happens when people identify supernatural events in the biblical narratives as the result of such things as the intervention of unidentified flying objects, or time machines from centuries future to our own, or supposed ancient secret scientific discoveries since lost to human knowledge. It is true that the Bible itself does not say *how* God did most of the miraculous things he brought to pass. But insatiable curiosity and desire to understand what the Bible has excluded, that is, exactly how such things occurred, can drive some people to accept absurd and farfetched explanations. A fascination with and awe of pseudoscience leads them to posit pseudoscientific explanations for the miraculous events of Scripture. God simply has not told us in the Bible how he did all that he did. A lust for an understanding of the process can result in explanations so wild and incompatible with the Bible narratives that they are in fact no explanations at all.

3. Old Testament narratives do not always teach *directly*. They emphasize God's nature and revelation in special ways that legal or doctrinal portions of the Bible never can, by allowing us vicariously to live through events and experiences rather than simply learning *about* the issues involved in those events and experiences. Modern clichés like "Don't knock it until you've tried it," or "To really understand something you have to experience it," are not always accurate. But they do contain a kernel of truth; knowledge sometimes comes better and affects behavior more permanently when it results from being involved *in* something. As you follow closely the action of Old Testament narratives, you naturally become involved vicariously, as you do in reading any story, no matter how much its participants differ from you and no matter how different their circumstances are. Narratives thus give you a kind of "hands on" knowledge of God's work in his world, and though this knowledge is secondary rather than primary, it is nevertheless a real knowledge that can help shape your behavior.

If you are a Christian, the Old Testament is *your* spiritual history. The promises and calling of God to Israel are *your* historical promises and calling (Gal. 3:29). In the best, most useful and practical sense, God allows you to follow the events he brought to pass in those past times, by his having inspired men and women to record them in the way that he wanted them recorded.

Although the Old Testament narratives do not necessarily teach directly, they often *illustrate* what is taught directly and categorically elsewhere. This represents an *implicit* kind of teaching, which in cooperation with the corresponding *explicit* teachings of Scripture, is highly effective in generating the sort of learning experience that the Holy Spirit can use positively. For example, in the narrative of David's adultery with Bathsheba (2 Sam. 11) you will not find any such statement as, "In committing adultery David did wrong." You are expected to know that adultery is wrong, because this is taught explicitly already in the Bible (Exod. 20:14). The narrative illustrates its harm to the personal life of King David and to his ability to rule. The narrative does not systematically teach about adultery and could not be used as the sole basis for such teaching. But as one illustration of the effects of adultery in a particular case, it conveys a powerful message that can imprint itself on the mind of the careful reader in a way that direct, categorical teaching might not do.

4. Each individual narrative or episode within a narrative does not necessarily have a moral all its own. Narratives cannot be interpreted atomistically, as if every statement, every event, every description could, independently of the others, have a special message for the reader. In fact, even in fairly lengthy narratives all the component parts of the narrative can work together to impress upon the reader a single major point. There is an overall drift or movement to a narrative, a kind of superstructure that makes the point, usually a single point.

In this way, narratives are analogous to parables (see chap. 8) in that the whole unit gives the message, not the separate individual parts. The punch, the effect, the impact, the persuasiveness—all come from the entire sequence of the events related. Many individual elements combine to constitute the narrative and to provide God's revelation via the narrative. To try to find a significance for each single bit of data or each single event in the narrative will not work. You have to evaluate the narrative as a unit, not atomistically.

Principles for Interpreting Narratives

To illustrate the points made in the discussion above we have selected two major Old Testament narratives for analysis in this chapter. But first, the following ten principles should help you to avoid obvious errors in interpretation whenever you seek to exegete these and other stories.

1. An Old Testament narrative usually does not directly teach a doctrine.
2. An Old Testament narrative usually illustrates a doctrine or doctrines taught propositionally elsewhere.

3. Narratives record what happened—not necessarily what should have happened or what ought to happen every time. Therefore, not every narrative has an individual identifiable moral of the story.

4. What people do in narratives is not necessarily a good example for us. Frequently, it is just the opposite.

5. Most of the characters in Old Testament narratives are far from perfect and their actions are, too.

6. We are not always told at the end of a narrative whether what happened was good or bad. We are expected to be able to judge that on the basis of what God has taught us directly and categorically elsewhere in the Scripture.

7. *All* narratives are selective and incomplete. Not all the relevant details are always given (cf. John 21:25). What does appear in the narrative is everything that the inspired author thought important for us to know.

8. Narratives are not written to answer all our theological questions. They have particular, specific limited purposes and deal with certain issues, leaving others to be dealt with elsewhere, in other ways.

9. Narratives may teach either explicitly (by clearly stating something) or implicitly (by clearly implying something without actually stating it).

10. In the final analysis, God is the hero of all biblical narratives.

Examples of Narrative Interpretation

The Joseph Narrative

The large block of narrative material that we call the Joseph narrative occupies chapters 37 and 39–50 of the book of Genesis. Read through those chapters and you will see that Joseph is the central *human* character at nearly every point. Indeed, he dominates the story.

We read of Joseph's rather haughty, critical style (chap. 37) stemming in part, perhaps, from his father's favoritism (37:3). Joseph's insistence on telling his arrogant dreams of superiority does not help his situation within the family (37:10, 11). The brothers sell Joseph into slavery, and trick their father Jacob into thinking that Joseph is dead. Sold as a slave in Egypt, Joseph becomes a successful administrator for Potiphar (chap. 39). Why? Was it because of his innate administrative skills? Hardly. The Bible very clearly identifies the reason: "The LORD was with Joseph. . . . The LORD was with him, and . . . the LORD caused all that he did to prosper. . . . The LORD blessed the Egyptian's house for Joseph's sake; the blessing of the LORD was upon all that he had" (Gen. 39:2–5 RSV). Whatever Joseph's managerial skills may have been, they clearly played a secondary role to *God's* intervention in his life. Unfairly jailed, Joseph rose to inmate-administrator. Why? The Bible again leaves no doubt: "The LORD was with Joseph, and showed him loyalty, and gave him favor" (39:21; cf. v. 23).

The inspired narrator is leaving no room for doubt as to the hero of the story or the moral of the story. God is the hero. And the moral is that God was with Joseph. If you seek to learn from this Joseph narrative, and you try to find a hero other than God, who will it be? Will it be Jacob, who shows favoritism among his own children? Will it be Potiphar or his wife, both unfair to Joseph? Will it be the unnamed Egyptian jailer? Will it be Joseph himself, the overconfident self-centered young man who seems to get into trouble so easily? If you choose any of these, you are sure to misplace the emphasis of the narrative, thus drawing attention away from God's sovereign guidance and manipulation of events.

And what of the moral of the story? Will you make the mistake, as so many preachers and teachers do, of looking for a self-contained lesson for living in each event in Joseph's life? If so, you may conclude that this narrative teaches: "Don't tell your dreams to others, lest you get in big trouble for it," or "Even slaves can get ahead if they pay attention to their administrative skills," or "You'll be better off in jail if you get some business experience before being arrested," or "Foreigners rise faster in positions of authority than natives do."

In other words, if you look for something that Joseph was or did that Christians today are supposed to copy to get a blessing, you will not find any such thing in the narrative. The narrative is telling you what God did with an *unlikely* candidate for success. It does not contain any rules for getting ahead in business or life in general. Joseph goes from bad to worse, and is in jail for many years before God (not Joseph) arranges his release.

Joseph's release from prison, because of his God-given dream interpretation skills (Gen. 40–41), his exaltation to power and the opportunity to help his family during the famine (Gen. 41–50), and the various details of the smaller narratives that make up the Joseph narrative as a whole, do not, in fact, point to anything intrinsic about Joseph or anything exemplary about his actions. You will look in vain for any other moral than the one the Bible itself supplies: "God was with Joseph." The entire process of Joseph's fall and rise to power was God's doing. Even his brothers' evil intent toward him was used in God's strategy. As Joseph himself says to his brothers: "Am I in the place of God? As for you, you meant evil against me; but God meant it for good, to bring it about that many people should be kept alive, as they are today" (50:19–20).

The entire chain of events and smaller narratives making up the larger compound Joseph narrative were part of a greater narrative still: God's plan for Israel as a nation, and for the preservation of Canaanites, Egyptians, and others with them during this time of famine. Egypt was the place where God built up and multiplied his people, preparing them for the exodus and conquest that he, God, would use to give them the land of Canaan as he had promised to Abraham.

Joseph's lifestyle, personal qualities, or actions do not tell us anything from which general moral principles may be derived. If you think you have found any, you are finding what *you* want to find in the text; you are *not* interpreting the text.

Joseph himself is eventually granted the ability to recognize that God has brought all the events of the Joseph narrative to pass for a greater purpose. Late in life he says to his brothers: "I am about to die; but God will visit you and bring you up out of this land to the land which he swore to Abraham, Isaac, and Jacob."

The focus is on God. He can accomplish what he wills. Using such unlikely vehicles as Joseph, his family, and the Pharaoh, God preserved many people and began to create for himself a special people. That is where we find the moral of the story, focusing on God's graciousness and providence, and leading us to be respectful of his ways and confident in his provision.

The Ruth Narrative

The book of Ruth is brief and self-contained, its plot easy to follow, and its main characters are not hard to get to know. This makes it a good candidate to illustrate the principles learned above, with a special emphasis on point 9 (above) of the list of principles: we want here to help you see that the Holy Spirit's teaching through narrative can be either *explicit* or *implicit*. Explicit teaching is that which the inspired narrator actually says ("God was with Joseph"). Implicit teaching is that which is clearly present in the story, but not stated in so many words. You must see it implied in the story, rather than just being able to read it right off the page.

Being able to distinguish what is explicitly taught can be fairly easy. Being able to distinguish what is implicitly taught can be difficult. It requires skill, hard work, caution, and a prayerful respect for the Holy Spirit's care in inspiring the text. After all, you want to read things *out of* the narrative, rather than *into* it.

Ruth's story may be summarized as follows. The widow Ruth, a Moabite, emigrates from Moab to Bethlehem with her Israelite mother-in-law, Naomi, who is also a widow (Ruth 1). Ruth gleans leftover grain in the field of Boaz, who befriends her, having heard of her faith and her kindness to Naomi, who is a relative of his (Ruth 2). At Naomi's suggestion, Ruth lets Boaz know that she loves him and hopes he would be willing to marry her (Ruth 3). Boaz undertakes the legal procedures necessary to marry Ruth and to protect the family property rights of her late husband, Mahlon. The birth of Ruth and Boaz's first son, Obed, is a great consolation to Naomi. Eventually, Obed's grandson turned out to be King David (Ruth 4).

If you are not familiar with the Ruth narrative, we suggest that you read the book through at least twice. Then, go back and take particular note of the following *implicit* points that the narrative makes.

1. The narrative tells us that Ruth converted to faith in the Lord, the God of Israel. It does this by reporting Ruth's words to Naomi, "Your people will be my people and your God my God" (1:17), rather than by telling us "Ruth was converted." We are expected to be able to recognize that because she took the Lord as her God, she was converted. The narrative also implicitly confirms Ruth's conversion as genuine and not just lip service, by reporting these words of Ruth: "May the LORD deal with me, be it ever so severely, if . . ." (1:17). These words clearly imply, though they do not state outright, that Ruth, a Moabite who once worshiped the gods of the Moabites, now believes in and lives by the standards of Yahweh, the Lord, Israel's God. There is no doubt that the narrative

tells us that Ruth converted to faith in the true God, even though this is nowhere explicitly stated.

2. The narrative tells us implicitly that Boaz was a righteous Israelite who kept the Mosaic Law, though many other Israelites did not. Where does it say that? Look carefully at 2:3–13, 22; 3:10–12; and 4:9–10. These portions of the narrative make clear that Boaz, by his speech, sees himself as loyal to and under the authority of the Lord, that Boaz is keeping the law of gleaning promulgated in Leviticus 19:9–10 (Ruth fits both categories of that law—she is poor *and* an alien), that he is keeping the law of redemption as promulgated in Leviticus 25:23–24, and that not all Israelites were so loyal to the law—indeed it was dangerous to glean in the fields of people who did not obey the law's gleaning obligations (2:22).

Again, we get a lot of important information *implicitly* from the narrative. This information is valuable to us, and helps us follow the narrative and interpret it. And yet it is information that is not made available to us *explicitly*.

3. The narrative tells us implicitly that this story is part of the background to the ancestry of King David—and by extension, therefore, to Jesus Christ. Look at 4:17–21. The brief genealogy in verse 17, and the fuller genealogy in verses 18–21 both end with the name David. This David is obviously the focus, the endpoint of this portion of the narrative. We know from several other genealogical lists in the Bible that this David is King David, the first great Israelite king. We also know from the New Testament genealogies that Jesus, humanly speaking, was descended from David. Ruth, then, was David's great-grandmother, and an ancestor of Jesus! This is an important part of the teaching of the entire narrative. It is a story not just about Ruth and Boaz in terms of their faithfulness to the Lord, but also in terms of their place in Israel's history. They had no way of knowing it, but these were people whom the Lord would use in the ancestry of David and "David's son," Jesus.

4. The narrative tells us implicitly that Bethlehem was an exceptional town during the Judges period by reason of the faithfulness of its citizenry. To spot this implicit thrust in the narrative is not easy or automatic. It requires a careful reading of the whole narrative, with special attention to the words and actions of *all* the participants in the story. It also requires a knowledge of what

things were generally like in other parts of Israel in those days in contrast to what they were like specifically in Bethlehem. The latter knowledge depends upon a familiarity with the main events and themes of the book of Judges, since Ruth is directly related to that time period by the narrator (1:1). If you have had the opportunity to read Judges carefully, you will have noticed that the Judges period (about 1240–1030 B.C.) was generally marked by such practices as widespread idolatry, syncretism (mixing features of pagan religions with those of Israel's true faith), social injustice, social turmoil, intertribal rivalries, sexual immorality, and other indications of unfaithfulness. The picture presented to us in the book of Judges is hardly a happy one, though there are individual cases where God, in his mercy, benefits Israel, or tribes within Israel, in spite of the general pattern of rebellion against him.

What in Ruth tells us that Bethlehem is an exception to the general picture of unfaithfulness? Practically everything except 2:22, which implies that not all Bethlehemites practice the gleaning laws as they should. Otherwise, the picture is remarkably consistent. The words of the characters themselves show just how consciously the people of this town manifest their allegiance to the Lord.

Remember that all the characters mentioned in the narrative, except for Ruth and her sister Orpah, are citizens of Bethlehem. Consider Naomi; whether in times of great bitterness (1:8–9, 13, 20–21) or in times of happiness (1:6; 2:19–20) she recognizes and submits to the Lord's will. Moreover, Boaz consistently shows himself by his words to be a worshiper and follower of the Lord (2:11–12; 3:10, 13), and his actions throughout confirm his words.

Even the way people greet one another shows a high degree of conscious allegiance to the Lord (2:4). Likewise, the elders of the town in their blessings on the marriage and its offspring (4:11–12), and the women of the town in their blessing on Naomi (4:14) show their faith. Their acceptance of the converted Moabite, Ruth, is further implicit testimony to their faith.

Finally, the inspired narrator attributes significant events to the Lord (1:6; 4:13)—though we have no way of knowing for sure if the narrator was a Bethlehemite or not, and it is not unexpected that the narrator would stand apart from the general unfaithfulness of the day.

The point is that one cannot read the narrative carefully (and in comparison with Judges) and not see again and again how exceptional Bethlehem was! Nowhere does the narrative actually say, "Bethlehem was a town remarkable for its piety in those days." But that is exactly what the narrative tells us—in ways just as forceful and convincing as the outright words could ever be.

These examples, we hope, will demonstrate that careful attention to details and to the overall movement of a narrative and its context are necessary if its full meaning is to be obtained. What is implicit can be every bit as significant as what is explicit.

Warning

Implicit does not mean secret! You will get into all sorts of trouble if you try to find meanings in the text that you think God has "hidden" in the narrative. That is not at all what is meant by *implicit*. *Implicit* means that the message is capable of being understood from what is said, though it is not stated in so many words. Your task is not to ferret out things that cannot be understood by everyone. Your task is to take note of *all* that the narrative actually tells you—directly and indirectly, but *never* mystically or privately. If you are not able confidently to express to others something taught implicitly, so that they can understand it and get the point, too, you probably are misreading the text. What the Holy Spirit has inspired is of benefit for *all* believers. Discern and relay what the story recognizably has in it—do not make up a new story (2 Peter 2:3)!

Some Final Cautions

Why is it that people so often find things in Bible narratives that are not really there—read into the Bible their own notions rather than read out of the Bible what God wants them to know? There are three main reasons. First, they are desperate—desperate for information that will help them, that will be of personal value, that will apply to their own situation. Second, they are impatient; they want their answers now, from *this* book, from *this* chapter. Third, they wrongly expect that everything in the Bible applies directly as instruction for their own individual lives. The Bible is a great resource. It contains all that a Christian really needs in terms of guidance from God for living. But it does not *always* contain answers as specific and personal as some people would wish, and it does not contain all its information in every chapter of every book! Too impatient to find God's will from the Bible as a whole, people make mistakes—they allow themselves to misinterpret individual parts of the Scriptures.

So that you might avoid this tendency, we list here eight of the most common errors of interpretation that people commit in looking for answers from parts of the Bible. While all of these apply to narratives, they are not limited to them.

1. *Allegorizing*. Instead of concentrating on the clear meaning, people relegate the text to merely reflecting another meaning beyond the text. There *are* allegorical portions of Scripture (e.g., Ezekiel 23 or parts of Revelation) but none of the scriptural allegories is simple narrative.

2. *Decontextualizing*. Ignoring the full historical and literary contexts, and often the individual narrative, people concentrate on small units only and thus miss interpretational clues. If you decontextualize enough, you can make almost any part of Scripture say anything you want it to.

3. *Selectivity*. This is analogous to decontextualizing. It involves picking and choosing specific words and phrases to concentrate on, ignoring the others, and ignoring the overall sweep of the passage being studied. Instead of balancing the parts and the whole, it ignores some of the parts and the whole entirely.

4. *False Combination*. This approach combines elements from here and there in a passage and makes a point out of their combination, even though the elements themselves are not directly connected in the passage itself. An extreme example of this all too common interpretational error would be the conclusion that one's real enemies are in the church rather than outside the church because in Psalm 23 David says that he will dwell in God's house forever, and that God has prepared him a table in the presence of his enemies. (The enemies must therefore be in God's house along with David, or else he could not be in their presence.)

5. *Redefinition*. When the plain meaning of the text leaves people cold, producing no immediate spiritual delight or saying something they do not want to hear, they are often tempted to redefine it to mean something else. For example,

they take Jesus' words, "Woe to you who are rich . . ." and "Woe to you when all people speak well of you . . ." (Luke 6:24, 26) and redefine them from their plain meaning to "Woe to you who love money so much you have renounced your faith in God" and "Woe to you who have become atheists in order to have cheap praise from worldly infidels." That is, these sayings are redefined in such a way that they are narrow enough no longer to be a threat to the people doing the redefinition.

6. *Extracanonical authority.* By using some sort of special external key to the Scriptures, usually a set of doctrines or a book that claims to reveal scriptural truths not otherwise knowable, people suppose that they can unlock the mysteries of the Bible. Cults usually operate on the basis of an extracanonical authority, treating the Bible somewhat like a series of riddles needing a special knowledge to solve.

7. *Moralizing.* This is the assumption that principles for living can be derived from all passages. The moralizing reader in effect asks the question, "What is the moral of this story?" at the end of every individual narrative. An example would be, "What can we learn about handling adversity from how the Israelites endured their years as slaves in Egypt?" The fallacy of this approach is that it ignores the fact that the narratives were written to show the progress of God's history of redemption, not to illustrate principles. They are historical narratives, not illustrative narratives.

8. *Personalizing.* Also known as individualizing, this is reading Scripture in a way that supposes that any or all parts apply to you or your group in a way that they do not apply to everyone else. People tend to be self-centered, even when reading the Bible. When the big picture of God's redemptive history fails to satisfy, they may fall prey to the temptation to look for something that will satisfy their personal needs, cravings, or problems. They can forget that all parts of the Bible are intended for everyone, not just them. Examples of personalizing would be, "The story of Balaam's talking donkey reminds me that I talk too much." Or, "The story of the building of the temple is God's way of telling us that we have to construct a new church building."

Perhaps the single most useful bit of caution we can give you about reading and learning from narratives is this: Do not be a monkey-see-monkey-do reader of the Bible. No Bible narrative was written specifically about *you*. The Joseph narrative is about Joseph, specifically how God did things through him—it is not a narrative directly about you. The Ruth narrative glorifies God's protection and benefit for Ruth and the Bethlehemites—not you. *You* can always learn a great deal from these narratives, and from all the Bible's narratives, but you can never assume that God expects you to do exactly the same thing that Bible characters did, or to have the same things happen to you that happened to them. For further discussion on this point, see chapter 6.

Bible characters are sometimes good, sometimes evil, sometimes wise, and sometimes foolish. They are sometimes punished, sometimes shown mercy, sometimes well off, and sometimes miserable.

Your task is to learn God's word from the narratives about them, not to try to do everything that was done in the Bible. Just because someone in a Bible story did something, that does not mean that you have either permission or obligation to do it too.

What you can and should do is to obey what God actually calls you to do in the Scripture. Narratives are precious to us because they so vividly *demonstrate* God's involvement in the world and *illustrate* his principles and calling. They thus teach us a lot—but what they directly teach us does not systematically include personal ethics. For that area of life, we must turn elsewhere in the Scriptures, to the various places where personal ethics are actually taught categorically and explicitly. The richness and variety of the Scriptures must be understood as our ally—a welcome resource, never a complicated burden.

6

Acts: The Question
of Historical Precedent

In one sense a separate chapter on the Acts of the Apostles is redundant, for almost everything that was said in the last chapter applies here as well. However, for a very practical, hermeneutical reason Acts requires a chapter of its own. The reason is simple; most Christians do not read Acts in the same way they read Judges or 2 Samuel, even if they are not fully aware of it.

When we read the Old Testament narratives we tend to do the things mentioned in the last chapter—moralize, allegorize, read between the lines, and so on. Seldom do we think of these narratives as serving as patterns for Christian behavior or church life. Even in the case of those few we do treat that way—for example, putting out a fleece to find God's will—we never do exactly what they did. That is, we never put out an actual fleece for God to make wet or dry. Rather we "fleece God" by setting up a set, or sets, of circumstances. "If someone from California calls us this week, then we'll let that be God's way of telling us that the move to California is the one he wants us to make." And never once, in using this "pattern," do we consider that Gideon's action was really not a good one, inasmuch as it showed his lack of trust in God's word that had already been given to him.

Thus we seldom think of the Old Testament histories as setting biblical precedents for our own lives. On the other hand, this is the normal way for Christians to read Acts. It not only tells us the history of the early church, but it also serves as the normative model

94

for the church of all times. And this is precisely our hermeneutical difficulty.

By and large, most sectors of evangelical Protestantism have a "restoration movement" mentality. We regularly look back to the church and Christian experience in the first century either as the norm to be restored or the ideal to be approximated. Thus we often say things like, "Acts plainly teaches us that. . . ." However, it seems obvious that not all of the "plain teaching" is equally plain to all.

In fact it is our lack of hermeneutical precision as to what Acts is trying to teach that has led to a lot of the division one finds in the church. Such diverse practices as the baptism of infants or of believers only, congregational and episcopalian church polity, the necessity of taking the Lord's Supper every Sunday, the choice of deacons by congregational vote, the selling of possessions and having all things in common, and even ritual snake handling (!) have been supported in whole or in part on the basis of Acts.

The main purpose of this chapter is to offer some hermeneutical suggestions for the problem of biblical precedents. What is said here, therefore, will also apply to all the historical narratives in Scripture, including some of the material in the Gospels. Before that, however, we need to say some things about how to read and study Acts.

In the discussion that follows, we will have occasion regularly to refer to Luke's intention or purpose in writing Acts. It must be emphasized that we always mean that the Holy Spirit lies behind Luke's intention. Just as we are "to continue to work out our salvation," yet "it is God who works in [us]" (Phil. 2:12–13), so Luke had certain interests and concerns in writing Luke-Acts. Yet behind it all, we believe, was the superintending work of the Holy Spirit.

The Exegesis of Acts

Although Acts is a readable book, it is also a difficult book for group Bible study. The reason is that people come to the book, and thus to its study, for a whole variety of reasons. Some are greatly interested in historical details, that is, what Acts can furnish about the history of the primitive church. The interest of others in the history is apologetic, proving the Bible to be true by showing Luke's accuracy as a historian. Most people, however, come to the book for purely religious or devotional reasons, wanting to know what the early Christians were like so that they may inspire us or serve as models.

The interest that brings people to Acts, therefore, causes a great deal of selectivity to take place as they read or study. For the person coming with devotional interests, for example, Gamaliel's speech in Acts 5 holds far less interest than Paul's conversion in chapter 9 or Peter's imprisonment in chapter 12. Such reading or study usually causes people to skip over the chronological or historical questions. As you read the first eleven chapters, for example, it is difficult to imagine that what Luke has included there has in fact covered a time span of ten to fifteen years.

Our interest here, therefore, is to help you read and study the book alertly, to help you to look at the book in terms of *Luke's* interests, and to ask some new kinds of questions as you read.

Acts as History

Most of the exegetical suggestions given in the preceding chapter hold true for Acts. What is important here is that Luke was a Gentile, whose inspired narrative is at the same time an excellent example of Hellenistic historiography, a kind of history writing that had its roots in Thucydides (ca. 460–400 B.C.) and flourished during the Hellenistic period (ca. 300 B.C.–A.D. 200). Such history was not written simply to keep records or to chronicle the past. Rather it was written *both* to encourage or entertain (i.e., to be good reading) *and* to inform, moralize, or offer an apologetic. At the same time, of course, Luke has been greatly influenced by his reading of, and living with, the Old Testament narratives, so that this kind of divinely inspired, religiously motivated history is also evident in his telling of the early Christian story.

Thus Luke's two volumes (Luke and Acts) fit both these kinds of history well. On the one hand, they are especially good reading; on the other hand, in keeping with both the best of Hellenistic historiography and the Old Testament histories, Luke at the same time has interests that go far beyond simply informing or entertaining. There is a divine activity going on in this story, and Luke is especially concerned that his readers understand this. For him the divine activity that began with Jesus and continues through the ministry of the Holy Spirit in the church is a continuation of God's story that began in the Old Testament. Therefore, making note of

Luke's own theological interests is of special importance as you read or study Acts. Exegesis of Acts, therefore, includes not only the purely historical questions like *What happened?* but also the theological ones such as *What was Luke's purpose in selecting and shaping the material in this way?*

The question of Luke's intent is at once the most important and the most difficult. It is the most important because it is crucial to our hermeneutics. If it can be demonstrated that Luke's intent in Acts was to lay down a pattern for the church at all times, then that pattern surely becomes normative, that is, it is what God requires of all Christians under any conditions. But if his intent is something else, then we need to ask the hermeneutical questions in a different way. To find Luke's intent, however, is especially difficult, partly because we do not know who Theophilus was, nor why Luke would have written to him, and partly because Luke seems to have so many different interests.

However, because of the significance of Luke's purpose for hermeneutics, it is especially important that you keep this question before you as you read or study at the exegetical level. In a way, this is much like thinking paragraphs when exegeting the Epistles. But in this case it moves beyond paragraphs to whole narratives and sections of the book.

Our exegetical interest, therefore, is both in *what* and *why*. As we have already learned, one must begin with *what* before we ask *why*.

The First Step

As always the first thing one does is to read, preferably the whole book in one sitting. And as you read, learn to make observations and ask questions. The problem with making observations and asking questions as you read Acts, of course, is that the narrative is so engrossing that one frequently simply forgets to ask the exegetical questions.

So again, if we were to give you an assignment here, it would look like this: (1) Read Acts all the way through in one or two sittings. (2) As you read make mental notes of such things as key people and places, recurring motifs (what really interests Luke?), natural divisions of the book. (3) Now go back and skim read, and jot down with references your previous observations. (4) Ask yourself Why did Luke write this book?

Since Acts is the only one of its kind in the New Testament, we will be more specific here in guiding your reading and study.

Acts: An Overview

Let us begin our quest of *what* by noting the natural divisions as Luke himself gives them to us. Acts has frequently been divided on the basis of Luke's interest in Peter (chaps. 1–12) and Paul 13–28), or in the geographical expansion of the Gospel (1–7, Jerusalem; 8–10, Samaria and Judea; 11–28, to the ends of the earth). Although both of these divisions are recognizable in terms of actual content, there is another clue, given by Luke himself, that seems to tie everything together much better. As you read, notice the brief summary statements in 6:7; 9:31; 12:24; 16:4; and 19:20. In each case the narrative seems to pause for a moment before it takes off in a new direction of some kind. On the basis of this clue, Acts can be seen to be composed of six sections, or panels, which give the narrative a continually forward movement from its Jewish setting based in Jerusalem with Peter as its leading figure toward a predominantly Gentile church, with Paul as the leading figure, and with Rome, the capital of the Gentile world, as the goal. Once Paul reaches Rome, where he once again turns to the Gentiles because they will listen (28:28), the narrative comes to an end.

You should notice, then, as you read how each section contributes to this "movement." In your own words, try to describe each panel, both as to its content and its contribution to the forward movement. What seems to be the key to each new forward thrust? Here is our own attempt to do this:

1:1–6:7. A description of the primitive church in Jerusalem, its early preaching, its common life, its spread and its initial opposition. Notice how Jewish everything is, including the sermons, the opposition, and the fact that the early believers continue associations with the temple and the synagogues. The panel concludes with a narrative indicating that a division had begun between Greek-speaking and Aramaic-speaking believers.

6:8–9:31. A description of the first geographical expansion, carried out by the "Hellenists" (Greek-speaking Jewish Christians) to diaspora Jews or "nearly Jews" (Samaritans and a proselyte). Luke also includes the conversion of Paul, who was (1) a Hellenist, (2) a Jewish opponent, and (3) the one who was to lead the specifically Gentile expansion. Stephen's martyrdom is the key to this initial expansion.

9:32–12:24. A description of the first expansion to the Gentiles. The key is the conversion of Cornelius, whose story is told twice. The significance of Cornelius is that his conversion was a direct act from God, who did not now use the Hellenists, in which case it would have been suspect, but Peter, the acknowledged leader of the Jewish-Christian mission. Also included is the story of the church in Antioch, where Gentile conversion is now carried out by the Hellenists in a purposeful way.

12:25–16:5. A description of the first geographical expansion into the Gentile world, with Paul in the leadership. Jews now regularly reject the Gospel because it includes Gentiles. The church meets in council and does not reject its Gentile brothers and sisters, nor does it lay Jewish religious requirements on them. The latter serves as the key to full expansion into the Gentile world.

16:6–19:20. A description of the further, ever westward, expansion into the Gentile world, now into Europe. Repeatedly the Jews reject and the Gentiles welcome the Gospel.

19:21–28:30. A description of the events that move Paul and the Gospel on to Rome, with a great deal of interest in Paul's trials, in which three times he is declared innocent of any wrongdoing.

Try reading Acts with this outline, this sense of "movement," in view to see for yourself whether this seems to capture what is going on. As you read you will notice that our description of the content omits one crucial factor—indeed *the* crucial factor—namely, the role of the Holy Spirit in all of this. You will notice as you read that at every key juncture, in every key person, the Holy Spirit plays the absolutely leading role. According to Luke, all of this forward movement did not happen by man's design; it happened because God willed it and the Holy Spirit carried it out.

Luke's Purpose

We must be careful that we do not move too glibly from this overview of what Luke did to an easy or dogmatic expression of what his inspired purpose in all of this was. But a few observations are in order, partly based also on what Luke did *not* do.

1. The key to understanding Acts seems to be in Luke's interest in this movement, orchestrated by the Holy Spirit, of the Gospel from its Jerusalem-based, Judaism-oriented beginnings to its be-

coming a worldwide, Gentile-predominant phenomenon. On the basis of structure and content alone, any statement of purpose that does not include the Gentile mission and the Holy Spirit's role in that mission will surely have missed the point of the book.

2. This interest in "movement" is further substantiated by what Luke does *not* tell us. First, he has no interest in the "lives," that is, biographies, of the apostles. James is the only one whose end we know (12:2). Once the movement to the Gentiles gets under way, Peter drops from sight except in chapter 15, where he certifies the Gentile mission. Apart from John, the other apostles are not even mentioned, and Luke's interest in Paul is almost completely in terms of the Gentile mission.

Second, he has little or no interest in church organization or polity. The Seven in chapter 6 are *not* called deacons, and in any case they soon leave Jerusalem. Luke never tells us why or how it happened that the church in Jerusalem passed from the leadership of Peter and the apostles to James, the brother of Jesus (12:17; 15:13; 21:18); nor does he ever explain how any of the local churches was organized in terms of polity or leadership, except to say that "elders" were "appointed" (14:23).

Third, there is no word about other geographical expansion except in the one direct line from Jerusalem to Rome. There is no mention of Crete (Titus 1:5), Illyricum (Rom. 15:19—modern Yugoslavia), or Pontus, Cappadocia, and Bithynia (1 Peter 1:1), not to mention the church's expansion eastward toward Mesopotamia or southward toward Egypt.

All of this together says that church history per se was simply *not* Luke's reason for writing.

3. Luke's interest also does not seem to be in standardizing things, bringing everything into uniformity. When he records individual conversions there are usually two elements included: gift of the Spirit and water baptism. But these can be in reverse order, with or without the laying on of hands, with or without the mention of tongues, and scarcely ever with a specific mention of repentance, even after what Peter says in 2:38–39. Similarly, Luke neither says nor implies that the Gentile churches experienced a communal life similar to that in Jerusalem in 2:42–47 and 4:32–35. Such diversity probably means that no specific example is being set forth as *the* model Christian experience or church life.

But is this to say that Luke is not trying to tell us something by these various specific narratives? Not necessarily. The real question is, What was he trying to tell his first readers?

4. Nonetheless, we believe that much of Acts is intended by Luke to serve as a model. But the model is not so much in the specifics as in the overall picture. By the very way God has moved him to structure and narrate this history it seems probable that we are to view this triumphant, joyful, forward-moving expansion of the Gospel into the Gentile world, empowered by the Holy Spirit and resulting in changed lives and local communities as God's intent for the continuing church. And precisely because this is God's intent for the church, nothing can hinder it, neither Sanhedrin nor synagogue, dissension nor narrow-mindedness, prison nor plot. Luke, therefore, probably intended that the church should be "like them," but in the larger sense, not by modeling itself on any specific example.

An Exegetical Sampling

With this overview of content and provisional look at intent before us, let us examine two narratives, 6:1–7 and 8:1–25, and note the kinds of exegetical questions one needs to learn to ask of the text of Acts.

As always, one begins by reading the selected portion and its immediate context over and again. As with the Epistles, the contextual questions you must repeatedly ask in Acts are, What is the point of this narrative or speech? How does it function in Luke's total narrative? Why has he included it here? You can usually provisionally answer that question after one or two careful readings. Sometimes, however, especially in Acts, you will need to do some outside reading to answer some of the *content* questions before you can feel confident that you are on the right track.

Let us begin with 6:1–7. How does this section function in the overall picture? Two things can be said right away. First, it serves to conclude the first panel, 1:1–6:7; second, it also serves as a transition to the second panel, 6:8–9:31. Note how Luke does this. His interest in 1:1–6:7 is to give us a picture both of the life of the primitive community and of its expansion *within Jerusalem*. This narrative, 6:1–7, includes both of those features. But it also hints of the first tension within the community itself, a tension based on traditional lines within Judaism between Jerusalem (or Aramaic-speaking) Jews and the Diaspora (Greek-speaking) Jews. In the church this tension was overcome by an official recognition of the leadership that had begun to emerge among the Greek-speaking Jewish Christians.

We have put the last sentence in that particular way because at this point one must also do some outside work on the historical context. By a little digging (articles in Bible dictionaries on "deacons" and "Hellenists," commentaries, and background books like J. Jeremias, *Jerusalem in the Time of Jesus* [Philadelphia: Fortress, 1967], you could discover the following important facts:

1. The Hellenists were almost certainly Greek-speaking Jews, that is, Jews from the Diaspora who were now living in Jerusalem.

2. Many such Hellenists returned to Jerusalem in their later years to die and be buried by Mount Zion. Since they were not *native* to Jerusalem, when they died, their widows had no regular means of sustenance.

3. These widows were cared for by daily subsidies; this care caused a considerable economic strain in Jerusalem.

4. It is clear from 6:9 that the Hellenists had their own Greek-speaking synagogue of which both Stephen and Saul, who was from Tarsus (located in Greek-speaking Cilicia, v. 9) were members.

5. The evidence of Acts 6 is that the early church had made considerable inroads into this synagogue—note the mention of "their widows," the fact that all seven chosen to handle this matter have Greek names and that the intense opposition comes from the Diaspora synagogue.

6. Finally, the seven men are never called deacons. They are simply "the Seven" (21:8), who to be sure are to oversee the daily food subsidies for the Greek-speaking widows, but who are also clearly ministers of the Word (Stephen, Philip).

This knowledge of content will especially help to make sense of what follows. For in 6:8–8:1 Luke focuses on one of the Seven as the key figure in the first expansion outside Jerusalem. He explicitly tells us that Stephen's martyrdom has this result (8:1–4). You should notice also from this latter passage how important this Greek-speaking community of Christians in Jerusalem is to God's plan. They are forced to leave Jerusalem because of persecution but they were not native there anyway. So they simply go out and share the Word "throughout Judea and Samaria."

The narrative in 6:1–7, therefore, is *not* given to tell us about the first organization of the church into clergy and lay deacons. It functions to set the scene for the first expansion of the church outside its Jerusalem base.

The narrative in 8:5–25 is of a different kind. Here we have the actual story of the first known spread of the early church. This narrative is especially important for our concerns because it contains several exegetical difficulties and because it has frequently served as something of a hermeneutical battleground.

As always, we must begin by doing our exegesis with care, and again, there is no substitute for reading the text over and again, making observations and notes. In this case, to get at the *what* of the narrative, try setting it out in your own words. Our summary observations are as follows:

The story is straightforward enough. It tells us of Philip's initial ministry in Samaria, which was accompanied by healings and deliverances from demons (8:5–7). Many Samaritans apparently became Christians, inasmuch as they believed and were baptized. Indeed, the miracles were so powerful that even Simon, a notorious purveyor of black magic, came to believe (8:9–13). When the Jerusalem church heard of this phenomenon, they sent Peter and John, and only then did the Samaritans receive the Holy Spirit (8:14–17). Simon now wanted to become a minister by buying what Peter and John had. Peter then rebuked Simon, but it is not clear from his final response (8:24) whether he was repentant or was to be the recipient of the judgment Peter spoke over him (8:20–23).

The way Luke has woven this narrative together makes it clear that two interests clearly predominate: the conversion of the Samaritans and the Simon matter. People's exegetical problems with these two matters basically stem from their prior knowledge and convictions. They tend to think that things just are not supposed to happen this way. Since Paul says in Romans 8 that without the Spirit one cannot be a Christian, how is it that these believers had not yet received the Spirit? And what about Simon? Was he really a believer who "fell away," or did he merely profess without having saving faith?

Probably the real problem stems from the fact that Luke himself does not try to harmonize everything for us. It is difficult to listen to a passage like this without our prior biases getting in the way, and the authors of this book are not immune. Nonetheless we will try to hear it from Luke's point of view. What interests *him* in presenting this story? How does it function in his overall concern?

About the Samaritan conversions, two things seem to be significant for him: (1) The mission to Samaria, which was the first geographical expansion of the Gospel, was carried out by one of the Hellenists quite apart from any design or program on the part of the apostles. (2) Nonetheless it is important for Luke's readers to know that the mission had both divine and apostolic approval, as evidenced by the withholding of the Spirit until the laying on of the apostles' hands. It is in keeping with Luke's overall concern to show that the missionary work of the Hellenists was not a maverick movement, although it happened quite apart from any apostolic conference on church growth.

Although we cannot prove this—because the text does not tell us and it lies apart from Luke's concerns—it is likely that what was withheld until the coming of Peter and John was the visible, charismatic *evidence* of the Spirit's presence. Our reasons for suggesting this are three: (1) All of the things said about the Samaritans before the coming of Peter and John are said elsewhere in Acts to describe genuine Christian experience. Therefore, they must have in fact begun the Christian life. (2) Elsewhere in Acts the presence of the Spirit—as here—is *the* crucial element in the Christian life. How then could they have begun Christian life without the crucial element? (3) For Luke in Acts the presence of the Spirit means power (1:8; 6:8; 10:38), which is usually manifested by some visible evidence. Therefore it is probably this powerful, visible manifestation of the Spirit's presence that had not yet occurred in Samaria that Luke equates with the "coming" or "receiving" of the Spirit.

The role of Simon in this narrative is equally complex. However, there is plenty of outside evidence that this Simon became a well-known opponent of the early Christians. Luke probably includes this material, therefore, to explain Simon's tenuous relationship with the Christian community and to indicate to his readers that Simon did *not* have divine or apostolic approval. Simon's final word seems ambiguous only if one is interested in early conversion stories. The whole of Luke's narrative in fact has a negative attitude toward Simon. Whether he was really saved or not is of no ultimate interest to the account. That he had a short time of contact with the church, at least as a professing believer, *is* of interest. But Peter's speech seems to reflect Luke's own judgment on Simon's Christianity—it was false!

We grant that exegesis of this kind that pursues the *what* and *why* of Luke's narrative is not necessarily devotionally exciting, but we would argue that it is the mandatory first step to the proper hearing of Acts as God's Word. Not every sentence in every narrative or speech is necessarily trying to tell *us* something. But every sentence in every narrative or speech contributes to what God is trying to say as a whole through Acts. In the process we can learn from the individual narratives of the variety of ways and people God uses to get his task accomplished.

The Hermeneutics of Acts

As noted previously, our concern here is with one question. How do the individual narratives in Acts, or any other biblical narrative for that matter, function as precedents for the later church, or do they? That is, does the book of Acts have a Word that not only *describes* the primitive church but *speaks as a norm* to the church at all times? If there is such a Word, how does one discover it or set up principles to aid in hearing it? If not, then what do we do with the concept of precedent? In short, just exactly what role does historical precedent play in Christian doctrine or in the understanding of Christian experience?

It must be noted at the outset that almost all biblical Christians tend to treat precedent as normative authority to some degree or another. But it is seldom done with consistency. On the one hand, people tend to follow some narratives as establishing obligatory patterns, while neglecting others; on the other hand, they sometimes tend to make one pattern mandatory when there is a complexity of patterns in Acts itself.

The following suggestions are not proposed as absolute, but we hope they will help you to come to grips with this hermeneutical problem.

Some General Principles

The crucial hermeneutical question here is whether biblical narratives that describe what *happened* in the early church also function as norms intended to delineate what *must happen* in the ongoing church. Are there instances from Acts of which one may appropriately say, "We *must* do this," or should one merely say, "We *may* do this"?

Our assumption, shared by many others, is that *unless Scripture explicitly tells us we must do something, what is only narrated or described does not function in a normative way—unless it can be demonstrated on other grounds that the author intended it to function in this way.* There are good reasons for making this assumption.

In general, doctrinal statements derived from Scripture fall into three (or four) categories: (1) Christian theology (what Christians believe), (2) Christian ethics (how Christians ought to behave), (3) Christian experience and Christian practice (what Christians do). Within these categories one might further distinguish two levels of statements, which we will call primary and secondary. At the primary level are those doctrinal statements derived from the explicit propositions or imperatives of Scripture (i.e., what Scripture *intends* to teach). At the secondary level are those statements derived only incidentally, by implication or by precedent.

For example, in the category of Christian theology such statements as, God is one, God is love, all have sinned, Christ died for our sins, salvation is by grace, and Jesus Christ is divine are derived from passages where they are taught by intent, and are therefore primary. At the secondary level are those statements that are the logical outflow of the primary statements or are derived by implication from Scripture. Thus the fact of the deity of Christ is primary; how the two natures concur in unity is secondary.

A similar distinction may be made with regard to the doctrine of Scripture. That it is the inspired Word of God is primary; the precise nature of inspiration is secondary. This is not to say that the secondary statements are unimportant. Often they will have significant bearing on one's faith with regard to the primary statements. In fact, their ultimate theological value may be related to how well they preserve the integrity of the primary statements.

What is important to note here is that almost everything Christians derive from Scripture by way of precedent is in our third category, Christian experience or practice, and always at the secondary level. For example, that the Lord's Supper should be a continuing practice in the church is a primary level statement. Jesus himself commands it; the Epistles and Acts bear witness to it. But the frequency of its observance, a place where Christians differ, is based on tradition and precedent; surely it is not binding. Scripture simply does not directly speak to that question. This also, we would argue, is the case with the necessity of baptism (primary) and its mode (secondary), or the practice of Christians "assembling themselves together" (primary) and the frequency or the day of the week (secondary). Again, this is not to say that the secondary statements are unimportant. For example, one is surely hard pressed to prove whether the day Christians meet to worship must be Saturday or Sunday, but in either case one is saying something of theological significance by one's practice.

Closely related to this discussion is the concept of intentionality. It is common among us to say, "Scripture teaches us that. . . ." Ordinarily people mean by that to say that something is "taught" by explicit statements. Problems with this arise when people move to the area of biblical history. Is something taught simply because it is recorded—even if it is recorded in what appears to be a favorable way?

It is a general maxim of hermeneutics that God's Word is to be found in the intent of the Scripture. This is an especially crucial matter to the hermeneutics of the historical narratives. It is one thing for the historian to include an event because it serves the greater purpose of his work and yet another thing for the interpreter to take that incident as having teaching value apart from the historian's larger intent.

Although Luke's inspired broader intent may be a moot point for some, it is our hypothesis, based on the preceding exegesis, that he was trying to show how the church emerged as a chiefly Gentile, worldwide phenomenon from its origins as a Jerusalem-based, Judaism-oriented sect of Jewish believers, and how the Holy Spirit was directly responsible for this phenomenon of universal salvation based on grace alone. The recurring motif that nothing can hinder this forward movement of the church empowered by the Holy Spirit makes us think that Luke also intended his readers to see this as a model for their existence. And the fact that Acts is in the canon further makes us think that surely this is the way the church was always intended to be—evangelistic, joyful, empowered by the Holy Spirit.

But what of the specific details in those narratives, which only when taken altogether help us to see Luke's larger intent? Do these details have the same teaching value? Do they also serve as normative models? We think not, basically because most such details are *incidental* to the main point of the narrative and because of the *ambiguity* of details from narrative to narrative.

Thus when we examined Acts 6:1–7, we saw how the narrative functioned in Luke's overall plan, as a conclusion to his first major section, which at the same time served to introduce the Hellenists. It might also have been a part of his intent to show the amicable resolution of the first tension within the Christian community.

From this narrative we might also incidentally learn several other things. For example, one might learn that a good way to help a minority group in the church is to let that group have its own leadership, selected by themselves. This is in fact what they did. *Must* we do it? Not necessarily, since Luke does not tell us so, nor is there any reason to believe that he had that in mind when he recorded the narrative. On the other hand, such a procedure makes such good sense one wonders why anyone would fight it.

Our point is, that whatever else anyone gleans from such a story, such gleanings are *incidental* to Luke's intent. This does not mean that what is incidental is false, nor that it has no theological value; it does mean that God's Word *for us* in that narrative is primarily related to what it was *intended* to teach.

On the basis of this discussion the following principles emerge with regard to the hermeneutics of historical narrative:

1. The Word of God in Acts that may be regarded as normative for Christians is related primarily to what any given narrative was *intended* to teach.

2. What is *incidental* to the primary intent of the narrative may indeed reflect an inspired author's understanding of things, but it does not have the same didactic value as what the narrative was *intended* to teach. This does not negate what is incidental nor imply that it has no word for us. What it does argue is that what is incidental must not become primary, although it may always serve as additional support to what is unequivocally taught elsewhere.

3. Historical precedent, to have normative value, must be related to *intent*. That is, if it can be shown that the purpose of a given narrative is to *establish* precedent, then such precedent should be regarded as normative. For example, if it could be demonstrated on exegetical grounds that Luke's intent in Acts 6:1–7 was to give the church a precedent for selecting its leaders, then such a selection process should be followed by later Christians. But if the establishing of precedent was *not* the intent of the narrative, then its value as

a precedent for later Christians should be treated according to the specific principles suggested in our next section.

The problem with all of this, of course, is that it tends to leave us with little that is normative for those broad areas of concern— Christian experience and Christian practice. There is *no* express teaching as to the *mode* of baptism, the *age* of those who are to be baptized, any specific charismatic phenomena that are to be in evidence when one receives the Spirit, or the frequency of the Lord's Supper, to cite but a few examples. Yet these are precisely the areas where there is so much division among Christians. Invariably, in such cases, people argue that this is what *they* did, whether they derive such practices from the narratives of Acts or by implication from what is said in the Epistles.

Scripture simply does not expressly command that baptism must be by immersion, nor that infants are to be baptized, nor that all genuine conversions must be as dramatic as Paul's, nor that Christians are to be baptized in the Spirit evidenced by tongues as a second work of grace, nor that the Lord's Supper is to be celebrated every Sunday. What do we do, then, with something like baptism by immersion? What *does* Scripture say? In this case it can be argued from the meaning of the word itself, from the one description of baptism in Acts of going "down into the water" and "coming up out of the water" (8:38–39), and from Paul's analogy of baptism as death, *burial,* and resurrection (Rom. 6:1–3), that immersion was the *presupposition* of baptism in the early church. It was nowhere commanded precisely because it was presupposed.

On the other hand, it can be pointed out that without a baptismal tank in the local church in Samaria, the people who were baptized there would have had great difficulty being immersed. There simply is no known supply of water there to have made immersion a viable option. Did they pour water over them, as that early church manual, the *Didache* (ca. A.D. 100), suggests should be done where there is not enough cold, running water or tepid, still water for immersion? We simply do not know, of course. The *Didache* makes it abundantly clear that immersion was the norm, but it also makes it clear that the act itself is far more important than the mode. Even though the *Didache* is not a biblical document, it is a very early, orthodox Christian document, and it may help us by showing how the early church made pragmatic adjustments in this area where Scripture is not explicit. The normal (regular) practice served as the norm. But because it was only *normal,* it did not become *normative.* We would probably do well to follow this lead and not confuse normalcy with normativeness, in the sense that all Christians must do a given thing or else they are disobedient to God's Word.

Some Specific Principles

With these general observations and principles in view, we would offer the following suggestions as to the hermeneutics of biblical precedents:

1. It is probably never valid to use an *analogy* based on biblical precedent as giving biblical authority for present-day actions. For example, Gideon's fleece has repeatedly been used as an analogy for finding God's will. Since God graciously condescended to Gideon's lack of trust, he may to other's as well but there is no biblical *authority* or encouragement for such actions.

Likewise, on the basis of the narrative of Jesus' reception of the Spirit at his baptism, two different analogies have been drawn that move in quite different directions. Some see this as evidence for the believer's reception of the Spirit at baptism and thus as support by way of analogy for baptismal regeneration; by contrast, others see it as evidence for a baptism of the Holy Spirit subsequent to salvation (since Jesus had been earlier born of the Spirit). There can be little question that Luke himself saw the event as the moment of empowering for Jesus' public ministry (cf. Luke 4:1, 14, 18 with Acts 10:38). But it is doubtful whether the narrative also functions well as an analogy for either of the later theological positions, especially when it is taken beyond mere analogy to become *biblical support* for either doctrine. If everything in Jesus' life were normative for us, we might all be expected to die by crucifixion and be raised three days later.

2. Although it may not have been the author's primary purpose, biblical narratives do have illustrative and, sometimes, "pattern" value. In fact, this is how the New Testament people occasionally used certain historical precedents from the Old Testament. Paul, for example, used some Old Testament examples as warnings to those who had a false security in their divine election (1 Cor. 10:1–13), and Jesus used the example of David as an historical precedent to justify his disciples' Sabbath actions (Mark 2:23–28 and parallels).

But none of us has God's authority to reproduce the sort of exegesis and analogical analyses that the New Testament authors occasionally applied to the Old Testament. It should be noted especially in cases where the precedent justifies a present action, that *the precedent does not establish a norm for specific action*. People are not to eat regularly of the showbread or to pluck grain on the Sabbath to show that the Sabbath was made for man. Rather, the precedent illustrates a principle with regard to the Sabbath.

A warning is in order here. If one wishes to use a biblical precedent to justify some present action, one is on safer ground if the principle of the action is taught elsewhere, where it is the primary intent so to teach. For example, to use Jesus' cleansing of the temple to justify one's so-called righteous indignation—usually a euphemism for selfish anger—is to abuse this principle. On the other hand, one may properly base the present-day experience of speaking in tongues not only on precedent (in Acts) but also on the teaching about spiritual gifts in 1 Corinthians 12–14.

3. In matters of Christian experience, and even more so of Christian practice, *biblical precedents may sometimes be regarded as repeatable patterns—even if they are not understood to be normative*. That is, for many practices there seems to be full justification for the later church's repeating of biblical patterns; but it is moot to argue that all Christians in every place and every time *must* repeat the pattern or they are disobedient to God's Word. This is especially true when the practice itself is mandatory but the mode is not. (It should be noted that not all Christians would be fully in agreement with this way of stating things. Some movements and denominations were founded partly on the premise that virtually all New Testament patterns should be restored as fully as possible in modern times and have over the years developed a considerable hermeneutic of the mandatory nature of much that is only narrated in Acts; others, similarly, would argue that Luke himself intended, for example, for the reception of the Spirit to be evidenced by the accompanying gift of tongues. But in both these cases the question rests finally not so much on the rightness or wrongness of this principle, but on the interpretation of Acts and of Luke's overall—as well as specific—intent in his telling of the story.)

The decision as to whether certain practices or patterns are repeatable should be guided by the following considerations. First, the strongest possible case can be made when only one pattern is found (although one must be careful not to make too much of silence), and when that pattern is repeated within the New Testament itself. Second, when there is an ambiguity of patterns or when a pattern occurs but once, it is repeatable for later Christians only if it appears to have divine approbation or is in harmony with what is taught elsewhere in Scripture. Third, what is culturally conditioned is either not repeatable at all, or must be translated into the new or differing culture.

Thus, on the basis of these principles, one can make a very strong case for immersion as the mode of baptism, a weaker case for the observance of the Lord's Supper each Sunday, but almost no case at all for infant baptism (this may, of course, be argued from historical precedent in the church, but not so easily from biblical precedent, which is the issue here). By the same token, the Christian minister's function as a priest fails on all counts, in terms of its biblical base.

We do not imagine ourselves hereby to have solved all the problems, but we think these are workable suggestions and we hope that they will cause you to think exegetically and with greater hermeneutical precision as you read the biblical narratives.

7

The Gospels: One Story, Many Dimensions

As with the Epistles and Acts, the Gospels seem at first glance easy enough to interpret. Since the materials in the Gospels may be divided roughly into sayings and narratives, that is, teachings *of* Jesus and stories *about* Jesus, one should theoretically be able to follow the principles for interpreting the Epistles for the one and the principles for historical narratives for the others.

In a sense this is true. However, it is not quite that easy. The four Gospels form a unique literary genre, for which there are few real analogies. Their uniqueness, which we will examine momentarily, is what presents most of our exegetical problems. But there are some hermeneutical difficulties as well. Some of these, of course, take the form of those several "hard sayings" in the Gospels. But the major hermeneutical difficulty lies with understanding "the kingdom of God," a term that is absolutely crucial to the whole of Jesus' ministry, yet at the same time is presented in the language and concepts of first-century Judaism. The problem is how to translate those ideas into our own cultural settings.

The Nature of the Gospels

Almost all the difficulties one encounters in interpreting the Gospels stem from two obvious facts: (1) Jesus himself did not write a gospel; they come from others, not from him. (2) There are four gospels.

The fact that the Gospels do not come from Jesus himself is a very important consideration. Had he written something, of course, it would probably have looked less like our Gospels and more like the Old Testament prophetic books, say, like Amos, a collection of spoken oracles and sayings plus a few brief personal narratives (like Amos 7:10–17). Our Gospels do indeed contain collections of sayings, but these are always woven, as an integral part, into a historical narrative of Jesus' life and ministry. Thus they are not books *by* Jesus but books *about* Jesus, which at the same time contain a large collection of his teaching.

The difficulty this presents to us should not be overdone, but it is there and needs to be addressed. The nature of this difficulty might best be seen by noting an analogy from Paul in Acts and his epistles. If we did not have Acts, for example, we could piece together some of the elements of Paul's life from the Epistles, but such a presentation would be meager. Likewise, if we did not have his epistles, our understanding of this theology based solely on his speeches in Acts would likewise be meager—and somewhat out of balance. For key items in Paul's life, therefore, we read Acts and feed into that the information he gives in his epistles. For his teaching we do not first go to Acts, but to the Epistles, and to Acts as an additional source.

But the Gospels are *not* like Acts, for here we have both a narrative of Jesus' life and large blocks of his sayings (teachings) as an absolutely basic part of that life. But the sayings were not *written* by him, as the Epistles were by Paul. Jesus' primary tongue was Aramaic; his teachings come to us only in a Greek translation. Moreover, the same saying frequently occurs in two or three of the Gospels, and even when it occurs in the exact chronological sequence or historical setting, it is seldom found with exactly the same wording in each.

To some this reality can be threatening, but it need not be. It is true, of course, that certain kinds of scholarship have distorted this reality in such a way as to suggest that nothing in the Gospels is trustworthy. But no such conclusion need be drawn. Equally good scholarship has demonstrated the historical reliability of the gospel materials.

Our point here is a simple one. God gave us what we know about Jesus' earthly ministry in *this* way, not in another way that might better suit someone's mechanistic, tape-recorder mentality. And in any case the fact that the Gospels were not written by Jesus, but about him, is a part of their genius, we would argue, not their weakness.

Then there are four of them. How did this happen, and why? After all, we do not have four Acts of the Apostles. Moreover, the materials in the first three Gospels are so often alike we call them the synoptic ("common-view") Gospels. Indeed, one might wonder why retain Mark at all, since the amount of material found exclusively in his gospel would scarcely fill two pages of print. But again, the fact that there are four, we believe, is a part of their genius.

So what is the nature of the Gospels, and why is their unique nature part of their genius? This can best be answered by first speaking to the question, Why four? We cannot give an absolutely certain answer to this, but at least one of the reasons is a simple and pragmatic one; different Christian communities each had need for a book about Jesus. For a variety of reasons the gospel written for one community or group of believers did not necessarily meet all the needs in another community. So one was written first (Mark, in the most common view), and that gospel was "rewritten" twice (Matthew and Luke) for considerably different reasons, to meet considerably different needs. Independently of them (again, in the most common view), John wrote a gospel of a different kind for still another set of reasons. All of this, we believe, was orchestrated by the Holy Spirit.

For the later church, none of the Gospels supersedes the other, but each stands beside the others as equally valuable and equally authoritative. How so? *Because in each case the interest in Jesus is at two levels.* First, there was the purely historical concern that this is who Jesus was and this is what he said and did; it is *this* Jesus, who was crucified and raised from the dead, whom we now worship as the risen and exalted Lord. Second, there was the existential concern of retelling this story for the needs of later communities that did not speak Aramaic but Greek, and that did not live in a basically rural, agricultural, and Jewish setting, but in Rome, or Ephesus, or Antioch, where the Gospel was encountering an urban, pagan environment.

In a certain sense, therefore, the Gospels are already functioning as hermeneutical models for us, insisting by their very nature that we, too, retell the same story in our own twentieth-century contexts.

Thus these books, which tell us virtually all we know about Jesus, are nonetheless not biographies—although they are partly biographical. Nor are they like the contemporary "lives" of great men—although they record the life of the greatest man. They are, to use the phrase of the second-century church father Justin Martyr, "the memoirs of the apostles." Four biographies could not stand side by side as of equal value; these books stand side by side because at one and the same time they record the facts *about* Jesus, recall the teaching *of* Jesus, and each bears witness *to* Jesus. This is their nature and their genius, and this is important both for exegesis and for hermeneutics.

Exegesis of the Gospels, therefore, requires us to think both in terms of the historical setting of Jesus and in terms of the historical setting of the authors.

The Historical Context

You will recall that the first task of exegesis is to have an awareness of the historical context. This means not only to know the historical context in general, but also to form a tentative, but informed, reconstruction of the situation that the author is addressing. This can become complex at times because of the nature of the Gospels as two-level documents. Historical context first of all has to do with Jesus himself. This includes both an awareness of the culture and religion of the first century, Palestinian Judaism in which he lived and taught, as well as an attempt to understand the particular context of a given saying or parable. But historical context also has to do with the individual authors (the evangelists) and their reasons for writing.

We are aware that trying to think about these various contexts can be an imposing task for the ordinary reader. Furthermore, we are aware that there is probably more speculative scholarship that goes on here than anywhere else in New Testament studies. Nonetheless, the *nature* of the Gospels is a given; they are two-level documents whether we like it or not. We do not begin to think that we can make you experts in these matters—indeed we sometimes wonder about the "experts" as well. Our hope here is simply to raise your awareness level so that you will have a greater appreciation for what the Gospels are, as well as a handle on the kinds of questions you need to ask as you read them.

The Historical Context of Jesus—in General

It is imperative to the understanding of Jesus that you immerse yourself in the first-century Judaism of which he was a part. And this means far more than knowing that the Sadducees did not believe in resurrection (they were "sad you see"). One needs to know why they do not believe and why Jesus had so little contact with them.

For this kind of background information there is simply no alternative to some good outside reading. Any one or all three of the following books would be of great usefulness in this regard: Joachim Jeremias, *Jerusalem in the Time of Jesus* (Philadelphia: Fortress, 1969); Eduard Lohse, *The New Testament Environment* (Nashville: Abingdon, 1976), pp. 11–196; J. Duncan M. Derrett, *Jesus's Audience* (New York: Seabury, 1973).

An especially important feature of this dimension of the historical context, but one that is often overlooked, has to do with the *form* of Jesus' teaching. Everyone knows that Jesus frequently taught in parables. What people are less aware of is that he used a whole variety of such forms. For example, he was a master of purposeful overstatement (hyperbole). In Matthew 5:29–30 (and the parallel in Mark 9:43–48) Jesus tells his disciples to gouge out an offending eye or cut off an offending arm. Now we all know that Jesus "did not really mean that." What he meant was that people are to tear anything out of their lives that causes them to sin. But how do we know that he did not really mean what he said? Because we can all recognize overstatement as a most effective teaching technique in which we are to take the teacher for what he *means* not for what he *says!*

Jesus also made effective use of proverbs (e.g., Matt. 6:21; Mark 3:24), similes and metaphors (e.g., Matt. 10:16; 5:13), poetry (e.g., Matt. 7:6–8; Luke 6:27–28), questions (e.g., Matt. 17:25), and irony (e.g., Matt. 16:2–3), to name a few. For further information on this as well as for other matters in this chapter, you would do well to read Robert H. Stein's *The Method and Message of Jesus' Teaching* (Philadelphia: Westminster, 1978).

The Historical Context of Jesus—in Particular

This is a more difficult aspect in the attempt to reconstruct the historical context of Jesus, especially so with many of his teachings, which are presented often in the Gospels without much context. The reason for this is that Jesus' words and deeds were handed on orally during a period of perhaps thirty years or more, and during this time whole gospels were not being passed on. It was the content of the Gospels that was being passed on in individual stories and sayings (pericopes). Many of these sayings were transmitted along with their original contexts. Scholars have come to call such pericopes *pronouncement stories,* because the narrative itself exists only for the sake of the saying that concludes it. A typical pronouncement story is Mark 12:13–17, where the context is a question about paying taxes to the Romans. It concludes with Jesus' famous pronouncement, "Give to Caesar what is Caesar's and to God what is God's." Can you imagine what we might have done in reconstructing an original context for that saying if it had not been transmitted with its original context?

The real difficulty, of course, comes with the fact that so many of Jesus' sayings and teachings were transmitted without their contexts. Paul himself bears witness to this reality. Three times he cites sayings of Jesus (1 Cor. 7:10; 9:14; Acts 20:35) without alluding to their original historical contexts—nor should we have expected him to. Of these sayings, the two in 1 Corinthians are also found in the Gospels. The divorce saying is found in two different contexts (that of teaching disciples in Matt. 5:31–32, and that of controversy in Matt. 10:1–19 and Mark 10:1–12). The "right to pay" saying is found in Matthew 10:10 and its parallel in Luke 10:7 in the context of sending out the Twelve (Matthew) and the seventy-two (Luke). But the saying in Acts is not found at all in the Gospels, so for us it is totally without an original context.

It should not surprise us, therefore, to learn that many such sayings (without contexts) were available to the evangelists, and that it was the evangelists themselves, under their own guidance of the Spirit, who gave these sayings their present contexts. That is one of the reasons we often find the same saying or teaching in different contexts in the Gospels. That is also why sayings with similar themes, or the same subject matter, are often grouped in the Gospels in a topical way.

Matthew, for example, has five large topical collections (each of these concludes with something like, "And when Jesus had finished all these sayings. . . ."): life in the kingdom (the so-called Sermon on the Mount, chaps. 5–7), instructions for the ministers of the kingdom (10:5–42), parables of the kingdom at work in the world (13:1–52), teaching on relationships and discipline in the kingdom (18:1–35), eschatology, or the consummation of the kingdom (chaps. 23–25).

That these are Matthean collections can be illustrated in two ways from the collection in chapter 10. (1) The context is the historical mission of the Twelve and Jesus' instructions to them as he sent them out (vv. 5–12). In verses 16–20, however, the instructions are for a much later time, since in verses 5–6 they had been told to go only to the lost sheep of Israel, while verse 18 prophesies of their being brought before "governors," "kings," and the "Gentiles," and none of these were included in the original mission of the Twelve. (2) These nicely arranged sayings are found scattered all over Luke's gospel in this order: 9:2–5; 10:3; 21:12–17; 12:11–12; 6:40; 12:2–9; 12:51–53; 14:25–27; 17:33; 10:16. This suggests that Luke also had access to most of these sayings as separate units, which he then put in different contexts.

Thus as you read the Gospels, one of the questions you will want to ask, even if it cannot be answered for certain, is whether Jesus' audience for a given teaching was his close disciples, the larger crowds, or his opponents. Discovering the historical context of Jesus, or who his audience was, will not necessarily affect the basic meaning of a given saying, but it will broaden your perspective and often will help in understanding *the point* of what Jesus said.

The Historical Context of the Evangelist

At this point we are not talking about the literary context in which each evangelist has placed his Jesus materials, but about the historical context of each author that prompted him to write a gospel in the first place. Again we are involved in a certain amount of scholarly guesswork since the Gospels themselves are anonymous (in the sense that their authors are not identified by name) and we cannot be sure of their places of origin. But we can be fairly sure of each evangelist's interest and concerns by the way he selected, shaped, and arranged his materials.

Mark's gospel, for example, is especially interested in explaining the nature of Jesus' messiahship. Although Mark knows that the Messiah is the strong Son of God (1:1), who moves through Galilee with power and compassion (1:1–8:26), he also knows that Jesus repeatedly kept his messiahship hidden (see, e.g., 1:34; 1:43; 3:12;

4:11; 5:43; 7:24; 7:36; 8:26; 8:30). The reason for this silence is that only Jesus understands the true nature of his messianic destiny—that of a suffering servant who conquers through death. Although this is explained three times to the disciples, they too fail to understand (8:27–33; 9:30–32; 10:32–45). Like the twice-touched man (8:22–26), they need a second touch, the Resurrection, for them to see clearly.

That Mark's concern is the suffering-servant nature of Jesus' messiahship is even more evident from the fact that he does not include any of Jesus' teaching of discipleship until *after* the first explanation of his own suffering in 8:31–33. The implication, as well as the explicit teaching, is clear. The cross and servanthood that Jesus experienced are also the marks of genuine discipleship. As the poet put it: "It is the way the Master trod. Should not the servant tread it still?"

All of this can be seen by a careful reading of Mark's gospel. This is his historical context. To place it specifically is more conjectural, but we see no reason not to follow the very ancient tradition that says that Mark's gospel reflects the "memoirs" of Peter and that it appeared in Rome shortly after the latter's martyrdom, at a time of great suffering among the Christians in Rome. In any case, such contextual reading and studying is as important for the Gospels as it is for the Epistles.

The Literary Context

We have already touched on this somewhat in the section on "the historical context of Jesus—in particular." The literary context has to do with the place of a given pericope in the context of any one of the Gospels. To some extent this context was probably already fixed by its original historical context, which may have been known to the evangelist. But as we have already seen, many of the materials in the Gospels owe their present context to the evangelists themselves, according to their inspiration by the Spirit.

Our concern here is twofold: (1) to help you exegete or read with understanding a given saying or narrative in its present context in the Gospels, and (2) to help you understand the nature of the composition of the Gospels as wholes, and thus to interpret any one of the Gospels itself, not just isolated facts about the life of Jesus.

Interpreting the Individual Pericopes

In discussing how to interpret the Epistles, we noted that you must learn to "think paragraphs." That is not quite so important with the Gospels, although it will still hold true from time to time, especially with the large blocks of teachings. As we noted at the outset, these teaching sections will indeed have some similarities to our approach with the Epistles. Because of the unique nature of the Gospels, however, one must do two things here: think horizontally, and think vertically.

This is simply our way of saying that when interpreting or reading one of the Gospels, one needs to keep in mind the two realities about the Gospels noted above: that there are four of them, and that they are "two-level" documents.

Think Horizontally. To think horizontally means that when studying a pericope in any one gospel, one should be aware of the parallels in the other gospels. To be sure, this point must not be overdrawn, since none of the evangelists intended his gospel to be read in parallel with the others. Nonetheless, the fact that God has provided four gospels in the canon means that they cannot legitimately be read in total isolation from one another.

Our first word here is one of caution. The purpose of studying the Gospels in parallel is not to fill out the story in one gospel with details from the others. Usually such a reading of the Gospels tends to harmonize all the details and thus blur the very distinctives in each gospel that the Holy Spirit inspired. Such "filling out" may interest us at the level of the historical Jesus, but that is *not* the canonical level, which should be our first concern.

The basic reasons for thinking horizontally are two. First, the parallels will often give us an appreciation for the distinctives of any one of the Gospels. After all, it is precisely their distinctives that are the reason for having four gospels in the first place. Second, the parallels will help us to be aware of the different kinds of contexts in which the same or similar materials lived in the ongoing church. We will illustrate each of these, but first, here is an important word about presuppositions.

It is impossible to read the Gospels without having some kind of presupposition about their relationships to one another—even if you have never thought about it. The most common presupposition, but the one that is the least likely of all, is that each gospel was written independently of the others. There is simply too much clear evidence against this for it to be a live option for you as you read.

Take, for example, the fact that there is such a high degree of verbal similarity among Matthew, Mark, and Luke in their *narratives,* as well as in their recording of the sayings of Jesus. Remarkable verbal similarities should not surprise us about the *sayings* of the one who "spake as never man spake." But for this to carry over to the narratives is something else again—especially so when one considers (1) that these stories were first told in Aramaic, yet we are talking about the use of Greek words, (2) that Greek word order is extremely free, yet often the similarities extend even to precise word order, and (3) that it is highly unlikely that three people in three different parts of the Roman Empire would tell the same story with the same words—even to such minor points of individual style as prepositions and conjunctions. Yet this is what happens over and again in the first three gospels.

This can easily be illustrated from the narrative of the feeding of the five thousand, which is one of the few stories found in all four gospels. Note the following statistics:

1. Number of words used to tell the story
   Matthew   157
   Mark   194
   Luke   153
   John   199

2. Number of words common to *all* of the first three gospels: 53

3. Number of words John has in common with all the others: 8 (five, two, five thousand, took loaves, twelve baskets of pieces)

4. Percentages of agreement
   Matthew with Mark   59%
   Matthew with Luke   44%
   Luke with Mark   40%
   John with Matthew   8.5%
   John with Mark   8.5%
   John with Luke   6.5%

The following conclusions seem inevitable: John represents a clearly *independent* telling of the story. He uses only those words absolutely necessary to be telling the same story, and even uses a different Greek word for *fish!* The other three are just as clearly *interdependent* in some way. Those who know Greek recognize how improbable it is for two people independently to tell the same story in narrative form and have a 60% agreement in the words used, and often in the exact word order.

Take as a further example the words from Mark 13:14 and the parallel in Matthew 24:15. ("Let the *reader* understand"). These words can hardly have been a part of the *oral* tradition (it says *reader,* not *hearer,* and since in its earliest form [Mark] there is no mention of Daniel, it is unlikely to be a word of Jesus referring to Daniel). The words were therefore inserted into the saying of Jesus by one of the evangelists for the sake of his readers. It seems highly improbable that exactly the same parenthesis would have been inserted independently at exactly the same point by two authors writing independently.

The best explanation of all the data is the one we suggested earlier, that Mark wrote his gospel first, probably in part at least from his recollection of Peter's preaching and teaching. Luke and Matthew had access to Mark's gospel and independently used it as the basic source for their own. But they also had access to all kinds of other material about Jesus, some of which they had in common. This common material, however, is scarcely ever presented in the same order in the two gospels, a fact that suggests that neither one had access to the other's writing. Finally, John wrote independently of the other three and thus his gospel has little material in common with them. This, we would note, is *how* the Holy Spirit inspired the writing of the Gospels.

That this will help you interpret the Gospels can be seen from the following brief sample. Notice how the sayings of Jesus on the "desolating sacrilege" appears when read in parallel columns:

Matt. 24:15–16	Mark 13:14	Luke 21:20–21
So when you see	But when you see	But when you see Jerusalem surrounded by armies, then know that
the desolating	the desolating	its desolation has come near.
sacrilege spoken of by the prophet Daniel, standing in the holy place	sacrilege set up where it ought not to be	

(let the reader under-
   stand),
	(let the reader under-
	   stand),	

then let	then let	Then let

those who are in Judea
  flee
	those who are in Judea
	  flee
		those who are in Judea
		  flee

to the mountains;	to the mountains;	to the mountains, and

It should be noted first of all that this saying is in the Olivet Discourse in exactly the same sequence in all three gospels. When Mark recorded these words, he was calling his readers to a thoughtful reflection as to what Jesus meant by "the desolating sacrilege set up where it ought not to be." Matthew, also inspired by the Spirit, helped his readers by making the saying a little more explicit. The "desolating sacrilege," he reminds them, was spoken about in Daniel, and what Jesus meant by "where it ought not to be" was "the holy place" (the temple in Jerusalem). Luke, equally inspired of the Spirit, simply interpreted the whole saying for the sake of his Gentile readers. He really lets them understand! What Jesus meant by all this was, "When Jerusalem is surrounded by armies, then know that its desolation is near."

Thus one can see how thinking horizontally and knowing that Matthew and Luke used Mark can help you to interpret any one of the Gospels as you read it. Similarly, awareness of Gospel parallels also helps one to see how the same materials sometimes came to be used in new contexts in the ongoing church.

Take, for example, Jesus' lament over Jerusalem, which is one of those sayings Matthew and Luke have in common that is not found in Mark. The saying appears nearly word for word in both gospels. In Luke 13:34–35 it belongs to a long collection of narratives and teaching as Jesus is on his way to Jerusalem (9:51– 19:10). It immediately follows the warning about Herod, which Jesus has concluded by his reply, "It cannot be that a prophet should perish away from Jerusalem." The rejection of God's messenger leads to judgment on Israel.

In Matthew 23:37–39 the lament concludes his collection of seven woes on the Pharisees, the final one of which reflects the theme of the prophets being killed in Jerusalem. In this case the saying has the same point in both gospels although it is placed in different settings.

The same thing is true of many other sayings as well. The

Lord's Prayer is set in both gospels (Matt. 6:7–13; Luke 11:2–4) in contexts of teaching on prayer, although the main thrust of each section is considerably different. Note also that in Matthew it serves as a model, "Pray then like this"; in Luke repetition is allowed, "When you pray, say." Likewise note the Beatitudes (Matt. 5:3–11; Luke 6:20–23). In Matthew the *poor* are "the poor in spirit"; in Luke they are simply "you poor" in contrast to "you that are rich" (6:24). On such points most people tend to have only half a canon. Traditional evangelicals tend to read only "the poor in spirit"; social activists tend to read only "you poor." We insist that *both* are canonical. In a truly profound sense the real poor are those who recognize themselves as impoverished before God. But the God of the Bible, who became incarnate in Jesus of Nazareth, is a God who pleads the cause of the oppressed and the disenfranchised. One can scarcely read Luke's gospel without recognizing his interest in this aspect of the divine revelation (see 14:12–14; cf. 12:33–34 with the Matthean parallel, 6:19–21).

A final word here. If you are interested in the serious study of the Gospels, you will need to refer to a synopsis (a presentation of the Gospels in parallel columns). The very best of these is edited by Kurt Aland, entitled *Synopsis of the Four Gospels* (New York: United Bible Societies, 1975).

Think Vertically. To think vertically means that when reading or studying a narrative or teaching in the Gospels, one should try to be aware of both historical contexts, that of Jesus and that of the evangelist.

Again, our first word here is one of caution. The purpose of thinking vertically is not primarily to study the life of the historical Jesus. That indeed should always be of interest to us. But the *Gospels in their present form* are the Word of God to us; our own *reconstructions* of Jesus' life are not. And again, one should not overdo this kind of thinking. It is only a call for the awareness that many of the gospel materials owe their present context to the evangelists, and that good interpretation may require appreciating a given saying first in its original historical context as a proper prelude to understanding that same word in its present canonical context.

We may illustrate this from a passage like Matthew 20:1–16, Jesus' parable of the laborers in the vineyard. Our concern is, What does this mean in its present context in Matthew? If we first think horizontally, we will note that on either side of the parable Matthew has long sections of material in which he follows Mark very closely (Matt. 19:1–30; 20:17–34 parallels Mark 10:1–52). At 10:31, Mark had the saying, "Many that are first will be last, and the last first," which Matthew kept intact at 19:30. But right at that point he then inserted this parable, which concluded with a repetition of this saying (20:16), only now in reverse order. Thus in Matthew's gospel the immediate context for the parable is the saying about the reversal of order between the first and the last.

When you look at the parable proper (20:1–15), you will note that it concludes with the landowner's justification of his generosity. Pay in the kingdom, Jesus says, is not predicated on what's fair, but on God's grace! In its original context this parable probably served to justify Jesus' own accepting of sinners in light of the Pharisees' cavil against him. They think of themselves as having "borne the burden of the day" and hence worthy of more pay. But God is generous and gracious, and he freely accepts sinners just as he does the "righteous."

Given that as its most likely original setting, how does the parable now function in Matthew's gospel? The point of the parable, God's gracious generosity to the undeserving, certainly remains the same. But that point is no longer a concern to justify Jesus' own actions. Matthew's gospel does that elsewhere in other ways. Here the parable functions in a context of discipleship, where those who have forsaken all to follow Jesus are the last who have become first (perhaps indeed in contrast to the Jewish leaders, a point Matthew makes over and again).

Many times, of course, thinking vertically will reveal that the same point is being made at both levels. But the illustration just given shows how fruitful such thinking can be for exegesis.

Interpreting the Gospels as Wholes

An important part of the literary context is to learn to see the kinds of concerns that have gone into the composition of each of the Gospels that make each of them unique.

We have noted throughout this chapter that in reading and studying the Gospels one must take seriously not only the evangelists' interest in Jesus per se, what he did and said, but also their reasons for retelling the one story for their own readers. The evangelists, we have noted, were authors, not merely compilers. But being authors does *not* mean they were creators of the material;

quite the opposite is true. Several factors prohibit greater creativity, including, we believe, the somewhat fixed nature of the material and the sovereign oversight of the Holy Spirit in the transmissional process. Thus they were authors in the sense that with the Spirit's help they creatively structured and rewrote the material to meet the needs of their readers. What concerns us here is to help you to be aware of each of the evangelist's compositional concerns and technique as you read or study.

There were three principles at work in the composition of the Gospels: selectivity, arrangement, and adaptation. On the one hand, the evangelists as divinely inspired authors selected those narratives and teachings that suited their purposes. It is true, of course, that simple concern for the preservation of what was available to them may have been one of those purposes. Nonetheless, John, who has fewer but considerably more expanded narratives and discourses, specifically tells us he has been very selective (20:30–31; 21:25). This last word (21:25), spoken in hyperbole, probably expresses the case for the others as well. Luke, for example, chose not to include a considerable section of Mark (6:45–8:26).

At the same time the evangelists and their churches had special interests that also caused them to arrange and adapt what was selected. John, for example, distinctly tells us that his purpose was patently theological, "that you may believe that Jesus is the Messiah, the Son of God" (20:31). This interest in Jesus as the Jewish Messiah is probably the chief reason that the vast majority of his material has to do with Jesus' ministry in Judea and Jerusalem, over against the almost totally Galilean ministry in the Synoptics. For Jews, the Messiah's true home was Jerusalem. Thus John knows of Jesus' having said that a prophet has no honor in his own home or country. This was originally said at the time of his rejection at Nazareth (Matt. 13:57; Mark 6:4; Luke 4:24). In John's gospel this saying is referred to as an explanation for the Messiah's rejection in Jerusalem (4:44)—a profound theological insight into Jesus' ministry.

The principle of adaptation is also what explains most of the so-called discrepancies among the Gospels. One of the most noted of these, for example, is the cursing of the fig tree (Mark 11:12–14, 20–25; Matt. 21:18–22). In Mark's gospel the story is told for its symbolic theological significance. Note that between the cursing and the withering Jesus pronounces a similar judgment on Judaism by his cleansing of the temple. However, the story of the fig tree had great meaning for the early church also because of the lesson on faith that concludes it. In Matthew's gospel the lesson on faith is the sole interest of the story, so he relates the cursing and the withering together in order to emphasize this point. Remember, in each case this telling of the story is the work of the Holy Spirit, who inspired *both* evangelists.

To illustrate this process of composition on a somewhat larger scale, let us look at the opening chapters of Mark (1:14–3:6). These chapters are an artistic masterpiece, so well constructed that many readers will probably get Mark's point even though not recognizing how he has done it.

There are three strands to Jesus' public ministry that are of special interest to Mark: popularity with the crowds, discipleship for the few, and opposition from the authorities. Notice how skillfully, by selecting and arranging narratives, Mark sets these before us. After the announcement of Jesus' public ministry (1:14–15), the first narrative records the call of the first disciples. This motif will be elaborated in the next sections (3:13–19; 4:10–12; 4:34–41; et al.); his greater concern in these first two chapters is with the other two items. Beginning with 1:21 to 1:45 Mark has just four pericopes, a day in Capernaum (1:21–28 and 29–34), a short preaching tour the next day (1:35–39), and the story of the healing of the leper (1:40–45). The common motif throughout is the rapid spread of Jesus' fame and popularity (see vv. 27–28, 32–33, 37, 45), which culminates with Jesus' not being able to "enter a town openly . . . yet people still came to him from everywhere." It all seems breathtaking; yet Mark has painted this picture with only four narratives, plus his repeated phrase "and immediately" (1:21, 23, 28, 29, 31, 42, a phrase that is unfortunately lost in the NIV) and his starting almost every sentence with "and" (which is also lost in the NIV).

With that picture before us Mark next selects five different kinds of narratives that, all together, paint the picture of opposition and give the reasons for it. Notice that the common denominator of the first four pericopes is the questions "Why?" (2:7, 16, 18, 24). Opposition comes because Jesus forgives sin, eats with sinners, neglects the tradition of fasting, and "breaks" the Sabbath. That this last item was considered by the Jews to be the ultimate insult to their tradition is made clear by Mark's appending a second narrative of this kind (3:1–6).

We do not mean to suggest that in all the sections of all the Gospels one will be able to trace the evangelist's compositional concerns so easily. But we do suggest that this is the kind of looking at the Gospels that is needed.

Some Hermeneutical Observations

For the most part the hermeneutical principles for the Gospels are a combination of what has been said in previous chapters about the Epistles and historical narratives.

The Teachings and Imperatives

Given that one has done exegesis with care, the teachings and imperatives of Jesus in the Gospels should be brought into the twentieth century in the same way as we do with Paul—or Peter or James—in the Epistles. Even the questions of cultural relativity need to be raised in the same way. Divorce is scarcely a valid option for couples who would both be followers of Jesus—a point repeated by Paul in 1 Corinthians 7:10–11. But in a culture such as modern America, where one out of two adult converts will have been divorced, the question of remarriage should probably not be decided mindlessly and without redemptive concern for new converts. One's early assumptions about the meaning of the words of Jesus spoken in an entirely different cultural setting must be carefully examined. Likewise, we will scarcely have a Roman soldier forcing us to go a mile (Matt. 5:41). But in this case Jesus' point, the "Christian extra," is surely applicable in any number of comparable situations.

An important word needs to be said here. Because many of Jesus' imperatives are set in the context of expounding the Old Testament Law and because to many people they seem to present an impossible ideal, a variety of hermeneutical ploys have been offered to "get around" these imperatives as normative authority for the church. We cannot take the time here to outline and refute these various attempts, but a few words are in order. An excellent overview is given in chapter 6 of Stein's *The Method and Message of Jesus' Teachings*.

Most of these hermeneutical ploys arose because the imperatives seem like law—and such an impossible law at that! And Christian life according to the New Testament is based on God's grace, not on obedience to law. But to see the imperatives as law is to misunderstand them. They are *not* law in the sense that one must obey them *in order to* become or remain a Christian; our salvation does not depend upon perfect obedience to them. They *are* descriptions, by way of imperative, of what Christian life should be like *because of* God's prior acceptance of us. A no-retaliation ethic (Matt. 5:38–42) *is* in fact the ethics of the kingdom—for this present age. But it is predicated on God's nonretaliatory love for us; and in the kingdom it is to be "like Father, like son." It is our experience of God's unconditional, unlimited forgiveness that comes first, but it is to be followed by our unconditional, unlimited forgiveness of others. Someone has said that in Christianity, religion is grace; ethics is gratitude. Hence Jesus' imperatives are a word for us; but they are not like the Old Testament Law. They describe the new life, which itself is not optional of course, that one is to live out as God's loved and redeemed child.

The Narratives

The narratives tend to function in more than one way in the Gospels. The miracle stories, for example, are not recorded to offer morals or to serve as precedents. Rather, they function in the Gospels as vital illustrations of the power of the kingdom breaking in through Jesus' own ministry. In a circuitous way they may illustrate faith, fear, or failure, but that is not their primary function. However, stories such as the rich young man (Mark 10:17–22 and parallels) or the request to sit at Jesus' right hand (Mark 10:35–45 and parallels) are placed in a context of teaching, where the story itself serves as an illustration of what is being taught. It seems to us to be the proper hermeneutical practice to use these narratives in precisely the same way.

Thus the *point* of the rich young man story is *not* that all Jesus' disciples must sell all their possessions to follow him. There are clear examples in the Gospels where that was not the case (cf. Luke 5:27–30; 8:3; Mark 14:3–9). The story instead illustrates the point of how difficult it is for the rich to enter the kingdom, precisely because they have prior commitments to mammon and are trying to secure their lives thereby. But God's gracious love can perform miracles on the rich, too, Jesus goes on to say. The Zacchaeus story (Luke 19:1–10) is an illustration of such.

Again, one can see the importance of good exegesis so that the point we make of such narratives is in fact the point being made in the Gospel itself.

A Final, Very Important Word

This word also applies to the prior discussion of the historical context of Jesus, but it is included here because it is so crucial to the hermeneutical question. The word is this: *One dare not think he or she can properly interpret the Gospels without a clear understanding of the concept of the kingdom of God in the ministry of Jesus.* For a brief, but good, introduction to this matter look at chapter 4 in Stein's *Method and Message.* Here we can give only a brief sketch, along with some words about how this affects hermeneutics.

First of all, you should know that the basic theological framework of the entire New Testament is eschatological. Eschatology has to do with the end, when God brings this age to its close. Most Jews in Jesus' day were eschatological in their thinking. That is, they thought they lived at the very brink of time, when God would step into history and bring an end to this age and usher in the age to come. The Greek word for the end they were looking for is *eschaton.* Thus to be eschatological in one's thinking meant to be looking for the end.

The Jewish Eschatological Hope
The Eschaton

This Age (Satan's Time)	The Age to Come (The Time of God's Rule)
characterized by:	characterized by:
sin	the presence of the Spirit
sickness	righteousness
demon possession	health
evil men triumph	peace

The earliest Christians, of course, well understood this eschatological way of looking at life. For them the events of Jesus' coming, his death and resurrection, and his giving of the Spirit were all related to their expectations about the coming of the end. It happened like this.

The coming of the end also meant a new beginning—the beginning of God's new age, the messianic age. The new age was also referred to as the kingdom of God, which meant "the time of God's rule." This new age would be a time of righteousness (e.g., Isa. 11:4–5), and people would live in peace (e.g., Isa. 2:2–4). It would be a time of the fullness of the Spirit (Joel 2:28–30) when the new covenant spoken of by Jeremiah would be realized (Jer. 31:31–34; 32:38–40). Sin and sickness would be done away with (e.g., Zech. 13:1; Isa. 53:5). Even the material creation would feel the joyful effects of this new age (e.g., Isa. 11:6–9).

Thus when John the Baptist announced the coming of the end to be very near and baptized God's Messiah, eschatological fervor reached fever pitch. The Messiah was at hand, the one who would usher in the new age of the Spirit (Luke 3:7–17).

Jesus came and announced that the coming kingdom was at hand with his ministry (e.g., Mark 1:14–15; Luke 17:20–21). He cast out demons, worked miracles, and freely accepted the outcasts and sinners—all signs that the end had begun (e.g., Luke 11:20; Matt. 11:2–6; Luke 14:21; 15:1–2). Everyone kept watching him to see if he really *was* the Coming One. Would he really bring in the messianic age with all of its splendor? Then suddenly he was crucified—and the lights went out.

But no! There was a glorious sequel. On the third day he was raised from the dead and he appeared to many of his followers. Surely *now* he would "restore the kingdom to Israel" (Acts 1:6). But instead he returned to the Father and poured out the promised Spirit. Here is where problems come for the early church and for us. Jesus announced the coming kingdom as having arrived with his own coming. The Spirit's coming in fullness and power, with signs and wonders, and the coming of the new covenant were signs that the new age had arrived. Yet the end of this age apparently had not yet taken place. How were they to understand this?

Very early, beginning with Peter's sermon in Acts 3, the early Christians came to realize that Jesus had not come to usher in the "final" end, but the "beginning" of the end, as it were. Thus they came to see that with Jesus' death and resurrection, and with the coming of the Spirit, the blessings and benefits of the future had already come. In a sense, therefore, the end had already come. But in another sense the end had not yet fully come. Thus it was *already*, but *not yet*.

The early believers, therefore, learned to be a truly eschatological people. They lived between the times—that is, between the *beginning* of the end and the *consummation* of the end. At the Lord's Table they celebrated their eschatological existence, by proclaiming "the Lord's death until he comes" (1 Cor. 11:26). *Already* they knew God's free and full forgiveness, but they had *not yet* been perfected (Phil. 3:7–14). *Already* victory over death was theirs (1 Cor. 3:22), *yet* they would still die (Phil. 3:20–22). *Already* they lived in the Spirit, *yet* they still lived in the word where Satan could attack (e.g., Eph. 6:10–17). *Already* they had been justified and faced no condemnation (Rom. 8:1), *yet* there was still to be a future judgment (2 Cor. 5:10). They were God's future people; they had been conditioned by the future. They knew its benefits, lived in light of its values, but they, as we, still had to live out these benefits and values in the present world. Thus the essential theological framework for understanding the New Testament looks like this:

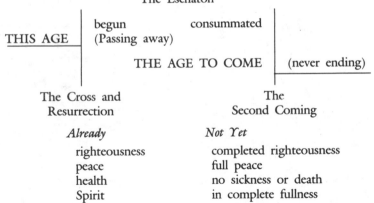

The New Testament Eschatological View
The Eschaton

	begun	consummated	
THIS AGE	(Passing away)		
	THE AGE TO COME		(never ending)

The Cross and Resurrection

The Second Coming

Already	*Not Yet*
righteousness	completed righteousness
peace	full peace
health	no sickness or death
Spirit	in complete fullness

The hermeneutical key to much in the New Testament, and especially the ministry and teaching of Jesus, is to be found in this kind of "tension." Precisely because the kingdom, the time of God's rule, has been inaugurated with Jesus' own coming we are called to *life* in the kingdom, which means life under his lordship, freely accepted and forgiven, but committed to the ethics of the new age, and to seeing them worked out in our own lives and world in this present age.

Thus when we pray, "Thy kingdom come," we pray first of all for the consummation. But because the kingdom we long to see consummated has already begun to come, the same prayer is full of implications for the present.

8

The Parables: Do You Get the Point?

It should be noted at the outset that everything said in chapter 7 about the teaching of Jesus in the Gospels holds true for the parables. Why then should the parables need a chapter of their own in a book like this? How could these simple, direct little stories Jesus told pose problems for the reader or the interpreter? It seems that one would have to be a dullard of the first rank to miss the point of the Good Samaritan or the Prodigal Son. The very reading of those stories pricks the heart or comforts it.

Yet a special chapter is necessary because, for all their charm and simplicity, the parables have suffered a fate of misinterpretation in the church second only to the Revelation.

The Parables in History

The reason for the long history of the misinterpretation of the parables can be traced back to something Jesus himself said, as recorded in Mark 4:10–12 (and parallels, Matt. 13:10–13; Luke 8:9–10). When asked about the purpose of parables, he seems to have suggested that they contained mysteries for those on the inside, while they hardened those on the outside. Because he then proceeded to "interpret" the parable of the Sower in a semi-allegorical way, this was seen to give license to the hardening theory and endless allegorical interpretations. The parables were considered to be simple stories for those on the outside, to whom the "real meanings," the "mysteries," were hidden; these belonged only to the church and could be uncovered by means of allegory.

Thus as great and brilliant a scholar as Augustine offers the following interpretation of the parable of the Good Samaritan:

> *A certain man went down from Jerusalem to Jericho* = Adam
> *Jerusalem* = the heavenly city of peace, from which Adam fell
> *Jericho* = the moon, and thereby signifies Adam's mortality
> *thieves* = the devil and his angels
> *stripped him* = namely, of his immortality
> *beat him* = by persuading him to sin
> *and left him half-dead* = as a man he lives, but he died spiritually, therefore he is half-dead
> *The priest and Levite* = the priesthood and ministry of the Old Testament
> *The Samaritan* = is said to mean Guardian; therefore Christ himself is meant
> *bound his wounds* = means binding the restraint of sin
> *oil* = comfort of good hope
> *wine* = exhortation to work with a fervent spirit
> *beast* = the flesh of Christ's incarnation
> *inn* = the church
> *the morrow* = after the Resurrection
> *two-pence* = promise of this life and the life to come
> *innkeeper* = Paul

As novel and interesting as all of this might be, one can be sure that it is not what Jesus intended. After all, the context clearly calls for an understanding of human relationships ("Who is my neighbor?"), not divine to human; and there is no reason to think that Jesus would *predict* the church and Paul in this obtuse fashion!

Indeed it is extremely doubtful whether most of the parables were intended for an inner circle at all. In at least three instances Luke specifically says that Jesus told parables *to* people (15:3; 18:9; 19:11) with the clear implication that the parables were to be understood. Moreover, the lawyer to whom Jesus told the parable of the Good Samaritan (Luke 10:25–37) understood the parable, as did the chief priests and Pharisees the parable of the tenants in Matthew 21:45.

If *we* have trouble at times understanding the parables, it is not because they are allegories for which we need some special interpretive keys. Rather it is related to some things we suggested in the previous chapter on the Gospels. One of the keys to understanding them lies in discovering the original audience to whom they were spoken; as we noted, many times they came down to the evangelists without a context.

If the parables, then, are not allegorical mysteries for the church, what did Jesus mean in Mark 4:10–12 by the mystery of the kingdom and its relationship to parables? Most likely the clue to this saying lies in a play on words in Jesus' native Aramaic. The word *methal* which was translated *parabolē* in Greek was used for a whole range of figures of speech in the riddle, puzzle, parable category, not just for the story variety called "parables" in English. Probably verse 11 meant that the meaning of Jesus' ministry (the secret of the kingdom) could not be perceived by those on the outside; it was like a *methal,* a riddle, to them. Hence his speaking in *mathelin* (parables) was part of the *methal* (riddle) of his whole ministry to them. They saw, but they failed to see; they heard—and even understood—the parables, but they failed really to appreciate the whole thrust of Jesus' ministry.

Our exegesis of the parables, therefore, must begin with the same assumptions that we have brought to every other genre so far. Jesus was not trying to be obtuse; he fully intended to be understood. Our task is first of all to try to hear what they heard. But before we can do that adequately, we must begin by looking at the question, What is a parable?

The Nature of the Parables

The Variety of Kinds

The first thing one must note is that not all the sayings we label as parables are of the same kind. There is a basic difference, for example, between the Good Samaritan (true parable), on the one hand, and the Leaven in the Meal (similitude), on the other, and both of these differ from the saying, "You are the salt of the earth" (metaphor), or "Do people pick grapes from thornbushes, or figs from thistles?" (epigram). Yet all of these can be found from time to time in discussions of the parables.

The Good Samaritan is an example of a *true parable*. It is a *story,* pure and simple, with a beginning and an ending; it has something of a "plot." Other such story parables include the Lost Sheep, the

Prodigal Son, the Great Supper, the Laborers in the Vineyard, the Rich Man and Lazarus, and the Ten Virgins.

The Leaven in the Meal, on the other hand, is more of a *similitude*. What is said of the leaven, or the sower, or the mustard seed was always true of leaven, sowing, or mustard seeds. Such "parables" are more like illustrations taken from everyday life that Jesus used to make a point.

Such sayings as "You are the salt of the earth," differ from both of these. These are sometimes called parabolic sayings, but in reality they are *metaphors* and *similes*. At times they seem to function in a way similar to the similitude, but their point—their reason for being spoken—is considerably different.

It should be noted further that in some cases, especially that of the Wicked Tenants (Mark 12:1–11; Matt. 21:33–44; Luke 20:9–18), a parable may approach something very close to allegory, where many of the details in a story are intended to represent something else (such as in Augustine's misinterpretation of the Good Samaritan). But *the parables are not allegories*—even if at times they have what appear to us to be allegorical features. The reason we can be sure of that has to do with their differing functions.

Because the parables are not all of one kind, one cannot necessarily lay down rules that will cover them all. What we say here is intended for the parables proper, but much of what is said will also cover the other types as well.

How the Parables Function

The best clues as to what the parables are is to be found in their *function*. In contrast to most of the parabolic sayings, such as the figs from thistles, the story parables do not serve to illustrate Jesus' prosaic teaching with picture words. Nor are they told to serve as vehicles for revealing truth—although they end up clearly doing that. Rather the story parables function as a means of *calling forth a response* on the part of the hearer. To paraphrase Marshall McLuhan's words, the parable itself *is* the message. It is told to address and capture the hearers, to bring them up short about their own actions, or to cause them to respond in some way to Jesus and his ministry.

It is this "call for response" nature of the parable that causes our great dilemma in interpreting them. For in some ways to interpret a parable is to destroy what it was originally. It is like interpreting a joke. The whole point of a joke and what makes it funny is that the hearer has an immediacy with it as it is being told. It is funny to the hearer precisely because he or she gets "caught," as it were. But it can only "catch" them if they understand the points of reference in the joke. If you have to interpret the joke by explaining the points of reference, it no longer catches the hearer and therefore usually fails to capture the same quality of laughter. When the joke is interpreted, it can then be understood all right, and may still be funny (at least one understands what one *should* have laughed at), but it ceases to have the same impact. Thus it no longer *functions* in the same way.

So with the parables. They were spoken, and we may assume that most of the hearers had an immediate identification with the points of reference that caused them to catch the point—or be caught by it. For us, however, the parables are written. We may or may not immediately catch the points of reference, therefore they can never function for us in quite the same way they did for the first hearers. But by interpreting we can understand what *they* caught, or what we would have caught had we been there. And this is what we must do in our exegesis. The hermeneutical task lies beyond that: How do we recapture the "punch" of the parables in our own times and our own settings?

The Exegesis of the Parables

Finding the Points of Reference

Let us go back to our analogy of the joke. The two things that capture the hearer of a joke and elicit a response of laughter are the same two things that captured the hearers of Jesus' parables, namely their knowledge of the points of reference and the unexpected turn in the story. The keys to understanding are the points of reference, those various parts of the story with which one identifies as it is being told. If one misses these in a joke, then there can be no unexpected turn, because the points of reference are what create the ordinary expectations. If one misses these in a parable, then the force and the point of what Jesus said is likewise going to be missed.

What we mean by "points of reference" can best be illustrated from a parable of Jesus that is recorded in its full original context— Luke 7:40–42. In the context Jesus has been invited to dinner by a

Pharisee named Simon. But the invitation was not to be considered as being in honor of a visiting famous rabbi. The failure to offer Jesus even the common hospitality of the day was surely intended as something of a put down. When the town prostitute finds her way into the presence of the diners and makes a fool of herself over Jesus by washing his feet with her tears and wiping them with her hair, it only fortifies the Pharisees' suspicions. Jesus could not be a prophet and leave uncondemned this kind of public disgrace.

Knowing their thoughts, Jesus tells his host a simple story. Two men owed money to a moneylender. One owed five hundred denarii (a denarius was a day's wage); the other owed fifty. Neither could pay, so he cancelled the debts of both. The point: Who, do you think, would have responded to the moneylender with the greater display of love?

This story needed no interpretation, although Jesus proceeded to drive the point home with full force. There are three points of reference: the moneylender and the two debtors. And the identifications are immediate. God is like the moneylender; the town harlot and Simon are like the two debtors. The parable is a word of judgment calling for response from Simon. He could scarcely have missed the point. When it is over, he has egg all over his face. Such is the force of a parable.

We should note further that the woman heard the parable as well. She, too, will identify with the story as it is being told. But what she will hear is not judgment but Jesus', and therefore God's, acceptance of her.

NOTE WELL: This is *not* an allegory; it is parable. A true allegory is a story where each element in the story means something quite foreign to the story itself. Allegory would give meaning to the five hundred denarii, the fifty denarii, as well as to any other details one might find. Furthermore, and this is especially important, the point of the parable is *not* in the points of reference as it would be in a true allegory. The points of reference are only those parts of the story that draw the hearer into it, with whom he or she is to identify in some way as the story proceeds. The *point* of the story is to be found in the intended response. In this parable it is a word of judgment on Simon and his friends or a word of acceptance and forgiveness to the woman.

Identifying the Audience

In the above illustration we also pointed out the significance of identifying the audience because the meaning of the parable has to do with how it was originally heard. For many of the parables, of course, the audience is given in the Gospel accounts. In such cases the task of interpretation is a combination of three things: (1) sit and listen to the parable again and again, (2) identify the points of reference intended by Jesus that would have been picked up by the original hearers, and (3) try to determine how the original hearers would have identified with the story, and therefore what they would have heard.

Let us try this on two well-known parables: the Good Samaritan (Luke 10:25–37) and the Prodigal Son (Luke 15:11–32). In the case of the Good Samaritan the story is told to an expert in the Law, who, wanting to justify himself, Luke says, had asked, "And who is my neighbor?" As you read the parable again and again, you will notice that it does not answer the question the way it was asked. But in a more telling way it exposes the smug self-righteousness of the lawyer. He knows what the Law says about loving one's neighbor as oneself, and he is ready to define "neighbor" in terms that will demonstrate that he piously obeys the Law.

There are really only two points of reference in the story, the man in the ditch and the Samaritan, although other details in the parable help to build the effect. Two things in particular need to be noted: (1) The two who pass by on the other side are priestly types, the religious order that stands over against the rabbis and the Pharisees, who are the experts in the Law. (2) Almsgiving to the poor was the Pharisees' big thing. This was how they loved their neighbors as themselves.

Notice, then, how the lawyer is going to get caught by this parable. A man falls into the hands of robbers on the road from Jerusalem to Jericho, a common enough event. Two priestly types next go down the road and pass by on the other side. The story is being told from the point of view of the man in the ditch, and the lawyer has now been "set up." "Of course," he would think to himself, "who could expect anything else from priests? The next person down will be a Pharisee, and he will show himself neighborly by helping the poor chap." But no, it turns out to be a

Samaritan! You will have to appreciate how contemptuously the Pharisees held the Samaritans if you are going to hear what he heard. Notice that he does not even bring himself to use the word Samaritan at the end.

Do you see what Jesus has done to this man? The second great commandment is to love one's neighbor as oneself. The lawyer had neat little systems that allowed him to love within limits. What Jesus does is to expose the prejudice and hatred of his heart, and therefore his real lack of obedience to this commandment. "Neighbor" can no longer be defined in limiting terms. His lack of love is not that he will not have helped the man in the ditch, but that he hates Samaritans (and looks down on priests). In effect, the parable destroys the question rather than answering it.

Similarly with the Prodigal Son. The context is the Pharisees' murmuring over Jesus' acceptance of and eating with the wrong kind of people. The three parables of lost things in Luke 15 are Jesus' justification of his actions. In the parable of the lost son there are just three points of reference, the father and his two sons. Here again, where one sat determined how one heard, but in either case the *point* is the same: God not only freely forgives the lost but accepts them with great joy. Those who consider themselves righteous reveal themselves to be unrighteous if they do not share the father's and the lost son's joy.

Jesus' table companions, of course, will identify with the lost son, as all of us well should. But that is not the real force of the parable, which is to be found in the attitude of the second son. He was "always with the father," yet he had put himself on the outside. He failed to share the father's heart with its love for a lost son. As a friend recently put it: Can you imagine anything worse than coming home and falling into the hands of the elder brother?

In each of these cases, and others, the exegetical difficulties you will encounter will stem mostly from the cultural gap between you and Jesus' original audience, which may cause you to miss some of the finer points that go into the makeup of the whole story. Here is where you will probably need outside help. But do not neglect these matters, for the cultural customs are what help to give the original stories their lifelikeness.

The "Contextless" Parables

But what of those parables that are found in the Gospels without their original historical context? Since we have already illustrated this concern in the previous chapter from the parable of the Laborers in the Vineyard (Matt. 20:1–16), we will only briefly review here. Again, it is a matter of trying to determine the points of reference and the original audience. The key is in the repeated rereading of the parable until its points of reference clearly emerge. Usually this will also give one an instant clue to its original audience.

Thus in the Laborers in the Vineyard, there are only three points of reference: the landowner, the full-day laborers and the one-hour laborers. This is easily determined, because these are the only people brought into focus as the story wraps up. The original audience is also easily determined. Who would have been "caught" by a story like this? Obviously the hearers who identify with the full-day laborers, since they alone are in focus at the end.

The point is similar to that of the Prodigal Son. God is gracious, and the righteous should not begrudge God's generosity. What has happened in its present Matthean context in this instance, however, is that the same point is now being made to a new audience. In the context of discipleship it serves as an assurance of God's generosity, despite the cavils or hatred of others.

One can see this same thing happening with the parable of the Lost Sheep in Matthew 18:12–14. In Luke's gospel this parable functions along with the Lost Coin and Prodigal Son as a word to the Pharisees. The lost sheep is clearly a sinner, whose finding brings joy in heaven. Again, as a word to the Pharisees, it justifies Jesus' acceptance of the outcasts; but when heard by the outcasts it assures them that they are the objects of the loving shepherd's search. In Matthew, the parable is a part of the collection of sayings on relationships within the kingdom. In this new context the same point is being made: God's care for the lost. But here the "lost" are sheep who have "wandered off." In Matthew's context it speaks to the question of what do we do for those "little ones" who are of weak faith, and who tend to go astray. In verses 6–9 Matthew's community is told that no one of them had better be responsible for causing a "little one" to go astray. In verses 10–14 the parable of the Lost Sheep tells them, on the other hand, they should seek out the wandering one and love him or her back into the fold. Same parable, same point, but to a brand new audience.

The Parables of the Kingdom

So far our illustrations have all been taken from parables of conflict between Jesus and the Pharisees. But there is a much larger group of parables—the parables of the kingdom—that need special mention. It is true that all of the parables we have already looked at are also parables of the kingdom. They express the dawning of the time of salvation with the coming of Jesus. But the parables we have in mind here are those that expressly say, "The kingdom of God is like. . . ."

First, it must be noted that the introduction, "The kingdom of God is like. . . ," is *not* to be taken with the first element mentioned in the parable. That is, the kingdom of God is *not* like a mustard seed, or a merchant, or treasure hidden in a field. The expression literally means, "It is like this with the kingdom of God. . . ." Thus the whole parable tells us something about the nature of the kingdom, not just one of the points of reference, or one of the details.

Second, it is tempting to treat these parables differently from those we have just looked at, as if they actually were teaching vehicles rather than stories calling for response. But that would be to abuse them. Granted, the divinely inspired collections in Mark 4 and Matthew 13 in their present arrangement are tended to teach *us* about the kingdom. But originally these parables were a part of Jesus' actual proclamation of the kingdom as dawning with his own coming. They are themselves vehicles of the message calling for response to Jesus' invitation and call to discipleship.

Take, for example, the interpreted parable of the Sower (Mark, 4:3–20; Matt. 13:3–23; Luke 8:5–15), which is rightfully seen by Mark as the key to the rest. You will notice that what Jesus has interpreted are the points of reference: The four kinds of soil are like four kinds of responses to the proclamation of the kingdom. But the *point* of the parable is the urgency of the hour: "Take heed how you hear. The word is being sown, the message of the Good News of the kingdom, the joy of forgiveness, the demand and gift of discipleship. It is before all, so listen, take heed; be fruitful soil." It will be noted, therefore, that most of these parables are addressed to the multitudes as potential disciples.

Since these parables are indeed parables of the *kingdom,* we find them proclaiming the kingdom as "already/not yet." But their main thrust is the *"already."* The kingdom has already come; God's hour is at hand. Therefore, the present moment is one of great urgency. Such urgency in Jesus' proclamation has a twofold thrust: (1) Judgment is impending; disaster and catastrophe are at the door. (2) But there is Good News; salvation is freely offered to all. Let us look at a couple of parables that illustrate these two aspects of the message.

1. In Luke 12:16–20 the parable of the Rich Fool has been set in a context of attitudes toward possessions in light of the presence of the kingdom. The parable is easy enough. A rich man, because of his hard work, thinks he has secured his life and is resting complacently. But as Jesus says elsewhere, "He who seeks to find (i.e., secure) his own life is in the process of losing it" (Mark 8:35 and parallels). Thus the man is a fool in the biblical sense—he tries to live without taking God into account. But sudden disaster is about to overtake him.

The *point* of the parable, you will note, is *not* the unexpectedness of death. It is the urgency of the hour. The kingdom is *at hand.* One is a fool to live for possessions, for self-security, when the end is right at the door. Note how this is supported by the context. A man wants his brother to divide the inheritance. But Jesus refuses to become involved in their arbitration. His point is that desire for possession of property is irrelevant in light of the present moment.

This is also how we should understand that most difficult of parables—the Unjust Steward (Luke 16:1–8). Again, the story is simple enough. A steward was embezzling, or otherwise squandering his master's money. He was called to produce accounts and knew his number was up; so he pulled off one more enormous rip-off. He let all the accounts adjust themselves, probably hoping to secure friends on the outside. The punch of this parable, and the part most of us have difficulty handling as well, is that the original hearers expect disapproval. Instead this monkey-business is *praised!*

What could possibly be Jesus' point in telling a story like that? Most likely he is challenging his hearers with the urgency of the hour. If they are properly indignant over such a story, how much more should they apply the lessons to themselves. They were in the same position as the steward who saw imminent disaster, but the crisis that threatened them was incomparably more terrible. That

man acted (note that Jesus does not excuse his action); he did
something about his situation. For you, too, Jesus seems to be
saying, the urgency of the hour demands action; everything is at
stake.

2. The urgent hour that calls for action, repentance, is also the
time of salvation. Thus the kingdom as present is also Good News.
In the twin parables of Matthew 13:44–46 (the Treasure in the
Field and the Pearl of Great Value), the emphasis is on the joy of
discovery. The kingdom overtakes the one; it is sought by the other.
In joy they liquidate their holdings for the treasure and the pearl.
The kingdom is not the treasure; and it is not the pearl. The
kingdom is God's gift. The discovery of the kingdom is unutterable
joy. You will notice how this same motif is thoroughgoing also in
the three parables of the lost things in Luke 15.

This, then, is how one needs to learn to read and study the
parables. They are not to be allegorized. They are to be heard—
heard as calls to response to Jesus and his mission.

The Hermeneutical Question

The hermeneutical task posed by the parables is unique. It has
to do with the fact that when they were originally spoken, they
seldom needed interpretation. They had immediacy for the hearers,
in that part of the effect of many of them was their ability to "catch"
the hearer. Yet they come to us in written form and in need of
interpretation precisely because we lack the immediate understanding of the points of reference the original hearers had. What, then,
do we do? We suggest two things.

1. As always, we concern ourselves basically with the parables
in their present biblical contexts. The parables *are* in a written
context and through the exegetical process just described we can
discover their meaning, their *point,* with a high degree of accuracy.
What we need to do then is what Matthew did (e.g., 18:10–14;
20:1–16): *Translate that same point into our own context.*

With the story parables one might even try retelling the story in
such a way that, with new points of reference, one's own hearers
might feel the anger, or joy, the original hearers experienced. The
following version of the Good Samaritan is not defended as
inspired! Hopefully it will illustrate a hermeneutical possibility. As

an audience it assumes a typical, well-dressed, middle-American Protestant congregation.

A family of dissheveled, unkempt individuals was stranded by the side of a major road on a Sunday morning. They were in obvious distress. The mother was sitting on a tattered suitcase, hair uncombed, clothes in disarray, with a glazed look to her eyes, holding a smelly, poorly clad, crying baby. The father was unshaved, dressed in coveralls, the look of despair as he tried to corral two other youngsters. Beside them was a run-down old car that had obviously just given up the ghost.

Down the road came a car driven by the local bishop; he was on his way to church. And though the father of the family waved frantically, the bishop could not hold up his parishioners, so he acted as if he didn't see them.

Soon came another car, and again the father waved furiously. But the car was driven by the president of the Kiwanis Club, and he was late for a statewide meeting of Kiwanis presidents in a nearby city. He too acted as if he did not see them, and kept his eyes straight on the road ahead of him.

The next car that came by was driven by an outspoken local atheist, who had never been to church in his life. When he saw the family's distress, he took them into his own car. After inquiring as to their need, he took them to a local motel, where he paid for a week's lodging while the father found work. He also paid for the father to rent a car so that he could look for work and gave the mother cash for food and new clothes.

One of the authors tried this once. The startled and angered response made it clear that his hearers had really "heard" the parable for the first time in their lives. You will notice how true to the original context this is. The evangelical Protestant was thinking, "Of course," about the bishop and the Kiwanis president. Surely one of his own would be next. After all, we have always talked about the *Good* Samaritan, as if Samaritans were the most respected of people. But nothing would be more offensive to the good churchgoer than to praise the actions of an atheist, which of course is precisely where the lawyer was at the original telling.

This may be a bit strong for some, and we insist that you make sure you have done your exegesis with great care before you try it. But our experience is that most of us are a bit high on ourselves, and the retelling of some of Jesus' parables would help to get at our own lack of forgiveness (Matt. 18:23–35), or our anger at grace when we want God to be "fair" (Matt. 20:1–6), or our pride in our own position in Christ as compared to the "bad guys" (Luke 18:9–14). We did not know whether to laugh or cry when we were told of a Sunday school teacher who after an hour of excellent instruction on this latter parable, in which he had thoroughly explained the abuses of Pharisaism, concluded in prayer—in all seriousness: "Thank you, Lord, that we are not like the Pharisee in this story"! And we had to remind each other not to laugh too hard, lest our laughter be saying, "Thank you, Lord, that we are not like that Sunday school teacher."

2. Our other hermeneutical suggestion is related to the fact that all of Jesus' parables are in some way vehicles, proclaiming the kingdom. Hence it is necessary for you to immerse yourself in the meaning of the kingdom in the ministry of Jesus. In this regard we highly recommend that you read George E. Ladd's *The Presence of the Future* (Grand Rapids: Eerdmans, 1974).

The urgent message of the kingdom as present and soon to be consummated is still needed in our own day. Those who are trying to secure their lives by possessions urgently need to hear the word of impending judgment, and the lost desperately need to hear the Good News. As Joachim Jeremias eloquently put it (*Rediscovering the Parables* [New York: Scribner, 1966], p. 181):

> The hour of fulfilment has come; that is the keynote of them all. The strong man is disarmed, the powers of evil have to yield, the physician has come to the sick, the lepers are cleansed, the heavy burden of guilt is removed, the lost sheep is brought home, the door of the Father's house is opened, the poor and the beggars are summoned to the banquet, a master whose kindness is undeserved pays wages in full, a great joy fills all hearts. God's acceptable year has come. For there has appeared the one whose veiled majesty shines through every word and every parable—the Saviour.

The Law(s): Covenant Stipulations for Israel

The Old Testament contains over six hundred commandments, which the Israelites were expected to keep as evidence of their loyalty to God. Only four of the thirty-nine Old Testament books contain these laws: Exodus, Leviticus, Numbers, and Deuteronomy. Although there is much other material in each of these books besides lists of commandments, these books are still referred to as books of the law. Genesis, which does not contain any commandments considered part of the Israelite legal system, was also traditionally called a book of the law. Thus we can begin to see immediately that there is not an exact correspondence between what we would call "laws" and what are called in the Old Testament "books of the law."

Further complicating the picture for most Christians is the occasional reference to all of the first five Old Testament books, Genesis through Deuteronomy, as a single "book." For example, Joshua, after the death of Moses, urges the people to remain faithful to the Lord their God, saying, "Do not let this Book of the Law depart from your mouth; meditate on it day and night, so that you may be careful to do everything written in it" (Josh. 1:8). Moreover, in the New Testament, reference is sometimes made to the "law" in a way that makes clear that the entire Old Testament is actually meant, inasmuch as the function of most Old Testament books is largely to illustrate and apply the Law found in the Pentateuch (see, e.g., Matt. 5:17–18; Luke 16:17; Titus 3:9).

However, in most instances when "the Law" is spoken of in the

Bible, it means the body of material that begins at Exodus 20 and goes through the end of Deuteronomy. Even a quick, skimming glance at this portion of Scripture will tell you at once that not everything contained there is in the form of commandments. But the majority of the contents of Exodus 20–Deuteronomy 33 *is* legal formulation, and therefore we will call it the Old Testament law.

The most difficult problem for most Christians with regard to these commandments is the hermeneutical one. How do these legal formulations apply to us, or do they? Because this is the crucial matter, we begin this chapter with some observations about Christians and the law(s), which in turn will aid in the exegetical discussion.

Christians and the Old Testament Law

If you are a Christian, are you expected to keep the Old Testament law? If you *are* expected to keep it, how can you possibly do so, since there is no longer any temple or central sanctuary on whose altar you can offer such things as the meat of animals (Lev. 1–5)? In fact, if you killed and burned animals as described in the Old Testament you would probably be arrested for cruelty to animals! But if you are *not* supposed to observe the Old Testament law any more, then, why would Jesus say, "I tell you the truth, until heaven and earth disappear, not the smallest letter, not the least stroke of a pen, will by any means disappear from the Law until everything is accomplished" (Matt. 5:18)? This question needs an answer, an answer that requires us to look at the way in which the Old Testament law still represents a responsibility incumbent upon Christians (i.e., the ways we still are obligated to obey any or all of the commandments in Exodus 20–Deuteronomy 33).

We suggest six initial guidelines for understanding the relationship of the Christian to the Old Testament law. These guidelines will require explanation, some of which we include immediately and some of which will appear more fully later in this chapter. The guidelines themselves are intended to help orient you in the direction of a proper appreciation for the Law.

1. *The Old Testament law is a covenant.* A covenant is a binding contract between two parties, both of whom have obligations specified in the covenant. In Old Testament times, many covenants were given generously by an all-powerful suzerain (overlord) to a

weaker, dependent vassal (servant). They guaranteed the vassal benefits and protection. But, in turn, the vassal was obligated to be loyal solely to the suzerain, with the warning that any disloyalty would bring punishments as specified in the covenant. How was the vassal to show loyalty? By keeping the stipulations (rules of behavior) specified in the covenant. As long as the vassal kept the stipulations, the suzerain knew that the vassal was loyal. When the stipulations were violated, however, the suzerain was required by the covenant to take action to punish the vassal.

God constructed the Old Testament law on the analogy of these ancient covenants and thereby constituted a binding contract between Yahweh, the Lord, and his vassal, Israel. In return for benefits and protection, Israel was expected to keep the more than six hundred stipulations (i.e., commandments) contained in the covenantal law as we find it in Exodus 20–Deuteronomy 33.

The covenant format had six parts to it: preamble, prologue, stipulations, witnesses, sanctions, and document clause. The preamble identified the parties to the agreement ("I am the Lord your God . . .") and the prologue gave a brief history of how the parties became connected to one another ("I brought you out of the land of Egypt . . ."). The stipulations, as we have noted, are the individual laws themselves. The witnesses are those who will enforce the covenant (the Lord himself, or sometimes "heaven and earth," a way of saying that all of God's creation is concerned with the covenant being kept—e.g., Deut. 4:26; 30:19). The sanctions are the blessings and curses that function as incentives for keeping the covenant (e.g., Lev. 26 and Deut. 28–33). The document clause is the provision for regular review of the covenant so that it will not be forgotten (e.g., Deut. 17:18–19; 31:9–13). Both the first statement of the Law (at Sinai, Exodus 20–Leviticus 27, with supplementation in Numbers) and the second statement of the Law (just prior to the conquest, as found in Deuteronomy) reflect this six-part format.

2. *The Old Testament is not our testament.* Testament is another word for covenant. The Old Testament represents an old covenant, which is one we are no longer obligated to keep. Therefore we can hardly begin by assuming that the Old Covenant should automatically be binding upon us. We have to assume, in fact, that none of its stipulations (laws) are binding upon us unless they are renewed in the New Covenant. That is, unless an Old Testament law is

somehow restated or reinforced in the New Testament, it is no longer directly binding on God's people (cf. Rom. 6:14–15). There have been changes from the Old Covenant to the New Covenant. The two are not identical. God expects of his people—us—somewhat different evidences of obedience and loyalty from those which he expected from the Old Testament Israelites. The *loyalty* itself is still expected. It is *how* one shows that loyalty that has been changed in certain ways.

3. *Some stipulations of the Old Covenant have clearly not been renewed in the New Covenant.* While a complete coverage of the categories of Old Testament law would take a book of its own, it is nevertheless possible to group together a majority of the Pentateuchal laws into two major categories, neither of which any longer applies to Christians. These are (1) the Israelite civil laws and (2) the Israelite ritual laws. The civil laws are those that specify penalties for various crimes (major and minor) for which one might be arrested and tried in Israel. Such laws apply only to citizens of ancient Israel, and no one living today is a citizen of ancient Israel. The ritual laws constitute the largest single block of Old Testament laws, and are found throughout Leviticus as well as in many parts of Exodus, Numbers, and Deuteronomy. These told the people of Israel how to carry on the practice of worship, detailing everything from the design of the implements of worship, to the priests' responsibilities, to what sorts of animals should be sacrificed, and how. The sacrificing (ceremonial killing, cooking, and eating) of animals was central to the Old Testament way of worshiping God. Without the shedding of blood, no forgiveness of sins was possible (Heb. 9:22). When Jesus' once-for-all sacrifice was accomplished, however, this Old Covenant approach immediately was outdated. It no longer figures in Christian practice, although worship—in the *New* Covenant manner—continues.

There are many modern analogies to this sort of change of stipulations from covenant to covenant. In the case of labor contracts, for example, a new contract may specify changes in working conditions, different staffing structures, different pay scales, etc. Yet it may also retain certain features of the old contract—seniority, work breaks, provisions against arbitrary firing, etc. Now a labor contract is hardly on the level of the covenant between God and Israel, but it is a type of covenant and therefore helps illustrate in a familiar way the fact that a new covenant can be

quite different from an old covenant, yet not necessarily totally different.
This is just the case with the biblical covenants.

To this one might ask, "Didn't Jesus say that we are still under
the Law, since no jot or tittle (the least stroke of a pen) would even
drop out of the Law?" The answer is, no, he did not say that. What
he said (see Luke 16:16–17) was that the Law cannot be changed.
The Law and prophets came to an end once John the Baptist began
to preach the New Covenant, and therefore Jesus emphasized that
people had better get into the kingdom of God, quickly, for
otherwise they would still be obliged to keep the old law, which was
impossible to amend. Jesus gave a new law, which did not abolish
the old, but fulfilled it. The new law or covenant could give those
who kept it a righteousness that exceeded that of the scribes and
Pharisees, who rigorously kept the Old Covenant. Jesus fulfilled the
whole Old Testament law and gave a new law, the law of love (see
below, #4).

4. *Part of the Old Covenant is renewed in the New Covenant.*
Which part do we refer to? The answer is that some *aspects* of the
Old Testament *ethical* law are actually restated in the New
Testament as applicable to Christians. These aspects of the old law
were obviously intended by God to continue to apply to all of his
people on through the New Covenant he would establish with
them. Actually such laws derive their continued applicability from
the fact that they serve to support the two basic laws of the New
Covenant, on which depend all the Law and the prophets (Matt.
22:40): "Love the LORD your God with all your heart, soul and
mind" (Deut. 6:5) and "Love your neighbor as yourself" (Lev.
19:18). Jesus thus excerpts some Old Testament laws, giving them
new applicability (read Matt. 5:21–48), and redefining them to
include more than their original scope. Thus we say that *aspects*
rather than simply the laws themselves are renewed from the Old
Covenant to the New, since it is only the aspects of those laws that
fall directly under the command to love God and neighbor that
constitute a continuing obligation for Christians.

5. *All of the Old Testament law is still the Word of God for us even
though it is not still the command of God to us.* The Bible contains all
sorts of commands that God wants us to know *about*, which are not
directed *toward* us personally. An example is Matthew 11:4, where
Jesus commands, "Go back and report to John what you hear and
see." The original audience of that command was the disciples of

John the Baptist. We read *about* the command; it is not a command to us. Likewise the original audience of the Old Testament law is ancient Israel. We read *about* that law; it is not a law to us.

6. *Only that which is explicitly renewed from the Old Testament law can be considered part of the New Testament "law of Christ"* (cf. Gal. 6:2). Included in such a category would be the Ten Commandments, since they are cited in various ways in the New Testament as still binding upon Christians (see Matt. 5:21–37; John 7:23), and the two great commandments from Deuteronomy 6:5 and Leviticus 19:18. No other specific Old Testament laws can be proved to be strictly binding on Christians, valuable as it is for Christians to know all of the laws.

The Role of the Law in Israel and in the Bible

It would be a mistake to conclude from what we have pointed out above that the Law is no longer a valuable part of the Bible. It functioned in the history of salvation to "bring us to Christ," as Paul says (Gal. 3:24), by showing how high God's standards of righteousness are and how impossible it is for anyone to meet those standards apart from divine aid. The Law functioned exactly this way for the ancient Israelites as well. The Law itself did not save them—that would be a notion incompatible with both the Pentateuch and the prophets. *God* saved Israel. He alone provided their means of rescue from slavery in Egypt, conquest of the land of Canaan, and prosperity as inhabitants of that promised land. The Law did none of that. The Law simply represented the terms of the agreement of loyalty that Israel had with God.

The Law in that sense stands as a paradigm (model). It is hardly a complete list of all the things one could or should do to please God in ancient Israel. The Law presents, rather, examples or samples of what it means to be loyal to God.

Apodictic Law

In light of what has just been said, consider the following passage:

> When you reap the harvest of your land, do not reap to the very edges of your field or gather the gleanings of your harvest. Do not go over your vineyards a second time or pick up the grapes

that have fallen. Leave them for the poor and the alien. I am the LORD your God. Do not steal. Do not lie. Do not deceive one another. Do not swear falsely by my name and so profane the name of your God. I am the LORD. Do not defraud your neighbor or rob him. Do not hold back the wages of a hired man overnight. Do not curse the deaf or put a stumblingblock in front of the blind, but fear your God. I am the LORD (Lev. 19:9–14).

Commands like these that begin with *do* or *do not,* are what we call apodictic laws. They are direct commands, generally applicable, telling the Israelites the sorts of things they are supposed to do to fulfill their part of the covenant with God. It is fairly obvious that such laws are not exhaustive, however. Look closely, for example, at the harvesting welfare laws in verses 9 and 10. Note that only field crops (wheat, barley, etc.) and grapes are actually mentioned. Does that mean that if you raised sheep or harvested figs or olives, you were under no obligation to share your produce with the poor and resident alien? Would others bear the burden of making the Old Testament divinely commanded welfare system work while you got off scot free? Of course not. The law is paradigmatic—it sets *a standard by an example,* rather than by mentioning every possible circumstance. Again, consider verses 13b and 14. The point of these statements is to prohibit holding up payment to day laborers, and abusing the handicapped. What if you withheld payment to a laborer almost all night but then gave it to him just before dawn? The scribes and Pharisees of Jesus' day might have argued that your actions were justified since the law plainly says "overnight." But narrow, selfish legalism of that sort is in fact a distortion of the law. The statements in the law were intended as a reliable *guide* with general applicability—not a technical description of *all* possible conditions one could imagine. Likewise, if you harmed a dumb person, or one crippled or retarded, would you still have kept the command in verse 14? Certainly not. The "deaf" and the "blind" are merely selected examples of *all* persons whose physical weaknesses demand that they be respected rather than despised.

Modern societies often have relatively exhaustive legal codes. The federal and state legal codes in the United States, for example, contain thousands of specific laws against all sorts of things. Even so, it always requires a judge (and often a jury) to determine whether a law has been violated by an accused individual, because it is impossible to write laws so comprehensive in wording that they specify every possible way of violating the intended rule. Accordingly, the Old Testament law is much closer to the U.S. *Constitution*—setting out in broad sweep and outline the characteristics of justice and freedom in the land—than it is to the U.S. federal/state codes.

Note that our explanation that the Old Testament apodictic (general, unqualified) laws are paradigmatic (examples rather than exhaustive) is no help to the person who wishes to make obedience to those laws easy. Rather we have pointed out that these laws, though limited in wording, are actually very comprehensive *in spirit*. If one therefore were to set out to keep the spirit of the Old Testament law, he or she would surely fail eventually. No human being can please God consistently in light of such high, comprehensive standards (cf. Rom. 8:1–11). Only the pharisaical approach—obeying the letter rather than the spirit of the Law—has much possibility of success. But it is a worldly success only, not one that results in actually keeping the Law as God intended it to be kept (Matt. 23:23).

Thus we make here a preliminary hermeneutical observation: *The Law shows us how impossible it is to please God on our own.* Now that is hardly a new observation. Paul said the same thing in Romans 3:20. But the point is applicable for *readers* of the Law, not just as a theological truth. When we read the Old Testament law, we ought to be humbled to appreciate how unworthy we are to belong to God. We ought to be moved to praise and thanksgiving that he provided for us a way to be accepted in his sight apart from humanly fulfilling the Old Testament law! For otherwise we would have no hope at all of pleasing him.

Casuistic Law

Apodictic law has a counterpart in another sort of law, which we call casuistic (case-by-case) law. Consider the following passage from Deuteronomy:

> If a fellow Hebrew, a man or a woman, is sold to you and he serves you six years, in the seventh year you must let him go free. And when you release him, do not send him away empty-handed. Supply him liberally from your flock, your threshing floor and your winepress. Give to him as the LORD your God has blessed you. Remember that you were slaves in Egypt and the LORD your God redeemed you. That is why I give you this command today.

But if your servant says to you, "I do not want to leave you," because he loves you and your family and is well off with you, then take an awl and push it through his ear lobe into the door, and he will become your servant for life. Do the same for your maidservant (Deut. 15:12–17).

The elements in a law like this are conditional. This law applies only in the case that (1) you, an Israelite, have at least one slave, or (2) you, an Israelite, have a slave who does or does not wish to remain as your slave voluntarily after the mandatory slavery deadline has passed. If you are *not* an Israelite or do *not* have slaves, the law does not apply to you. If you yourself are a slave, the law, because it is directed to your owner, applies only *indirectly* to you in that it protects your rights. But the law does not pertain to everyone. It is conditional—based on a possible condition that may or may not apply to a given person at a given time.

Such casuistic or case-by-case laws constitute a large portion of the more than six hundred commandments found in the Old Testament pentateuchal law. Interestingly, none of them is explicitly renewed in the New Covenant. Because such laws apply specifically to Israel's civil, religious, and ethical life, they are by their very nature limited in their applicability and therefore unlikely to apply to the Christian. What hermeneutical principles then can a Christian learn from the casuistic laws? Looking at Deuteronomy 15:12–17 we note several items.

First, although we personally might not keep slaves, we can see that God's provision for slavery under the Old Covenant was hardly a brutal, harsh regulation. We could scarcely justify the sort of slavery practiced in most of the world's history—including American history, for example—from such a law. Letting slaves go free after only six years of service provided a major limitation on the practice of slavery, so that the practice could not be abused beyond reasonable limits.

Second, we learn that God loves slaves. His love is seen in the stringent safeguards built into the law, as well as in verses 14 and 15, which demand generosity toward the slaves, inasmuch as God himself considers Israel, his people, a group of former slaves.

Third, we learn that slavery could be practiced in such a benign fashion that slaves were actually better off in bondage than free. That is, the slave owner, by assuming the obligation to provide food, clothing, and housing for his or her slaves, was in many cases keeping them alive and well. On their own, they might die of starvation, or perhaps exposure, if they lacked the resources to survive in the harsh economic conditions that prevailed in ancient Palestine.

Fourth, the slave owner did not really own the slave in a total sense. He owned the slave subject to a host of restrictions spelled out or alluded to in a number of other laws on slavery. His power over the slave was not absolute under the Law. God was the owner of both the slave owner and the slave. God had redeemed (bought back) all the Hebrews, as verse 15 states, and had owner's claim on all of them, slave or free.

These four observations are valuable lessons for us. It does not matter that the law of Deuteronomy 15:12–17 is not a command directly to us or about us. What matters is how much we can learn from this law about God, his demands of fairness, his ideals for the Israelite society, and his relationship to his people, especially as regards the meaning of "redemption." This law, then, provides us with (1) an important part of the background for the New Testament teaching on redemption, (2) a clearer picture of how Old Testament slavery was quite different from what we usually think of as slavery, and (3) a perspective on the love of God that we might not otherwise have had. This legal passage, in other words, is still the precious Word of God for us, though it is obviously not a command from God to us.

Not everything, however, about slavery in ancient Israel can be learned from this law. For example, certain rules for slaves of foreign origin are different in scope. Indeed, all the laws on slavery in the Pentateuch put together still only touch the surface. It should be obvious that a few hundred laws can function only paradigmatically, that is, as examples of how people should behave, rather than exhaustively. If even the modern criminal and civil codes with their thousands of individual statutes cannot exhaustively give guidance to a society, then the Old Testament law cannot be understood as all-encompassing. Nevertheless, because it does contain the *sorts* of standards God set for his Old Covenant people, it should be enormously instructive to us as we seek to do his will.

The Old Testament Law and Other Ancient Law Codes

The Israelites were not the first people to live by laws. Several other law codes have survived from ancient nations from times even earlier than the time the Law was given to Israel through Moses (1440 B.C. or later, depending on the date of the exodus from Egypt). When these earlier laws are compared to the Old Testament law, it becomes evident that the Old Testament law represents a definite advancement over its predecessors. One can more fully appreciate the Old Testament law if one recognizes the difference between it and the other ancient laws it improved upon. We do not mean by this to suggest that the Old Testament law represents the highest possible standard of moral or ethical teaching. This indeed comes only with the teaching of Christ himself in the New Testament. But the Old Testament law does show a remarkable degree of progress beyond the standards set prior to it.

Consider, for example, the following two sets of laws. The first is from the *Laws of Eshnunna,* an Akkadian law code that is dated about 1800 B.C.:

> If a free man has no claim against another free man, but seizes the other free man's slave girl, detains the one seized in his house and causes her death, he must give two slave girls to the owner of the slave girl as a compensation. If he has no claim against him but seizes the wife or child of an upper class person and causes their death, it is a capital crime. The one who did the seizing must die (Eshnunna, laws 23, 24, author's translation; cf. J. B. Pritchard, ed. *Ancient Near Eastern Texts Relating to the Old Testament.* 3d ed.; Princeton: University Press, 1969, p. 162).

The second is from the famous *Law Code of Hammurabi,* a Babylonian king who "enacted the law of the land" in 1726 B.C.:

> If a free nobleman hit another free nobleman's daughter and caused her to have a miscarriage, he must pay ten shekels of silver for her fetus. If that woman died, they must put his daughter to death. If by a violent blow he caused a commoner's daughter to have a miscarriage, he must pay five shekels of silver. If that woman died, he must pay ½ mina of silver. If he hit a free nobleman's female slave and caused her to have a miscarriage, he must pay two shekels of silver. If that female slave died, he must pay ⅓ mina of silver (Hammurabi, laws 209–14, author's translation; cf. J. B. Pritchard, ed. *Ancient Near Eastern Texts*

Relating to the Old Testament. 3d ed.; Princeton: University Press, 1969, p. 175).

There are several issues in these laws that might bear looking at, but we wish to draw attention to one in particular—class distinctions built into them. Note that the laws provide only for fines as punishment for causing the death of a slave or a commoner whereas the penalty for causing the death of a member of the nobility is death. Note also that male members of the nobility were practically immune from personal punishment so long as the harm they brought was to a woman. Thus in the second group of laws (Hammurabi, laws 209–14) even when the nobleman causes the death of another nobleman's daughter, he himself does not suffer. Rather, his daughter is put to death. In the first set of laws (Eshnunna, laws 23, 24), likewise, the death of a slave is simply compensated for by the payment of two slaves. The killer goes free.

In such laws, then, women and salves are treated like property. Harm to either of them is handled in the same way that harm to an animal or a material possession is handled in other laws in these law codes.

The Old Testament law represents a quantum jump ahead ethically over such codes. The prohibition against murder is absolutely unqualified by sex or social status: "You shall not murder" (Exod. 20:13). "Anyone who strikes someone and kills him shall surely be put to death" (Exod. 21:12). As regards compensation for injury to slaves, there has been an advance as well: "If someone knocks out the tooth of a male servant or female servant, he must let the servant go free to compensate for the tooth" (Exod. 21:27). Slaves, in general, had very different status in the Old Testament law from their status under the earlier laws. "If a slave has taken refuge with you, do not hand him over to his master. Let him live among you wherever he likes and in whatever town he chooses" (Deut. 23:15–16). And in contrast to the provision in the laws of Hammurabi that allowed a nobleman to force his daughter to be put to death for a death he had caused, the Old Testament law is explicit that "fathers shall not be put to death for their children, nor children put to death for their fathers; each is to die for his own sin" (Deut. 24:16).

The Old Testament Law As Benefit to Israel

In terms of its ability to provide eternal life and true righteousness before God, the Law was quite inadequate. It was not designed for such purposes. Anyone who tried to gain salvation and acceptance by God exclusively through the Law was bound to fail, since the Law was ultimately unkeepable—at least one of its rules was bound to be broken sometime during one's life (Rom. 2:17–27; 3:20). And breaking even one law makes one, by definition, a "law breaker" (cf. James 2:10).

Yet when its own purposes are properly understood, the Law can be seen as beneficial to the Israelites, a marvelous example of God's mercy and grace to his people. Read it in that light when you come across the kinds of laws which we have sampled here.

The Food Laws

Example: "And the pig, because it parts the hoof and is cloven-footed, but does not chew the cud, is unclean to you" (Lev. 11:7).

The food laws, such as this prohibition against pork (Lev. 11:7), are not intended by God to represent arbitrary and capricious restrictions on Israelite tastes. Rather, they have a serious protective purpose. The vast majority of the foods prohibited are those which (1) are more likely to carry disease in the arid climate of the Sinai desert and/or the land of Canaan; or (2) are foolishly uneconomical to raise as food in the particular agrarian context of the Sinai desert and/or the land of Canaan; or (3) are foods favored for religious sacrifice by groups whose practices the Israelites were not to copy. Moreover, in light of the fact that medical research has now indicated that food allergies vary according to ethnic populations, the food laws undoubtedly kept Israel away from certain allergies. The desert did not contain many pollens to bother the Israelite pulmonary tract, but it did contain some animals whose meat would irritate the nervous system. It is especially interesting to note that the main source of Israel's meat—lamb—is the least allergenic of all major meats, according to specialists in food allergies.

Laws About the Shedding of Blood

Example: "Then you shall bring the bull before the tent of meeting. Aaron and his sons shall lay their hands on the head of the bull, and you shall kill the bull before the LORD, at the door of the tent of meeting, and shall take part of the blood of the bull, and put it on the horns of the altar with your finger, and the rest of the blood you shall pour out at the base of the altar" (Exod. 29:10–12).

Such laws as this set an important standard for Israel. Sin deserves punishment. God revealed to his people through the Law that the one who sins against God does not deserve to live. But he also provided a procedure by which the sinner might escape death: a substitute's blood could be shed. Thus God offered to accept the death of another living thing—an animal—in place of the death of the sinner among his people. The sacrificial system of the Law incorporated this procedure into the life of Israel. It was a necessary part of the survival of the people. "Without the shedding of blood, there is no remission of sins" (Heb. 9:22). Most importantly, the laws that required a substitutionary sacrifice set a precedent for the work of Christ's substitutionary atonement. The principle stated in Hebrews 9:22 is a thoroughly biblical one. Christ's death provides a fulfillment of the Law's demand and is the basis for our acceptance with God. The Old Testament law serves as a vivid background for that great event in history.

Unusual Prohibitions

Example: "Do not cook a young goat in its mother's milk" (Deut. 14:21).

"What's wrong with that?" you may ask. And why are this and other laws like "Do not mate different kinds of animals," or "Do not plant your field with two kinds of seed," or "Do not wear clothing woven of two kinds of material" (Lev. 19:19) in the Old Testament law?

The answer is that these and other prohibitions were designed to forbid the Israelites to engage in the fertility cult practices of the Canaanites. The Canaanites believed in what is called sympathetic magic, the idea that symbolic actions can influence the gods and nature. They thought that boiling a goat kid in its mother's milk would magically insure the continuing fertility of the flock. Mixing animal breeds, seeds, or materials was thought to "marry" them so as magically to produce "offspring," that is, agricultural bounty in the future. God could not and would not bless his people if they practiced such nonsense. Knowing the intention of such laws—to keep the Israelites from being led into the Canaanite religion where salvation was not available—helps you see that they are not arbitrary, but crucial—and graciously beneficial.

Laws Giving Blessings to Those Who Keep Them

Example: "At the end of every three years, bring all the tithes of that year's produce and store it in your towns, so that the Levites (who have no allotment or inheritance of their own) and the aliens, the orphans and the widows who live in your towns may come and eat and be satisfied, so that the LORD your God may bless you in all the work of your hands" (Deut. 14:28–29).

Of course, all of Israel's laws were designed to be a means of blessing for the people of God (Lev. 26:3–13). Some specifically mention, however, that keeping them will provide a blessing. The third-year tithe law of Deuteronomy 14:28–29 predicates blessing upon obedience. If the people do not care for the needy among them—the Levites, orphans, and widows, God cannot give prosperity. The tithe belongs to him, and he has delegated how it is to be used. If this command is violated, it is a theft of God's money. This law provides benefit for the needy (the Old Testament welfare system was well-established), and benefit for those who benefit the needy. Such a law is neither restrictive nor punitive. It is instead a vehicle for good practice, and as such is instructive to us as well as to ancient Israelites.

In Summary: Some Dos and Don'ts

As a distillation of some of the things we have talked about in this chapter, we present here a brief list of hermeneutical guidelines that we hope will serve you well whenever you read the Old Testament pentateuchal law. Keeping these principles in mind when you read may help you to avoid mistaken applications of the Law, while seeing in the Law its instructive and faith-building character.

1. Do see the Old Testament law as God's fully inspired word *for* you.
   Don't see the Old Testament law as God's direct command *to* you.

2. Do see the Old Testament law as the basis for the Old Covenant, and therefore for Israel's history.
   Don't see the Old Testament law as binding on Christians in the New Covenant except where specifically renewed.

3. Do see God's justice, love, and high standards revealed in the Old Testament law.
   Don't forget to see that God's mercy is made equal to the severity of the standards.

4. Don't see the Old Testament law as complete. It is not technically comprehensive.
   Do see the Old Testament law as a paradigm—providing examples for the full range of expected behavior.

5. Don't expect the Old Testament law to be cited frequently by the prophets or the New Testament.
   Do remember that the *essence* of the Law (Ten Commandments and the two chief laws) is repeated in the prophets and renewed in the New Testament.

6. Do see the Old Testament law as a generous gift to Israel, bringing much blessing when obeyed.
   Don't see the Old Testament law as a grouping of arbitrary, annoying regulations limiting people's freedom.

10

The Prophets: Enforcing the Covenant in Israel

More individual books of the Bible come under the heading of prophecy than under any other heading. Four major prophets (Isaiah, Jeremiah, Ezekiel, Daniel) and twelve minor prophets (the final twelve books of the Old Testament), written in ancient Israel between about 760 and 460 B.C., contain a vast array of messages from God. The minor prophets are so-called only because these books are relatively short in length; the major prophets are relatively long books. The terms imply absolutely nothing about importance.

The Nature of Prophecy

We should note at the outset that the prophetical books are among the most difficult parts of the Bible to interpret or read with understanding. The reasons for this are related to misunderstandings as to their *function* and *form*. But before we discuss these two matters, some preliminary comments are in order.

The Meaning of Prophecy

The primary difficulty for most modern readers of the Prophets stems from an inaccurate prior understanding of the word *prophecy*. For most people this word means what appears as the first definition in most dictionaries: "Foretelling or prediction of what is to come." It often happens, therefore, that many Christians refer to the Prophets *only* for predictions about the coming of Jesus and/or certain features of the New Covenant age—as though prediction of events far distant from their own day was the main concern of the Prophets. In fact, using the Prophets in this way is highly selective. Consider in this connection the following statistics: Less than 2 percent of Old Testament prophecy is messianic. Less that 5 percent specifically describes the New Covenant age. Less that 1 percent concerns events yet to come.

The prophets *did* indeed announce the future. But it was usually the immediate future of Israel, Judah, and other nations surrounding them that they announced, rather than *our* future. One of the keys to understanding the Prophets, therefore, is that for us to see their prophecies fulfilled, we must look back upon times which for them were still future but for us are past.

The Prophets as Spokespersons

To see the prophets as primarily predicters of future events is to miss their primary function, which was to *speak* for God to their own contemporaries. It is the "spoken" nature of their prophecies that causes many of our difficulties in understanding.

For example, of the hundreds of prophets in ancient Israel in Old Testament times, only sixteen were chosen to speak oracles (messages from God) that would be collected and written up into books. We know that other prophets, such as Elijah and Elisha, played a very influential role in delivering God's Word to his people and to other nations than Israel as well. But we know more about these prophets than we do of their actual words. What they *did* was described in far greater length than what they *said*—and what they said was placed very specifically and clearly in the context of their times by the writers of the Old Testament narratives in which they appear. Of a few prophets such as God (1 Sam. 22; 2 Sam. 24; et al.), Nathan (2 Sam. 7, 12; 1 Kings 1; et al.) or Huldah (2 Kings 22) we have a combination of prophecy and biography—a situation paralleled in the case of Jonah and to a lesser extent Daniel. But generally in the narrative books of the Old Testament we hear *about* prophets and very little *from* prophets. In the prophetical books, however, we hear *from* God *via* the prophets and very little about the prophets themselves. That single difference accounts for most of the problem people have making sense of the prophetical books in the Old Testament.

Furthermore, have you ever noticed how difficult it is to read any of the longer prophetic books through in one sitting? Why do you suppose that is? Primarily, we think, because they were probably not intended to be read that way. For the most part these longer books are *collections of spoken oracles,* not always presented in their original chronological sequence, often without hints as to where one oracle ends and another begins, and often without hints as to their historical setting. And most of the oracles were spoken in poetry! We will say more about this below.

The Problem of History

Another matter complicates our understanding of the Prophets, and that is the problem of historical distance. Indeed, by the very nature of things, we modern readers will find it much harder to understand in our own time the Word of God as it was spoken by the prophets than did the Israelites who heard those same words in person. Things clear to them tend to be opaque to us. Why? Partly, it is because those in a speaker's audience have certain obvious advantages over those who read a speaker's words second hand (cf. what was said about the parables in chap. 8). But that is not really where the difficulties lie for the most part. Rather, as people far removed from the religious, historical, and cultural life of ancient Israel, we simply have great trouble putting the words spoken by the prophets in their proper context. It is often hard for us to see what they are referring to and why.

The Function of Prophecy

To understand what God would say to us through these inspired books, we must first have a clear understanding as to the role and function of the prophet in Israel. Three things must be emphasized:

The Prophets were covenant enforcement mediators. We explained in the preceding chapter how Israel's law constituted a covenant between God and his people. This covenant contains not only rules to keep, but describes the sorts of punishments that God will necessarily apply to his people if they do not keep the Law, as well as the sorts of benefits he will impart to them if they do. The punishments are often called "curses" of the covenant, and the benefits "blessings." The name is not important. What is important is that God does not merely give his law, but he enforces it. Positive enforcement is blessing; negative enforcement is curse. This is where the prophets come in. God announced the enforcement (positive or negative) of his law through them, so that the events of blessing or curse would be clearly understood by his people. Moses was the mediator for God's law when God first announced it, and thus is a paradigm (model) for the prophets. They are God's mediators, or spokespersons, for the covenant. Through them God reminds people in the generations after Moses that if the Law is kept, blessing will result; but if not, punishment will ensue.

The kinds of blessings that will come to Israel for faithfulness to the covenant are found especially in Leviticus 26:1–13; Deuteronomy 4:32–40; and 28:1–14. But these blessings are announced with a warning; if Israel does *not* obey God's law, the blessings will cease. The sorts of curses (punishments) that Israel may expect if it violates the Law are found especially in Leviticus 26:14–39; Deuteronomy 4:15–28; and throughout Deuteronomy 28:15–32:42.

Therefore, one must always bear in mind that the prophets did not invent the blessings or curses they announced. They may have worded these blessings and curses in novel, captivating ways, as they were inspired to do so. But they reproduced *God's* word, not their own. Through them God announced his intention to enforce the covenant, for benefit or for harm depending on the faithfulness of Israel, but always on the basis of and in accordance with the categories of blessing and curse already contained in Leviticus 26, Deuteronomy 4, and Deuteronomy 28–32. If you will take the trouble to learn those chapters from the Pentateuch, you will be rewarded with a much better understanding of why the prophets say the things that they do.

Briefly, what one finds is this. The law contains certain categories of corporate blessings for covenant faithfulness: life, health, prosperity, agricultural abundance, respect, and safety. Most of the specific blessings mentioned will fall under one of these six general groupings. As regards curses, the law describes corporate punishments, which we happen to find convenient (and memorizable) to group under ten headings which begin with the letter "d": death, disease, drought, dearth, danger, destruction, defeat, deportation, destitution, and disgrace. Most of the curses will fit under one of these categories.

These same categories apply in what God communicates through the prophets. For example, when he wishes to predict future blessing for the nation (not any given individual) through the prophet Amos, he does so in terms of metaphors of agricultural abundance, life, health, prosperity, respect, and safety (Amos 9:11–15). When he announces doom for the disobedient nation of Hosea's day, he does so according to one or more of the ten "d's" listed above (e.g., destruction in Hos. 8:14, or deportation in Hos. 9:3). These curses are often metaphorical, though they can be literal as well. They are always corporate, referring to the nation as a whole. Blessings or curses do not guarantee prosperity or dearth to any *specific* individual. Statistically, a majority of what the prophets announce in the eighth, seventh, and early sixth centuries B.C. is curse, because the major defeat and destruction of the northern kingdom did not occur until 722 B.C.; that of the southern kingdom (Judah) did not occur until 587 B.C. The Israelites, north and south, were heading for punishment during that era, so naturally warnings of curse rather than blessing predominate as God seeks to get his people to repent. After the destruction of both north and south, that is, after 587 B.C., the prophets were moved more often to speak blessings than curses. That is because once the punishment of the nation is complete, God resumes his basic plan, which is to show mercy (see Deut. 4:25–31 for a nutshell description of this sequence).

As you read the Prophets, look for this simple pattern: (1) an identification of Israel's sin *or* of God's love for her; (2) a prediction of curse or blessing depending on the circumstance. Most of the time, that is what the prophets are conveying, according to God's inspiration to them.

The prophets' message was not their own, but God's. It is God who raised up the prophets (cf. Exod. 3:1f.; Isa. 6; Jer. 1; Ezek. 1–3; Hos. 1:2; Amos 7:14–15; Jonah 1:1; et al.). If a prophet presumed to take the office of prophet upon himself or herself, this would be good cause to consider such a one a false prophet (cf. Jer. 14:14; 23:21). The prophets responded to a divine call. The Hebrew word for prophet (*nābî'*) comes in fact from the Semitic verb "to call" (*nabû*). You will note as you read the Prophets that they preface, or conclude, or regularly punctuate their oracles with reminders like "Thus says the LORD" or "Says the LORD." A majority of the time, in fact, the prophetic message is relayed directly as received from the LORD, in the first person, so that God speaks of himself as "I" or "Me."

Read, for example, Jeremiah 27 and 28. Consider Jeremiah's difficult task in relaying to the people of Judah that it would be necessary for them to submit to the imperial armies of their enemy, Babylon, if they wished to please God. His hearers, most of them, considered this message to be the equivalent of treason. When he delivers the message, however, he makes it abundantly clear that they are not hearing *his* views on the matter, but God's. He begins by reminding them, "This is what the LORD said to me. . ." (27:2), and then quotes God's command, "Then send word . . ." (27:3); "Give them a message . . ." (27:4), and adds "says the LORD" (27:11). His word is God's Word. It is delivered on God's authority (28:15–16), not his own.

As vehicles through whom God delivered his Word both to Israel and other nations, the prophets held a kind of societal office. They were like ambassadors from the heavenly court, who relayed the divine sovereign's will to the people. The prophets were, on their own, neither radical social reformers nor innovative religious thinkers. The social reforms and the religious thought which God wished to impart to the people had already been revealed in the covenantal law. No matter which group broke those laws, God's Word through the prophet held punishment. Whether the guilt for covenant violations lay with the royalty (e.g., 2 Sam. 12:1–14; 24:11–17; Hos. 1:4), or with the clergy (Hos. 4:4–11; Amos 7:17; Mal. 2:1–9), or any other group, the prophet conveyed God's message of national curse faithfully. Indeed, by God's word prophets even installed or deposed kings (1 Kings 19:16; 21:17–22) and declared war (2 Kings 3:18–19; 2 Chron. 20:14–17; Hos. 5:5–8) or against war (Jer. 27:8–22).

What we read in the prophetical books then, is not merely God's Word as the prophet saw it, but God's Word as God wished the prophet to present it. The prophet does not act or speak independently.

The prophets' message is unoriginal. The prophets were inspired by God to present the essential content of the covenant's warnings and promises (curses and blessings). Therefore, when we read the prophets' words, what we read is nothing genuinely new, but the same message in essence delivered by God originally through Moses. The form in which that message is conveyed may, of course, vary substantially. God raised up the prophets to gain the attention of the people to whom they were sent. Gaining people's attention may involve rephrasing and restructuring something that they have already heard many times, so that it has a certain kind of "newness." But that is not at all the same as actually initiating any new message or altering the old message. The prophets are not inspired to make any points or announce any doctrines that are not already contained in the Pentateuchal covenant. As a first example of this conservation of the message, consider the first half of Hosea 4:2: "There is only cursing, lying and murder, stealing and adultery."

In this verse, which is part of a long description of Israel's sinfulness in Hosea's day (750–722 B.C.), five of the Ten Commandments are summarized, each by a single term. These terms are: "Cursing," the third commandment, "Do not use the LORD's name wrongly . . ." (Exod. 20:7; Deut. 5:11). "Lying," the ninth commandment, "Do not give dishonest testimony . . ." (Exod. 20:16; Deut. 5:20). "Murder," the sixth commandment, "Do not murder" (Exod. 20:13; Deut. 5:17). "Stealing," the eighth commandment, "Do not steal" (Exod. 20:15; Deut. 5:18). "Adultery," the seventh commandment, "Do not commit adultery" (Exod. 20:14; Deut. 5:18).

It is as interesting to note what the inspired prophet does *not* do as what he does do. That is, Hosea does not cite the Ten Commandments verbatim. He mentions five of them in a one-word summary fashion much as Jesus does in Luke 18:20. But mentioning five, even out of their usual order, is a very effective way of communicating to the Israelites that they have broken the Ten Commandments. For upon hearing five of the commandments, the hearer would think, "And what of the others? What of the usual order? The original wording is. . . ." The audience would begin thinking of all ten, reminding *themselves* of what the covenant law calls for in terms of basic righteousness. Hosea did not change a thing in the Law, any more than Jesus did, in citing five of the commandments for a similar effect. But he did impress the Law upon his hearers in a way that simply repeating it word for word might never have done.

A second example concerns the messianic prophecies. Are these new? Not at all. Certainly, the kind of *detail* about the life and role of the Messiah that we find in the Servant Songs of Isaiah 42, 49, 50, and 53 may be considered new. But God did not bring the notion of a Messiah to the people for the first time through the prophets. It had in fact originated with the Law. Otherwise how could Jesus have described his life as fulfilling what was written "in the Law of Moses, the Prophets, and the Psalms" (Luke 24:44)? Among other portions of the Mosaic Law that foretell the Messiah's ministry, Deuteronomy 18:18 is prominent: "I will raise up for them a prophet like you from among their brothers. I will put my words in his mouth, and he will tell them everything I command him."

As John 1:45 also reminds us, the Law already spoke of Christ. It was hardly a new thing for the prophets to speak of him. The mode, the style, and the specificity with which they made their inspired predictions did not need to be restricted to what the Pentateuch already contained. But the essential fact that there would be a New Covenant ushered in by a new "Prophet" (using the language of Deut. 18) was, in fact, an old story.

The Exegetical Task

The Need for Outside Help

We noted in chapter 1 that there is a popular notion that everything in the Bible ought to be clear to everyone who reads it, without study or outside help of any kind. The reasoning is that if God wrote the Bible for *us* (for all believers), we should be able to understand it completely the first time we read it, since we have the Holy Spirit in us. Such a notion is simply incorrect. Parts of the Bible are obvious on the surface, but parts are not. In accordance with the fact that God's thoughts are profound compared with human thoughts (Ps. 92:5; Isa. 55:8) it should not be surprising that some parts of the Bible will require time and patient study to understand.

The prophetical books require just such time and study. People often approach these books casually, as if a surface reading through the Prophets will yield a high level of understanding. This cannot be done with school textbooks, and it does not work with the Prophets either.

We need to repeat here, specifically for the interpretation of the Prophets, the three kinds of helps that are available to you. The first source would be *the Bible dictionaries,* which provide articles on the historical setting of each book, its basic outline, the special features it contains, and issues of interpretation of which the reader must be aware. We recommend that you make it a practice to read a Bible dictionary article on a given prophetical book before you start to study that book. You need to know the background information before you will be able to catch the point of much of what a prophet conveys. God's Word came through the prophets to people in *particular* situations. Its value to us depends partly on our ability to appreciate those situations so that we can in turn apply it to our own.

A second source of help would be *the commentaries*. These provide lengthy introductions to each book, somewhat on the manner of the Bible dictionaries though often less usefully organized. But more importantly, they provide explanations of the meaning of the individual verses. They may become essential if you are studying carefully a relatively small portion of a prophetical book, that is, less than a chapter at a time (see Appendix).

A third source of help would be *the Bible handbooks*. The best of these combine features of both the Bible dictionaries and the commentaries, though they do not go into as great detail on either the introductory materials or the verse-by-verse explanations. When one is reading through several chapters at a time of a prophetical book, however, a Bible handbook can yield a lot of helpful guidance in a minimal amount of time.

The Historical Context

In the study of Jesus (chap. 7), "historical context," you will recall, referred both to the larger arena into which Jesus came and to the specific context of any one of his deeds and sayings. In the study of the Prophets, the historical context can likewise be larger (their era) or specific (the context of a single oracle). To do good exegesis you need to understand both kinds of historical context for all the prophetical books.

The Larger Context. It is interesting to note that the sixteen prophetical books of the Old Testament come from a rather narrow band in the whole panorama of Israelite history, i.e., about 760–460 B.C. Why do we have no books of prophecy from Abraham's day (about 1800 B.C.) or Joshua's day (about 1400 B.C.) or David's day (about 1000 B.C.)? Didn't God speak to his people and their world before 760 B.C.? The answer is, of course, that he did, and we have much material in the Bible about those ages, including some that deals with prophets (e.g., 1 Kings 17–2 Kings 13). Moreover, remember that God spoke especially to Israel in the Law, which was intended to stand for the entire remaining history of the nation, until it would be superseded by the New Covenant (Jer. 31:31–34).

Why then is there such a concentrated writing down of prophetic word during the three centuries between Amos (ca. 760 B.C., the earliest of the "writing prophets") and Malachi (ca. 460 B.C. the latest)? The answer is that this period in Israel's history called especially for *covenant enforcement mediation*, the task of the prophets. A second factor was the evident desire of God to record for all subsequent history the warnings and blessings that those prophets announced on his behalf during those pivotal years.

Those years were characterized by three things: (1) unprecedented political, military, economic, and social upheaval, (2) an enormous level of religious unfaithfulness and disregard for the original Mosaic covenant, and (3) shifts in populations and national boundaries. In these circumstances God's Word was needed anew. God raised up prophets and announced his Word accordingly.

As you make use of dictionaries, commentaries, and handbooks you will note that by 760 B.C. Israel was a nation divided permanently by a long ongoing civil war. The northern tribes, called "Israel," or sometimes "Ephraim," were separated from the southern tribe of Judah. The north, where disobedience to the covenant far outstripped anything yet known in Judah, was slated for destruction by God because of its sin. Amos, beginning around 760, and Hosea, beginning around 755, announced the impending destruction. The north fell to the superpower in the Middle East at that time, Assyria, in 722 B.C. Thereafter, the mounting sinfulness of Judah and the rise of another superpower, Babylon, constituted the subject of many prophets, including Isaiah, Jeremiah, Joel, Micah, Nahum, Habakkuk, and Zephaniah. Judah, too, was destroyed for its disobedience in 587 B.C. Afterward, Ezekiel, Daniel, Haggai, Zechariah, and Malachi announced God's will for the restoration of his people (beginning with a return from the Exile in 538 B.C.), the rebuilding of the nation, and the reinstitution of orthodoxy. All of this follows the basic pattern laid out in Deuteronomy 4:25–31.

The prophets speak in large measure directly to *these* events. Unless you know these events and others within this era too numerous to mention here, you probably will not be able to follow very well what the prophets are saying. God spoke in history and about history. To understand his Word we must know something of that history.

Specific Contexts: An Example. Each prophetic oracle was delivered in a specific historical setting. God spoke through his prophets to people in a given time and place, and under given circumstances. A knowledge of the date, audience, and situation, therefore, when they are known, contributes substantially to a reader's ability to comprehend an oracle.

Read Hosea 5:8–10, a brief, self-contained oracle grouped with several other oracles in that chapter. A good contemporary will identify for you the fact that this oracle is in the form of a war oracle, one of a type (form) that announces the judgment of God as carried out through battle. The usual elements of such a form are: the call to alarm, the description of attack, and the prediction of defeat. In the same way that it is helpful to recognize the form, it is also helpful to recognize the specific content.

The *date* is 734 B.C. The *audience* is the northern Israelites (called here "Ephraim") to whom Hosea preached. Specifically the message was to certain cities on the road from the Judean capital, Jerusalem, to the center of Israelite false worship, Bethel. The *situation* is war. Judah counterattacked Israel after Israel and Syria had invaded Judah (see 2 Kings 16:5). The invasion had been beaten back with the help of the superpower Assyria (2 Kings 16:7–9). God through Hosea sounds the alarm metaphorically in cities located in the territory of Benjamin (v. 8), which was part of the northern kingdom. Destruction is sure (v. 9), because Judah will capture the territory it invades ("moving the boundary stones" as it were). But Judah, too, will get its due. God's wrath will fall upon them both for this act of war and for their idolatry (cf. 2 Kings 16:2–4). Judah and Israel were under obligation to the divine covenant that forbade such internecine war. So God would punish this violation of his covenant.

Knowing these few facts makes a great deal of difference in one's ability to appreciate the oracle in Hosea 5:8–10. Refer to the commentaries or handbooks as you read the Prophets, and as always, try to be aware of the date, audience, and situation of the oracles you read.

The Isolation of Individual Oracles

When one comes to the actual study or exegetically informed reading of the prophetical books, the first thing one must learn to do is to THINK ORACLES (as one must learn to think paragraphs in the Epistles). This is not always an easy task, but to know the difficulty and the need to do this is the beginning of some exciting discovery.

Most of the time what the prophets said is presented in their books in run-on fashion. That is, the words they spoke at various times and places over the years of their ministry have been collected and written down together without any divisions to indicate where one oracle ends and another begins. Moreover, even when one can assume by a major change of subject that a new oracle has probably begun, the lack of explanation (i.e., editorial remarks or transitions) still leaves one asking, "Was this said on the same day to the same audience, or was it said years later—or earlier—to a different group under different circumstances?" The answer can make a big difference as to one's understanding.

Some parts of the prophetical books provide exceptions. In Haggai and the early chapters of Zechariah, for example, each prophecy is dated. With the help of your Bible dictionary, handbook, or commentary, you can follow the progression of those prophecies in their historical context rather easily. And *some* of the prophecies in other books, notably Jeremiah and Ezekiel, are likewise dated and placed in a setting by the inspired author.

But it simply does not work that way most of the time. For example, read Amos chapter 5 in a version of the Bible which does not insert explanatory titles (these headings are only scholarly opinion), and ask yourself whether the chapter is all one prophecy (oracle) or not. If it is a single oracle, why does it have so many changes of subject (lament over Israel's destruction, vv. 1–3; invitation to seek God and live, vv. 5–6, 14; attacks on social injustice, vv. 7–13; prediction of miseries, vv. 16–17; description of the Day of the Lord, vv. 18–20; criticism of hypocritical worship, vv. 21–24; and a brief overview of Israel's sinful history culminating in a prediction of exile, vv. 25–27)? If it is not a single oracle, how are its component parts to be understood? Are they all independent of one another? Are some to be grouped together? If so, in what ways?

In fact, chapter 5 contains what are generally agreed to be three oracles. Verses 1–3 form a single short lament oracle announcing punishment, verses 4–17 form a single (though complex) oracle of invitation to blessing and warning of punishment, and verses 18–27 from a single (though complex) oracle warning of punishment. The smaller changes of subject, then, do not each indicate the beginning of a new oracle. On the other hand, the chapter divisions do not correspond with individual oracles either. Oracles are isolated by attention to their known *forms* (see below). All three of the oracles in chapter 5 were given late in the reign of King Jeroboam of Israel (793–753 B.C.), to a people whose relative prosperity caused them to consider it unthinkable that their nation would be so devastated as to cease to exist in just a generation. A good commentary, Bible dictionary, or Bible handbook will explain such things to you as you read. Do not handicap yourself needlessly by trying to do without one.

The Forms of Prophetic Utterance

Since the isolation of individual oracles is one key to understanding the prophetical books, it is important for you to know something about the different *forms* the prophets used to compose their oracles. Just as the whole Bible is composed of many different kinds of literature and literary forms, so also the prophets employed a variety of literary forms in the service of their divinely inspired messages. The commentaries can identify and explain these forms. We have selected three of the most common forms to help alert you to the importance of recognizing and rightly interpreting the literary techniques involved.

The lawsuit. First, we suggest you read Isaiah 3:13–26, which constitutes an allegorical literary form called a "covenant lawsuit" (Hebrew, *rîb*). In this and the scores of other lawsuit allegories in the Prophets (e.g., Hos. 3:3–17; 4:1–19, etc.), God is portrayed imaginatively as the plaintiff, prosecuting attorney, judge, and bailiff in a court case against the defendant, Israel. The full lawsuit form contains a summons, a charge, evidence, and a verdict, though these elements may sometimes be implied rather than explicit. In Isaiah 3 the elements are incorporated as follows: The court convenes and the lawsuit is brought against Israel (vv. 13–14a). The indictment or accusation is spoken (vv. 14b–16). Since the evidence shows that Israel is clearly guilty, the judgment sentence is announced (vv. 17–26). Because the covenant has been violated, the sorts of punishments listed in the covenant will come upon Israel's women and men: disease, destitution, deprivation, death. The figurative style of this allegory is a dramatic and effective way of communication to Israel that it is going to be punished because of its disobedience, and that the punishment will be severe. The special literary form helps get the special message across.

The woe. Another common literary form is that of the "woe oracle." "Woe" was the word ancient Israelites cried out when facing disaster or death, or when they mourned at a funeral. Through the prophets, God makes predictions of imminent doom using the device of the "woe," and no Israelite could miss the significance of the use of that word. Woe oracles contain, either explicitly or implicitly, three elements that uniquely characterize this form: an *announcement* of distress (the word "woe," for example), the *reason* for the distress, and a *prediction* of doom. Read Habakkuk 2:6–8 to see one of several instances in this prophetic book of a "woe oracle" spoken against the nation of Babylon. Babylon, a brutal, imperialistic superpower in the ancient Fertile Crescent, was making plans to conquer and crush Judah at the end of the seventh century B.C. when Habakkuk spoke God's words against it. Personifying Babylon as a thief and extortionist (the *reason*), the oracle *announces* woe, and *predicts* disaster (when all those Babylon has oppressed will one day rise against it). Again, this form is allegorical (though not all woe oracles are; cf. Micah 2:1–5; Zeph. 2:5–7).

The promise. Yet another common prophetic literary form is the promise or "salvation oracle." You will recognize this form whenever you see these elements: reference to the future, mention of radical change, and mention of blessing. Amos 9:11–15, a typical promise oracle, contains these elements. The *future* is mentioned as "In that day" (v. 11). The *radical change* is described as the restoration and repair of "David's fallen tent" (v. 11), the exaltation of Israel over Edom (v. 12), and the return from the Exile (vv. 14, 15). *Blessing* comes via the covenantal categories mentioned (life, health, prosperity, agricultural abundance, respect, and safety). All these items are included in Amos 9:11–15, though health is implicit rather than explicit. The central emphasis is upon agricultural abundance. Crops, for example, will be so enormous that the harvesters still will not be finished by the time the sowers start planting again (v. 13)! For other examples of promise oracles, see Hosea 2:16–20 and 2:21–23; Isaiah 45:1–7; and Jeremiah 31:1–9.

From these brief examples, we hope that you can gain a sense of how an informed sense of prophetic literary devices will help you comprehend the message of God more accurately. Learn the forms by referring to the commentaries (see the appendix), and you will be glad you did!

The Prophets as Poets

The average American has little appreciation for poetry. Poetry seems a strange and confusing way to express things, as if it were designed to make ideas less, rather than more, intelligible. Our culture places little emphasis on poetry, except in popular music, which normally contains the sort of poor quality poetry called doggerel. In some present-day cultures, however, and in most ancient ones, poetry was a highly prized mode of expression. Whole national epics and key historical and religious memories were preserved in poetry. We say "preserved" because one major advantage of poetry over prose is that it is more readily memorizable. A poem has a certain rhythm (also called meter), certain balances (also called parallelism or stichometry), and a certain overall structure. It is relatively regular and orderly. Once learned well, poetry is not as easily forgotten as is prose.

The poetic prose sometimes used by the prophets is a special, formal style employing these same characteristics, though less consistently. Because it is so much more regular and stylized than common spoken language (colloquial prose), it, too, is better remembered. For convenience, let us also speak of it with the general term "poetry."

In ancient Israel poetry was widely appreciated as a means of learning. Many things that were important enough to be remembered were considered appropriate for composition in poetry. Just as we can reproduce from memory the words of songs (i.e., the poems called "lyrics") much more easily than we can reproduce sentences from books or speeches, the Israelites found it relatively simple to commit to memory and to recall things composed in poetry. Making good use of this helpful phenomenon in an age where reading and writing were rare skills and where the private ownership of books was virtually unknown, God spoke through his prophets largely by poems. People were used to poetry, and could remember those prophecies; they would ring their ears.

All the prophetic books contain a substantial amount of poetry, and several are exclusively poetic. Before you read the prophetic books, therefore, you might find it very helpful to read an introduction to Hebrew poetry. We especially recommend the article by Norman Gottwald entitled "Poetry, Hebrew" in the *Interpreter's Dictionary of the Bible* (Nashville: Abingdon, 1962). But any Bible dictionary will have at least one informative article on poetry. As a small hint of the benefits to be realized from knowing how Hebrew poetry functions we suggest you learn these three features of the repetitive style of Old Testament poetry. They are:

1. *Synonymous parallelism*. The second or subsequent line repeats or reinforces the sense of the first line, as in Isaiah 44:22:

   > "I have swept your offenses like a cloud,
   >   your sins like the morning mist."

2. *Antithetical parallelism*. The second or subsequent line contrasts the thought of the first, as in Hosea 7:14:

   > "They do not cry out to me from their hearts,
   >   but wail upon their beds."

3. *Synthetic parallelism*. The second or subsequent line adds to the first line in any manner which provides further information, as in Obadiah 21:

   > "Deliverers will go up from Mount Zion
   >   to govern the mountains of Esau.
   > And the kingdom will be the LORD's."

Remember that the presentation of ideas in poetry need not confuse you as long as you read carefully and knowledgeably. Poetry is just as comprehensible as prose if you know the rules.

Some Hermeneutical Suggestions

If the task of exegesis is to set the Prophets within their own historical contexts and to hear what God was saying to Israel through them, then what can be said at the hermeneutical level? What is God's Word to us through these inspired poetic oracles, spoken in another time to God's ancient people? First, we would point out that much of what was said in chapter 4 about the hermeneutics of the Epistles applies here as well. Once we hear what God said to them, even if our circumstances differ considerably, we will often hear it again in our own settings in a rather direct way. We would argue that God's judgment always awaits those who "sell the needy for a pair of shoes" (Amos 2:6), or who use religion as a cloak for greed and injustice (cf. Isa. 1:10–17), or who have mixed modern idolatries (such as self-justification) with the Gospel of Christ (cf. Hos. 13:2–4). These sins are sins in the New Covenant, too. They violate the two great commandments that both the Old and New Covenant share (see chap. 9).

But beyond these kinds of applications, there are three further matters that must be addressed: one a caution, another a concern, and still another a benefit.

A Caution: The Prophet as Foreteller of the Future

Toward the beginning of this chapter we noted that it was not the prophets' primary task to predict the distant future. They did indeed predict future events, but for the most part *that* future is now past. That is, they spoke of coming judgment or salvation in the relatively immediate future of Israel, not of our own future. We cautioned that to see their prophecies fulfilled we must look *back* upon times that for them were still future, but for us are past. This hermeneutical principle needs to be illustrated.

As an example of the prophets' messages being concentrated on the near rather than the distant future, we suggest you read through Ezekiel 25–39. Notice that the various oracles contained in that large block of material concern mostly the fate of nations other than Israel, though Israel is also included. It is important to see that God refers to the fate of those nations, and that the fulfillment came *within decades* of the time the prophecies were delivered, that is, mostly during the sixth century B.C. There are individual exceptions to this, of course. Ezekiel 37:15–28 describes the New Covenant age, and the blessings God will pour out on the church via the Messiah. But most of the prophecies, including those of chapters 38 and 39 (consult a commentary on these chapters) concern Old Testament times and events.

Too great a zeal for identifying New Testament events in Old Testament prophetic oracles can yield strange results. The reference in Isaiah 49:23 to kings who "will bow down before you with their faces to the ground" has sounded just enough like the three Magi who visited the infant Jesus (Matt. 2:1–11) to encourage many to assume that Isaiah's words are messianic. Such an interpretation embarrassingly ignores the *context* (both kings *and* queens are mentioned; the issue of the passage is the restoration of Israel after its Babylonian exile), the *intent* (the language of the oracle intends to show how great Israel's respect will be when God restores it), the *style* (the poetry symbolizes the respect of the nations via images of their rulers as foster parents to Israel, and licking the dust at the feet of the nation), and the *wording* (*Magi* are wise men/astrologers, not kings). We must be careful that we do not make prophetic oracles, or any part of Scripture, say what we would like it to say. We must hear what *God* intends it to say.

It should be noted, of course, that some of the prophecies of the near future were set against the background of the great, eschatological future, and sometimes they seem to blend. We will speak to this again in chapter 13. For now let it be noted that the reason for this is that the Bible regularly sees God's acts in temporal history in light of his overall plan for all of human history. Thus the temporal is to be seen in light of the eternal plan. It is something like looking at two discs, with a smaller one in front of a larger, straight on; then from the perspective of subsequent history to see them from a side view and thus see how much distance there is between them.

Prophetic Perspective of Chronological Events

Straight on view   Side view

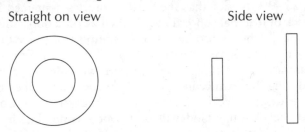

Thus there are some things in the prophets that may belong to the final events of the age (e.g., Joel 3:1–3; Zeph. 3:8–9; Zech. 14:9). But the temporal judgments that are often spoken of in conjunction with those final events must not be pushed into the future as well.

One further point should be mentioned. Eschatological language by its very nature is often metaphorical. Sometimes those metaphors express poetically the *language* of the final events, but are not necessarily intended to be predictions of those events per se. An example is found in Ezekiel 37:1–14. Using the language of the resurrection of the dead, an event we know will occur at the *end* of the age, God predicts through Ezekiel the return of the nation of Israel from the exile in Babylon *in the sixth century* B.C. (vv. 12–14). Thus an event that to us is past (as described in Ezra 1–2) is predicted metaphorically with eschatological language as if it were an end-time event.

A Concern: Prophecy and Second Meanings

At a number of places in the New Testament, reference is made to Old Testament passages that do not appear to refer to what the New Testament says they do. That is, these passages seem to have a clear meaning in their original Old Testament setting and yet are used in connection with a different meaning by a New Testament writer.

As an example, consider the two stories of how Moses and the Israelites were miraculously given water from rocks in the wilderness: once at Rephidim (Exod. 17:1–7) and once at Kadesh (Num. 20:1–13). The stories are, it appears, simple enough and abundantly clear in their original contexts. But in 1 Corinthians 10:4, Paul seems to identify the experience of the Israelites as an encounter with Christ. He says that "they drank from the spiritual rock that accompanied them, and that rock was Christ." In each Old Testament story there is no hint that the rock is anything other than a rock. Paul gives the rock a second meaning, identifying it as "Christ." This second meaning is commonly called the *sensus plenior* (fuller meaning).

Upon reflection, one can see that Paul is drawing an analogy. He is saying, in effect, "That rock was to them as Christ is to us—a source of sustenance in the same way that spiritual things are a sustenance for us." Paul's language in verses 2–4 is highly metaphorical. He wants the Corinthians to understand that the experience of the Israelites in the wilderness can be understood as an allegory of their own experience with Christ, especially at the Lord's Table.

Now we modern readers are quite unlikely on our own to

notice that analogy in the way that Paul described it. If Paul had never written these words, would we have made the identification of cloud and sea with baptism (v. 2) or the rock with Christ (v. 4)? In other words, would we, on our own, be able with any degree of certainty to determine the *sensus plenior* or secondary meaning? The answer is no. The Holy Spirit inspired Paul to write about that analogical connection between the Israelites in the wilderness and life in Christ without following the usual rules about *context, intent, style,* and *wording* (see above, *The Prophet as Foreteller of the Future*). The Holy Spirit directed Paul to describe the fact that the Israelites got water more than once from rocks, with the figurative, unusual language that a rock had "accompanied them." Other details of the descriptive language Paul uses in 1 Corinthians 10:1–4 (nonliteral terms like "all our forefathers" in v. 1 and "spiritual" food and drink in vv.3–4) are likewise strikingly unusual.

We, however, are simply not inspired writers of Scripture. What Paul did we are not authorized to do. The allegorical connections he was inspired to find between the Old Testament and the New Testament are trustworthy. But nowhere does the Scripture say to us: "Go and do likewise." Thus the principle: *Sensus plenior (fuller meaning) is a function of inspiration, not illumination.* The same Holy Spirit who inspired an Old Testament author to write a certain set of words or a passage, can inspire a New Testament writer to by-pass the usual considerations of context, intent, style, and wording and identify that set of words or that passage as having a second meaning. But *we* are not inspired writers. We are illumined readers. Inspiration is the original motivation to record the Scripture in a certain way. Illumination is the insight to understand what the Scripture's authors wrote. We cannot rewrite or redefine Scripture by our illumination. We can only perceive a *sensus plenior* with any certainty, therefore, *after the fact*. Unless it is identified as a *sensus plenior* in the New Testament, it cannot confidently be identified as such from the Old Testament by us on our own authority.

Study Bibles, commentaries, handbooks, and Bibles with reference columns will all tend to identify Old Testament prophetic passages that have a second meaning in the New Testament. Some typical instances where the New Testament gives a second meaning are: Matthew 1:22–23 (Isa. 7:14); 2:15 (Hos. 11:1); 2:17–18 (Jer. 31:15); John 12:15 (Zech. 9:9).

We need take only one of these to illustrate the phenomenon of a second meaning being assigned to a prophetic passage: Matthew 2:15. In Hosea 11:1, we read:

> When Israel was a child I loved him
> and out of Egypt I called my son.

In Hosea, the *context* is Israel's rescue from Egypt by way of the Exodus. The *intent* is to show how God loved Israel even as his own child. The *style* is synonymous, poetic parallelism whereby "my son" is linked with the nation Israel. The *wording* is metaphorical: Israel is unquestionably personified as a "child" in the verse. The second person of the Trinity, Christ, is not referred to by the "plain" meaning of this Scripture.

If we did not have Matthew 2:15 in our Bibles, we would not likely be inclined to identify this verse from Hosea as a prophecy of Jesus of Nazareth. But Matthew had something we do not have. He had authoritative inspiration from the same Spirit who inspired Hosea to compose Hosea 11:1. This same Spirit moved him to decide that the words Hosea used could be *reused* with a different context, intent, and style, and in connection with other wordings about the Messiah. The Holy Spirit had, as it were, "planted" those choice words in the book of Hosea to be ready for reuse in connection with the events in Jesus' life. Matthew does *not* apply those words to Jesus on the basis of a typical exegetical-hermeneutical principle or process. Rather, he takes those words out of their original context and gives them a whole new meaning. He has the authority to do this. We can only read and appreciate what he has done. We cannot, however, do this same sort of thing on our own with any given passage.

A Final Benefit: The Dual Emphasis on Orthodoxy and Orthopraxy

Orthodoxy is correct belief. Orthopraxy is correct action. Through the prophets God calls the people of ancient Israel and Judah to a balance of right belief and action. This, of course, remains the very balance that the New Covenant requires as well (cf. James 1:27; 2:18; Eph. 2:8–10). What God wants of Israel and Judah is in a general sense the same as what he wants of us. The Prophets can serve constantly as reminders to us of God's determination to enforce his covenant. For those who obey the stipulations of the New Covenant (loving God and loving one's neighbor), the final, eternal, result will be blessing, even though the results in this world are not guaranteed to be so encouraging. For those who disobey, the result can be only curse, regardless of how well one fares during life on earth. Malachi's warning (Mal. 4:6) still stands.

11

The Psalms: Israel's Prayers and Ours

The book of Psalms, a collection of inspired Hebrew prayers and hymns, is probably for most Christians the best-known and most-loved portion of the Old Testament. The fact that the Psalms are often appended to copies of the New Testament and that they are used so often in worship and meditation has given this particular book a certain prominence. Yet despite all this, the Psalms are also frequently misunderstood and thus frequently misused.

The problem with interpreting the Psalms arises primarily from their nature—what they are. Because the Bible is God's Word, most Christians automatically assume that all it contains are words *from* God *to* people. Thus many fail to recognize that the Bible also contains words spoken *to* God or *about* God, and that these words, too, are God's Word.

The Psalms are just such words. That is, because psalms are basically prayers and hymns, by their very nature they are addressed to God or express truth about God in song. This presents us with a unique problem of hermeneutics in Scripture. *How* do these words spoken *to* God function as a Word *from* God to us? Because they are not propositions, or imperatives, or stories that illustrate doctrines, they do not function primarily for the teaching of doctrine or moral behavior. Yet they are profitable when used for the purposes intended by God who inspired them: for helping us (1) to express ourselves to God, and (2) to consider his ways. The Psalms, therefore, are of great benefit to the believer who wishes to have help from the Bible in expressing joys and sorrows, successes and failures, hopes and regrets.

But the Psalms are frequently misapplied, precisely because they are so often poorly understood. Not all of them are as easy to follow logically, or to apply to the twentieth century, as in the Twenty-third Psalm, for example. In its symbolism God is portrayed as a shepherd, and the psalmist (and thus ourselves) as his sheep. His willingness to care for us by pasturing us in the appropriate places, i.e., meeting our every need, generously protecting us and benefiting us, is evident to those who are familiar with the psalm.

But other psalms do not yield their meaning at first glance. For example, how is one to use a psalm that seems to be negative throughout and seems to express the misery of the speaker? Is this something that should be used in a church service? Or is it for private use only? And what of a psalm that tells about the history of Israel and God's blessings on it? Can an American Christian make good use of this sort of psalm? Or is it reserved only for Jews? Or how about psalms that predict the work of the Messiah? Or what of psalms that laud the benefits of wisdom? What about the several psalms that discuss the glory of Israel's human kings? Since very few people in the world now live under royalty, it would seem especially difficult to make sense of this latter sort of psalm. And, finally, what does one do with the desire that Babylonian infants should be dashed against the rocks (137:8–9)?

While it would require a lengthy book to discuss all the types of psalms and all the possible uses they might be put to, in this chapter we provide some guidelines by which you will be in a better position to appreciate and use the Psalms both in your personal life, and also in the life of the church where you worship.

Some Preliminary Exegetical Observations

As with the other biblical genres, because the Psalms are a special kind of literature, they require special care in reading and interpreting. In the case of the Psalms this means an understanding of their *nature*, including their various *types*, as well as their *forms* and *function*.

The Psalms as Poetry

Perhaps the most important thing to remember in reading or interpreting the Psalms should also be the most obvious: they are poems—musical poems. We have already briefly discussed the nature of Hebrew poetry in the preceding chapter, but there are three additional points that we need to make in connection with the Psalms.

1. One needs to be aware that Hebrew poetry, by its very nature, was addressed, as it were, to the mind through the heart (i.e., much of the language is intentionally emotive). Therefore, one needs to be careful of over-exegeting the Psalms by finding special meanings in every word or phrase, where the poet may have intended none. For example, you will recall that the nature of Hebrew poetry always involves some form of parallelism and that one common form is that called *synonymous parallelism* (where the second line repeats or reinforces the sense of the first line). In this type of parallelism, then, the two lines *together* express the poet's meaning; and the second line is not trying to say some new or different thing. Consider, for example, the opening of Psalm 19:1:

> The heavens declare the glory of God;
>   the skies proclaim the work of his hands.
> Day after day they pour forth speech;
>   night after night they display knowledge.

Here in two sets of synonymous parallelism the inspired poet is glorifying God as Creator. Notice how the NIV has tried to help you see the parallels, by capitalizing only the first line in each and using a semicolon between the two lines.

The poet's point in plain prose is: "God is revealed in his creation, especially in the heavenly bodies." But our plain prose sentence is colorless next to the magnificent poetry of the psalm. The exalted language of the poem both says it better and says it in a more memorable way. You will notice that the four lines are not trying to say four different things, although the second set adds the new idea that during both the day and the night the heavens reveal their maker. But in the first set the psalmist is not bent on saying that the "heavens" do one thing and the "skies" another; together the two lines speak of one glorious reality.

2. One must also remember that the Psalms are not just any kind of poems; they are *musical* poems. A musical poem cannot be

read in the same way that an epistle or a narrative or a section of law can be read. It is intended to appeal to the emotions, to evoke feelings rather than propositional thinking, and to stimulate a response on the part of the individual that goes beyond a mere cognitive understanding of certain facts. While the Psalms contain and reflect doctrine, they are hardly repositories for doctrinal exposition. It is dangerous to read a psalm as if it taught a system of doctrine, in the same way that it is dangerous to do this with narrative. The fact that the Psalms touch upon certain kinds of issues in their musical, poetical way does not allow one to assume that the way that they express the matter is automatically a subject for rational debate.

Who of us in singing the song "A Mighty Fortress Is Our God" would assume that God is in fact some kind of a fortification or impenetrable building or wall? We understand that "Mighty Fortress" is a figurative way of thinking about God. In the same way, when the psalmist says, "In sin did my mother conceive me" (Ps. 51:5) he is hardly trying to establish the doctrine that conception is sinful, or that all conceptions are sinful, or that his mother was a sinner by getting pregnant, or that original sin applies to unborn children, or any such thing. The psalmist has employed hyperbole—purposeful exaggeration—in order to express strongly and vividly that he is a sinner. When you read a psalm, be careful that you do not derive from it notions that were never intended by the musical poet who was inspired to write it.

3. It is likewise important to remember that the *vocabulary* of poetry is purposefully metaphorical. Thus one must take care to look for the *intent* of the metaphor. In the Psalms mountains skip like rams (114:4; what a marvelous way to sing about the miracles that accompanied the Exodus!); enemies spew out swords from their lips (59:7; who has not felt the sharp pain of calumny or lies?); and God is variously seen as a shepherd, fortress, shield, and rock. It is extremely important that you learn to "listen" to the metaphors and understand what they signify.

It is likewise important that one not press metaphors or take them literally. If a person took Psalm 23 literally, for example, he or she might make the rather excessive mistake of assuming that God wants us to be and act like sheep, or else wants us to live a rural, pastoral life. Thereby the psalm becomes a treatise against city life. An inability to appreciate symbolic language (metaphor and simile) and to translate into actual fact the more abstract symbolic notions of the psalm could lead a person to misapply it almost entirely.

The Psalms as Literature

Because the Psalms, as musical poems, are also a form of literature, it is important to recognize certain literary features of the Psalms as you read or study them. Failure to note these features can lead one to several errors of interpretation and application.

1. The Psalms are of several different *types*. This is so important to your understanding that we will elaborate on the basic types later on in the chapter. For now it is important to remember that the Israelites knew all these types. They knew the difference between a psalm of lament (whereby an individual or a group could express grief before the Lord and make appeal for help) and a psalm of thanksgiving (whereby individuals or groups expressed joy in the mercy God had already shown them). In our culture, we do not routinely use psalms as the Israelites did. It can be hard, therefore, for a person to understand a psalm, if one is not aware of the type of psalm he or she is reading.

2. Each of the Psalms also is characterized by its *form*. By form we mean the *particular* type, as determined by the characteristics (especially structure) that it shares with all other psalms of its particular type. When one understands the structure of a psalm, one can follow what is happening within the psalm. One can recognize, for example, the transitions from subject to subject, and the way the psalmist apportions the attention paid to given issues, so as to have an appreciation for the message the psalm conveys. You will see this especially in our exegetical sampling given later on.

3. Each of the types of psalms is also intended to have a given *function* in the life of Israel. This matter is also so important as to receive special attention below. For now one must remember that each psalm has an intended purpose. It is not reasonable, for example, to take a royal psalm, which had as its original function the celebration of Israel's kingship as God endowed it, and read this at a wedding. The psalm was simply not designed to have application at a wedding ceremony.

4. One must also learn to recognize various *patterns* within the Psalms. The psalmists frequently took delight in certain arrangements or repetitions of words and sounds, as well as stylistic plays upon words. Moreover, some psalms are acrostic; that is, the initial

letters of each line or verse work through the letters of the alphabet. Psalm 119 is an example of an acrostic psalm. Its pattern of enumeration and repetition effectively guides the reader through a long list of the believers' benefits from and responsibilities toward the law of God.

5. Finally, each psalm must be read as a *literary unit*. The Psalms are to be treated as wholes, not atomized into single verses or thought of, as often happens with the Proverbs, as so many pearls on a string, each to be enjoyed for its own delight apart from its relationship to the whole. It is helpful in reading to follow the flow and balance of a psalm. Each psalm has a pattern of development by which its ideas are presented, developed, and brought to some kind of conclusion.

Because of the literary unity of any given psalm, therefore, one must be especially careful not to take individual verses out of context from a psalm, seeing them only in their own light, as if they did not need a context in which to be interpreted. For example, consider Psalm 105:34: "He spoke and the locusts came, grasshoppers without number." Taken out of context, this verse might seem to suggest that God has generally intended grasshoppers and locusts as his special agents to do certain things in the earth, or that his word is somehow carried out by grasshoppers and locusts. How does this then compare with Psalm 85:12: "The LORD will indeed give what is good and our land will yield its harvest," since the grasshoppers and locusts are destroyers of the land (cf. Joel 2:25)? How can it be that God's Word is what brings them forth and yet he also guarantees that he will give good to the land and that it will yield its harvest? The answer is of course that in the full context of the musical poems in which each of these verses belongs, there is a framework of meaning which helps us to define the words in these verses, and to understand them according to their real intent rather than according to some intent we may assign them because we do not know the context. Psalm 85 is a discussion of the benefits that God gives to the land of Israel, as an example of how he is faithful to his promises. And Psalm 105 describes the way in which God used grasshoppers and locusts in the plague by which he helped to force the Pharaoh to let the Israelites go free from Egypt. Decontextualizing parts of these psalms leads to wrong conclusions. Whenever one takes a piece of literature and uses it wrongly, that literature will be unable to do what it was intended to do. If even only a part of a psalm is misapplied, then indeed God's purposes in inspiring it are thwarted.

The Use of the Psalms in Ancient Israel

The Psalms were functional songs, composed for use in worship by the ancient Israelites. By *functional* we mean that they were not simply used as hymns are sometimes used today, spacing material to separate out parts of a worship service in preparation for the sermon. Rather, the Psalms served the crucial function of making connection between the worshiper and God.

It is not possible to date with certainty most of the Psalms. This is not, however, a significant exegetical problem. The Psalms are remarkably applicable to *all* ages. Their uses in ancient Israel are instructive to us, but hardly confine us to the worship and prayer of a past age. As they speak to the heart of a believer or group of believers gathered together in worship, the pan-cultural, pan-geographic value of the Psalms is demonstrated.

In ancient times the Psalms were commonly used as worship aids by Israelites when they brought sacrifices to the temple in Jerusalem. It is possible that professional singers sometimes sang the Psalms during the time that people were worshiping, though this cannot be proved. However, it is obvious that the knowledge of the Psalms spread widely beyond the temple, and that people began to sing them in all sorts of situations where the wordings expressed their own attitudes and circumstances. The Psalms were eventually collected into groupings called "books." There are five such books (Book 1: Pss. 1–41; Book 2: Pss. 42–72; Book 3: Pss. 73–89; Book 4: Pss. 90–106; Book 5: Pss. 107–150). Because certain groups of the Psalms have special characteristics, it is likely that they were collected originally into subcategories, which have now been included within the five major books. But these categories are not significant in terms of the present organization of the book of Psalms, because so many different types are scattered among the various ones we find in the present order.

According to the titles, which are not part of the original psalms and therefore are not considered inspired, David wrote almost half the Psalms, seventy-three in all. Moses wrote one (Ps. 90), Solomon wrote two (Pss. 72 and 127), the sons of Asaph wrote several, the sons of Korah several, etc.

After the Israelites returned from exile and rebuilt the temple, the book of Psalms was apparently made a formal collection, almost a "temple hymnal," with Psalm 1 being placed at the beginning as an introduction to the whole, and Psalm 150 at the end as a conclusion. From the New Testament we see that Jews in general, and Jesus and his disciples in particular, knew the Psalms well. The Psalms were part of their worship. Paul encourages the early Christians to encourage one another with "psalms and hymns and spiritual songs" (Eph. 5:19; Col 3:16). All three of these terms can refer to the Psalms, although in giving this advice Paul may also have had in mind other types of early Christian music.

The Types of Psalms

It is possible to group the Psalms into seven different categories. Though these categories may overlap somewhat, or have subcategories, they serve well to classify the Psalms and thus to guide the reader toward good use of them.

Laments

Laments constitute the largest group of psalms in the Psalter. There are more than sixty, including individual and corporate laments. *Individual* laments (e.g., 3, 22, 31, 39, 42, 57, 71, 120, 139, 142) help a person to express struggles, suffering, or disappointment to the Lord. *Corporate* laments (e.g., 12, 44, 80, 94, 137) do the same for a group of people rather than for an individual. Are you discouraged? Is your church going through a difficult period? Are you part of a group, small or large, that wonders why things are not going as well as they should? If so, the use of laments is potentially a valuable adjunct to your own expression of concern to the Lord. Times were often hard for the ancient Israelites. The laments in the book of Psalms express with a deep, honest fervor the distress that people felt.

Thanksgiving Psalms

These psalms were used, as the name suggests, in circumstances very opposite from those of the laments. Such psalms expressed joy to the Lord because something had gone well, because circumstances were good, and/or because people had reason to render thanks to God for his faithfulness, protection, and benefit. The thanksgiving psalms help a person or a group express thoughts and feelings of gratefulness. In all, there are six community (group) psalms of thanksgiving (65, 67, 75, 107, 124, 136), and ten individual psalms of thanksgiving (18, 30, 32, 34, 40, 66, 92, 116, 118, 138) in the Psalter.

Hymns of Praise

These psalms, without particular reference to previous miseries or to recent joyful accomplishments, center on the praise of God for who he is, for his greatness and his beneficence toward the whole earth, as well as his own people. God may be praised as Creator of the universe as in Psalms 8, 19, 104, and 148. He may be praised as the protector and benefactor of Israel, as in Psalms 66, 100, 111, 114, and 149. He may be praised as the Lord of history as in Psalms 33, 103, 113, 117, 145–147. God deserves praise. These psalms are especially adapted for individual or group praise in worship.

Salvation History Psalms

These few psalms (78, 105, 106, 135, 136) have as their focus a review of the history of God's saving works among the people of Israel, especially his deliverance of them from bondage in Egypt and his creation of them as a people. Israel, from whom eventually came Jesus the Christ and through whom the Word of God was mediated, is of course a special nation in human history, and its story is celebrated in these salvation history psalms.

Psalms of Celebration and Affirmation

In this category are included several kinds of psalms. A first group is the *covenant renewal liturgies,* such as Psalms 50 and 81, which are designed to lead God's people to a renewal of the covenant he first gave to them on Mount Sinai. These psalms can serve effectively as worship guidelines for a service of renewal. Psalms 89 and 132 are often categorized as Davidic covenant psalms, which praise the importance of God's choice of the lineage of David. Inasmuch as this lineage eventually leads into the birth of our Lord, these psalms provide background for his messianic ministry. There are nine psalms in the Psalter that deal especially with the kingship. These we call *royal psalms* (2, 18, 20, 21, 45, 72, 101, 110, 144). One of them (18) is a royal thanksgiving psalm and one of them (144) a royal lament. The kingship in ancient Israel was an important institution, because through it God provided stability and protection. Though most of Israel's kings were unfaithful to God, he nevertheless could use any of them for good purposes. God works through intermediaries in society, and the praise of the function of these intermediaries is what we find in the royal psalms.

Related to the royal psalms are the so-called *enthronement psalms* (24, 29, 47, 93, 95–99). It is likely that these psalms celebrated the enthronement of the king in ancient Israel, a ceremony that may have been repeated yearly. Some scholars have argued that they represent also the enthronement of the Lord himself, and were used as liturgies for some sort of ceremony which celebrated this, although the evidence is scant.

Finally, there is a category called the *Songs of Zion* or *Songs of the City of Jerusalem* (46, 48, 76, 84, 87, 122). According to the predictions of God through Moses to the Israelites while they were yet in the wilderness (e.g., Deut. 12), Jerusalem became the central city of Israel, the place where the temple was built, and from which the kingship of David exercised authority. Jerusalem as the "holy city" receives special attention and celebration in these songs. Inasmuch as the New Testament makes much of the symbol of a New Jerusalem (heaven) these psalms remain useful in Christian worship.

Wisdom Psalms

Eight psalms can be placed in this category: 36, 37, 49, 73, 112, 127, 128, 133. We may note also that Proverbs chapter 8 is itself a psalm, praising, as these others do, the merits of wisdom and the wise life. These psalms may be read profitably along with the book of Proverbs (cf. chap. 12).

Songs of Trust

These ten psalms (11, 16, 23, 27, 62, 63, 91, 121, 125, 131) center their attention upon the fact that God may be trusted, and that even in times of despair, his goodness and care for his people ought to be expressed. God delights in knowing that those who believe in him trust him for their lives and for what he will choose to give them. These psalms help us to express our trust in God, whether we are doing well or not.

For those who would wish to be able to explore further the

different categories of the Psalms and to understand the characteristics that determine how psalms are categorized, we recommend a book titled *Out of the Depths: The Psalms Speak for Us Today*, 2d ed., by Bernhard Anderson (Louisville: Westminster/John Knox, 1983). This book not only contains additional details of how the Psalms functioned in ancient Israel, but it also makes further suggestions for the way that they might also function in the lives of believers today.

An Exegetical Sampling

In order that we might illustrate how knowing a psalm's form and structure helps us appreciate its message, we have chosen two psalms for close examination. One is a personal lament; the other, a thanksgiving psalm.

Psalm 3: A Lament

By carefully comparing all the lament psalms, scholars have been able to isolate six elements that appear in one way or another in virtually all of them. These elements, in their typical order, are:

1. *Address.* The psalmist identifies the one to whom the psalm is prayed. This is, of course, the Lord.
2. *Complaint.* The psalmist pours out, honestly and forcefully, a complaint, identifying what the trouble is and why the Lord's help is being sought.
3. *Trust.* The psalmist immediately expresses trust in God. (Why complain to God if you don't trust him?) Moreover, you must trust him to answer your complaint in the way he sees fit, not necessarily as you would wish.
4. *Deliverance.* The psalmist pleads for God to deliver from the situation described in the complaint.
5. *Assurance.* The psalmist expresses the assurance that God will deliver. This assurance is parallel somewhat to the expression of trust.
6. *Praise.* The psalmist offers praise, thanking and honoring God for the blessings of the past, present, and/or future.

Psalm 3

¹O Lord, how many are my foes!
How many rise up against me!
²Many are saying of me,
"God will not deliver him."
³But you are a shield around me, O Lord,
my Glorious One, who lifts up my head.
⁴To the Lord I cry aloud,
and he answers me from his holy hill.

⁵I lie down and sleep;
I wake again, because the Lord sustains me.
⁶I will not fear the tens of thousands
drawn up against me on every side.

⁷Arise, O Lord!
Deliver me, O my God!
For you have struck all my enemies on the jaw;
you have broken the teeth of the wicked.

⁸From the Lord comes deliverance.
May your blessings be on your people.

In this psalm, the six elements of a lament are to be identified as follows:

1. *Address*. This is the "O Lord" of verse 1. Note that the address need not be lengthy or fancy. Simple prayers are just as effective as oratorical ones. We do not need to "butter up" God.
2. *Complaint*. This comprises the remainder of verse 1 and all of verse 2. David describes the foes (which can stand in these psalms as personified symbols of virtually any misery or problem), and how bleak his situation seems. *Any* difficulty can be expressed this way.
3. *Trust*. Here, verses 3–6 are all part of the expression of trust in the Lord. Who God is, how he answers prayer, how he keeps his people secure even when their situation is apparently hopeless—all this represents evidence that God is trustworthy.
4. *Deliverance*. In verse 7a ("Arise, O Lord! Deliver me, O my God!") David expresses his (and *our*) plea for help. Notice how the direct request for aid is held until this point in the

psalm, coming *after* the expression of trust. This order is not required, but is normal. A balance between asking and praising seems to characterize the laments, and this should be instructive to us in our own prayers.

5. *Assurance*. The remainder of verse 7 ("For you have struck. . . ," etc.) constitutes the statement of assurance. You may ask, "What sort of assurance is communicated by this pugilistic picture of God?" In fact the language is, again, metaphorical rather than literal. "You have already knocked out all my real problems" would be a suitable paraphrase, since the "enemies" and the "wicked" stand for the problems and distresses David felt then and we feel now. By this vivid picture, the defeat of that which oppresses us is envisioned. But remember that this part of the psalm does not promise that God's people will be trouble free. It expresses the assurance that God in his own time will have taken care of our really significant problems according to his plan for us.

6. *Praise*. Verse 8 lauds God for his faithfulness. He is declared to be one who is a deliverer, and in the request for his blessing, he is implicitly declared one who blesses. (You wouldn't ask for blessing from one who couldn't deliver it.)

Much can be learned from a lament such as Psalm 3. The importance of balanced prayer (requests should be balanced by appreciation; complaints by expressions of confidence) is perhaps at the top of the list. The evidence of honesty (note how freely and strongly David is inspired to word the complaint and the appeal) leads us to be more willing to express ourselves to God openly without covering over our problems.

However, the psalm is not designed specifically to instruct, but as a guide. We can use this very psalm when we are at wit's end, discouraged, seemingly surrounded by problems, feeling defeated. It will help us to express our thoughts and feelings and to rely upon God's faithfulness, just as it did for the ancient Israelites. God has placed it in the Bible so that it may help us commune with him, "casting all our cares upon him because he cares for us" (1 Peter 5:7).

The *group* lament psalms, sometimes called "community laments," follow the same six-step pattern. A church or other group facing difficult circumstances can use these psalms in a way analogous to the way the individual uses a psalm like Psalm 3.

Psalm 138: A Thanksgiving Psalm

Thanksgiving psalms have a different structure, as might be expected, because they have a different purpose in what they express. The elements of the thanksgiving psalm are as follows:

1. *Introduction.* Here the psalmist's testimony of how God has helped is summarized.
2. *Distress.* The situation from which God gave deliverance is portrayed.
3. *Appeal.* The psalmist reiterates the appeal that he or she made to God.
4. *Deliverance.* The deliverance God provided is described.
5. *Testimony.* A word of praise for God's mercy is given.

As you can see from this outline, the thanksgiving psalms concentrate on appreciation for past mercies. A thanksgiving psalm usually thanks God for what he *has* done. The order of these five elements may vary considerably. A firmly fixed order would unduly limit the creativity of the inspired author.

Psalm 138

¹I will praise you, O LORD, with all my heart;
  before the "gods" I will sing your praise.
²I will bow down toward your holy temple
  and will praise your name
  for your love and your faithfulness,
for you have exalted above all things
  your name and your word
³When I called, you answered me;
  you made me bold and stouthearted.

⁴May all the kings of the earth praise you, O LORD,
  when they hear the words of your mouth.
⁵May they sing of the ways of the LORD,
  for the glory of the LORD is great.

⁶Though the LORD is on high, he looks upon the lowly,
  but the proud he knows from afar.
⁷Though I walk in the midst of trouble,
  you preserve my life:

you stretched out your hand against the anger of my foes,
   with your right hand you save me.
⁸The LORD will fulfill his purpose for me;
   your love, O LORD, endures forever—
   do not abandon the works of your hands.

1. *Introduction*. In verses 1–2 David expresses his intention to praise God for the love and faithfulness he has shown, as well as for the fact that God's greatness in and of itself deserves acclamation.
2. *Distress*. In verse 3 the distress is unspecified—it may be any sort of difficulty in which David called to the Lord. Accordingly, the psalm is of use to any Christian who wishes to thank God for any sort of help.
3. *Appeal*. The appeal is also contained in verse 3. God is praised for having graciously responded to David's (unspecified) distress.
4. *Deliverance*. Here verse 6–7 are most pertinent. The fact that God paid attention to his undeserving supplicant, preserved his life in the midst of trouble (perhaps many times, since "preserve" is in the present tense), and rescued David from his "foes" serves to express for us our own appreciation for God's faithful help to us in the past.
5. *Testimony*. Verses 4–5, and 8 all constitute David's (and our) testimonial to God's goodness. God is so beneficent that he deserves praise from even the great of the earth (vv. 4–5). He may be counted upon and appealed to in connection with carrying out his promises and intentions. His love never stops (v. 8).

What grand expectations of our relationship to God a thanksgiving song like Psalm 138 contains! How useful it can be in marshalling our own thoughts and feelings when we reflect on the faithfulness God has shown us over the years.

If you wish to pursue the contents of the other types of psalms than those discussed here, you will find Anderson's book a big help. Many of the same results can be obtained, however, from simply reading several psalms of a given type and then analyzing on your own the common characteristics they contain. The most important thing is to realize that the psalms do differ from one another, and that a wise discernment of the types will lead to a wise use of the psalms themselves.

A Special Note on the "Imprecatory Psalms"

One reason the Psalms have had so much appeal to God's people in all ages is their comprehensiveness of language. A full range of human emotion, even extreme emotion, is found. No matter how sad you are, the psalmist helps you express your sadness, with abject pathos if necessary (e.g., Ps. 69:7–20 or 88:3–9). No matter how glad you are, the psalmist helps you express that (e.g., Ps. 98 or 133 or 23:5–6). The obviously exaggerated language (hyperbole) is hard to outdo!

Now sadness and gladness are not sinful. But bitterness, anger, and hatred may lead one to sinful thoughts or actions, such as the desire or the attempt to harm others. It is surely true that expressing one's anger verbally—letting it out in words as it were—is better than letting it out in violent actions. Parts of certain psalms help us in just this way, and with an added dimension. They guide or channel our anger *to and through* God verbally, rather than to or at anyone else, verbally or physically. Psalms that contain verbalizations to God of anger at others are called imprecatory psalms.

It would be both useless and dishonest to try to deny that we sometimes have negative thoughts about others, whether such thoughts are always sinful or not. God, through the imprecatory psalms, invites us to "be angry but not to sin" (Ps. 4:4). We must fulfill the New Testament teaching, "Do not let the sun go down while you are angry, and do not give the devil a foothold" (Eph. 4:25–26), by expressing our anger directly to and through God rather than by seeking to return evil to those who have done evil to us. Imprecatory psalms harness our anger and help us express it (to God) using the same sorts of obvious, purposeful exaggeration known to us from other types of psalms.

The imprecatory parts of psalms are virtually always found in laments. Psalm 3, described in detail above, contains in verse 7 an imprecation that, like most others found in the Psalms, is brief and therefore not likely to be highly offensive. But some imprecations are rather lengthy and harsh (see parts of Pss. 12, 35, 58, 59, 69, 70, 83, 109, 137, 140). Consider, for example, Psalm 137:7–9:

7Remember, O LORD, what the Edomites did
 on the day Jerusalem fell.
"Tear it down," they cried,
 "tear it down to its foundations."

8O Daughter of Babylon, doomed to destruction,
 happy is he who repays you
 for what you have done to us—
9he who seizes your infants
 and dashes them against the rocks.

Psalm 137 is a lament for the suffering endured by the Israelites in the Exile; their capital, Jerusalem, had been destroyed, and their land had been taken from them by the Babylonians, aided and encouraged by the Edomites (cf. the book of Obadiah). Heeding God's Word, "It is mine to avenge, I will repay" (Deut. 32:35; cf. Rom. 12:19) the composer of this lament calls for judgment *according to the covenant curses* (see chap. 10). Included in these curses is provision for the annihilation of the whole wicked society, including family members (Deut. 32:25; cf. Deut. 28: 53–57). Nothing in the Scripture teaches, of course that this *temporal* judgment should be seen as indicating anything about the *eternal* destiny of such family members.

What the psalmist has done in Psalm 137 is to tell God about the feelings of the suffering Israelites, using hyperbolic language of the same extreme sort found in the covenant curses themselves. The fact that the psalmist seems to be addressing the Babylonians directly is simply a function of the style of the psalm—he also addresses Jerusalem directly in verse 5. It is God who is the actual hearer of these angry words (v. 7), just as it should be God, and God alone, who hears *our* angry words. Understood in their context as part of the language of the laments, and used rightly to channel and control our potentially sinful anger, the imprecatory psalms can indeed help keep us from sin. To harbor or display anger against others is something we should all avoid (Matt. 5:22).

The imprecatory psalms do not contradict Jesus' teaching to love our enemies. We tend wrongly to equate "love" with "having a warm feeling toward." Jesus' teaching, however, defines love actively. It is not so much how you *feel* about a certain person, but what you *do* for that person that shows love (Luke 10:25–37). The biblical command is to *do* love, not to *feel* love. In a related way, the imprecatory psalms help us, when we feel anger, not to do anger.

We should honestly express our anger to God, no matter how bitterly and hatefully we feel it, and let God take care of justice against those who misuse us. The foe who continues evil in the face of our forbearance is in big trouble indeed (Rom. 12:20). The proper function of these psalms, then, is to help us not to be "overcome by evil," but to help free us from our anger, that we might "overcome evil with good" (Rom. 12:21).

A final word: The term "hate" in the Psalms has been commonly misunderstood. When the psalmist says, "I have nothing but hatred for them" (Ps. 139:22), he is not expressing sin. Otherwise God's declaration, "Esau have I hated" (Mal. 1:2; cf. Rom. 9:13), would prove him a sinner. The Hebrew word translated "hate" does in some contexts mean "despise." But it can also mean "be unwilling or unable to put up with" or "reject," both standard definitions in the Hebrew lexicons for this word. Therefore, on this account as well there should be no presumption that the language of the imprecatory psalms violates the Scriptures' teaching elsewhere, including Matthew 5:22.

Some Concluding Hermeneutical Observations

Since Christians for generations have almost instinctively turned to the Psalter in times of need, perplexity, or joy, we hesitate to offer a "hermeneutics" of the Psalms lest we somehow make them too pedestrian. Nonetheless, some observations are in order— hopefully so as to make them still a greater joy to read, sing, or pray.

First, we should note that the Christian "instinct" (common sense) just alluded to provides the basic answer to the question with which we began this chapter: *How* do these words spoken *to* God function for us as a Word *from* God? The answer? Precisely in the ways they functioned in Israel in the first place—as opportunities to speak to God in words he inspired others to speak to him in times past.

Three Basic Benefits of the Psalms

From the use of the Psalms both in ancient Israel and in the New Testament church we can see three important ways in which Christians can use the Psalms. First, it must be remembered that the Psalms are a *guide to worship*. By this we mean that the worshiper who seeks to praise God, or to appeal to God, or to remember God's benefits, can use the Psalms as a formal means of expression of his or her thoughts and feelings. A psalm is a carefully composed literary preservation of words designed to be spoken. When a psalm touches upon a topic or a theme that we wish to express to the Lord, our ability to do so may be enhanced by employing a psalm as an aid. It can help us express our concerns in spite of our own lack of skill to find the right words.

Second, the Psalms demonstrate to us how we can *relate honestly* to God. Although they do not so much provide doctrinal instruction on this point, they do give, *by example,* a true sort of instruction. One can learn from the Psalms how to be honest and open in expressing joy, disappointment, anger, or other emotions.

Third, the Psalms demonstrate the importance of *reflection and meditation* upon things that God has done for us. They invite us to prayer, to controlled thinking upon God's Word (that is what meditation is), and to reflective fellowship with other believers. Such things help shape in us a life of purity and charity. The Psalms, like no other literature, lift us to a position where we can commune with God, capturing a sense of the greatness of his kingdom and a sense of what living with him for eternity will be like. Even in our darkest moments, when life has become so painful as to seem unendurable, God is with us. "Out of the depths" (Ps. 130:1) we wait and watch for the Lord's deliverance, knowing we can trust him in spite of our feelings. To cry to God for help is not a judgment on his faithfulness, but an affirmation of it.

A Caution

We conclude this chapter with a very important caution: *The Psalms do not guarantee a pleasant life.* It is a misunderstanding—an overliteralization—of the language of the Psalms to infer from some of them that God promises to make his believers happy and their lives trouble-free. David, who expresses in the Psalms God's blessing in the strongest terms, lived a life that was filled with almost constant tragedy and disappointment; as 1 and 2 Samuel describe. Yet he praises and thanks God enthusiastically at every turn, even in laments, just as Paul advises us to do even in the midst of hard times (Eph. 1:16; 5:20). God deserves praise for his greatness and goodness in spite of and in the midst of our misery. This life holds no certainty of freedom from distress.

12

Wisdom: Then and Now

Hebrew wisdom is a category of literature that is unfamiliar to most modern Christians. Though a significant portion of the Bible is devoted to wisdom writings, Christians often either misunderstand or misapply this material, losing benefits that God intended for them. When properly understood and used, however, wisdom is a helpful resource for Christian living. When misused, it can provide a basis for selfish, materialistic, short-sighted behavior—just the opposite of what God intended.

Three Old Testament books are commonly known as "wisdom" books: Ecclesiastes, Proverbs, and Job. In addition, as we noted in chapter 11, a number of the Psalms are often classified in the wisdom category. Finally, there is the Song of Songs, also commonly called the Song of Solomon. We think it fits properly under the category of wisdom, as we will discuss below. Not everything in these books is, strictly speaking, concerned with wisdom. But in general they contain the type of material that fits the wisdom label.

The Nature of Wisdom

What exactly is wisdom? A brief definition runs as follows: Wisdom is the ability to make godly choices in life. That sounds reasonable enough, and not the sort of thing that should confuse Christians. The problem is, however, that the wisdom material of the Old Testament seems all too often to end up being misunderstood, with the result that the choices people make are not all that godly. This chapter intends to help you refine your understanding and application of wisdom.

Abuse of Wisdom Literature

Traditionally, the wisdom books have been misused in three ways.

First, people often read these books only in part. They fail to see that there is an overall message according to the inspired author's intentions. Bits and snatches of wisdom teaching taken out of context can sound profound and seem practical, but they can be easily misapplied. For example, the teaching in Ecclesiastes that there is a "time to be born and a time to die" (3:2) is intended in its context to be a cynical teaching on the futility of all life (i.e., no matter how bad or good your life is, you still will die whenever your "time" comes). Many Christians have thought that the verse intended to teach that God protectively picks out our lifespan for us; in context, this is definitely *not* what Ecclesiastes 3:2 is saying.

Second, people often misunderstand wisdom terms and categories as well as wisdom styles and literary modes. Thus they misdefine the terms used in the Bible in wisdom contexts. For example, consider Proverbs 14:7, "Stay away from a fool for you will not find knowledge on his lips." Does this mean that Christians should choose not to associate with the retarded, the uneducated, or the mentally ill? Not at all. In Proverbs, "fool" means basically "infidel"—it refers to an unbeliever who lives life according to selfish, indulgent whims, and who acknowledges no higher authority than himself. And the "staying away" is inextricably linked with the purpose ("for you will not find"). In other words, the proverb teaches that if you are seeking knowledge, you should not seek it from an infidel.

Third, people often fail to follow the line of argument in a wisdom discourse. Accordingly, they try to live by what was intended to be understood as *incorrect*. Consider Job 15:20, "All his days the wicked person suffers torment, the ruthless person through all the years stored up for him." Would you take this to be an inspired teaching that evil people cannot really be happy? Job did not! He energetically refuted it. This verse is part of a speech by Job's self-appointed "comforter" Eliphaz, who is trying to convince Job that the reason he is suffering so much is that he has been evil.

Later in the book God vindicates the words of Job and condemns the words of Eliphaz. But unless you follow the *whole* argument, you cannot know that.

Our procedure in this chapter will be to discuss what wisdom literature is and what it is not, and then to make some useful observations on it. We will sample some wisdom books to show how they must be understood, and finally present some guidelines for correctly interpreting them. We will pay most attention to Proverbs, because that is the book we judge to be most often abused.

Who Is Wise?

We stated above that wisdom is the ability to make godly choices in life. There is thus a personal side to wisdom. Wisdom is not something theoretical and abstract—it is something that exists only when a *person* thinks and acts according to the truth as he or she makes the many choices that life demands. The Old Testament recognizes therefore that some people have more wisdom than others and that some people have so devoted themselves to gaining wisdom that they themselves can be called "wise" (Hebrew *ḥākām*). The wise person was highly practical, not merely theoretical. He or she was interested in being able to formulate the sorts of plans— that is, make the sorts of choices—that would help produce the desired results in life.

There is a very real sense in which the entire progress of our lives may be viewed as the result of choices. In fact, almost everything we do is to some degree a matter of choice. When to get up in the morning, what to do first, where to work, whom to speak to, how to speak to them, what to accomplish, when to start and stop things, what to eat, what to wear, whom to associate with, where to go, with whom to go—all these actions are the result of decisions. Some of the decisions are made on the spot (what to have for lunch, for example), others may have been made long ago so that they need not be remade daily (where to live, whom to marry, what kind of work to engage in), and others may be the result of God's choices and not our own (Gen. 45:8), while yet others may be only partly voluntary on our part (Prov. 16:33). Nevertheless, choices chart the course of life.

The ancients knew this, and wisdom literature, which is found all over ancient culture—not just in Israel—sought to evaluate how best to make life's choices. Non-Israelite wisdom had as its goal the making of the best choices, the purpose being to achieve the best life. What the inspired biblical wisdom added to this was the crucial idea that the only good choices are godly choices. Thus "the fear of the LORD is the beginning of wisdom"—a basic theme of Proverbs. After all, how can you make godly choices if you do not believe and obey God? The very first step, then, in biblical wisdom is knowing God—not abstractly or theoretically, but in the concrete sense of committing your life to him. Then your general direction will be correct, and as you learn specific rules and perspectives for making godly choices, a more precise sense of direction for wise living can follow.

Wisdom, therefore, as the Bible defines it (Hebrew *ḥokmáh*) has nothing to do with I.Q. It is not a matter of cleverness and quickness or skill in expression or age, even though personal experience is a valuable teacher if interpreted in light of revealed truth. It is a matter of orientation to God, out of which comes the ability to please him. That is why James 1:5 says that God gives wisdom to those who ask for it. This is a promise not that we can become smarter by prayer, but that God will help us to become more godly if we ask. James defines the kind of wisdom that God gives in James 3:13–18, in contrast to the worldly wisdom by which a person seeks to know how to get ahead of others.

Responsible, successful living was the goal. Sometimes such wisdom was applied to technical matters like construction (cf. Bezaleel, the tabernacle architect, called "wise" in Exod. 31:3) or navigation (Ezek. 27:8–9). Wisdom was also sought by people who had to make decisions affecting the welfare of others. Political leaders such as Joshua (Deut. 34:9), David (2 Sam. 14:20), and Solomon (1 Kings 3:9 et al.) were described as having been given wisdom by God, so that their rule might be effective and successful. We are reminded of the personal side of the skill of wise people by the fact that the human heart is described as the focal point of wisdom (cf. 1 Kings 3:9, 12). The "heart" in the Old Testament refers to the moral and volitional faculties, as well as the intellectual.

Wisdom literature, then, tends to focus on people and their behavior, how successful they are at making godly choices and whether or not they are learning how to apply God's truth to the experiences they have. It is not so much the case that people seek to learn how to *be* wise, but rather that they seek to *get* wise. Anyone who seeks to apply God's truth daily and learn from his or her experience can become wise eventually. But there is a great danger in seeking wisdom simply for one's own advantage or in a way that does not honor God above all; "Woe to those who are wise in their own eyes!" (Isa. 5:21). Moreover, God's wisdom always excels human wisdom (Isa. 29:13–14).

Teachers of Wisdom

In ancient Israel some people devoted themselves not only to gaining wisdom, but also to teaching others how to gain it. These wisdom instructors were simply called "wise men," though they eventually occupied a position in Israelite society somewhat parallel to that of the priest and the prophet (Jer. 18:18). This special class of wise men and women arose at least as early as the beginning of the kingship period in Israel (i.e., about 1000 B.C.; cf. 1 Sam. 14:2), and functioned as teacher-counselors to those who sought their wisdom. Some were inspired by God to help write portions of the Old Testament. We note that the wise person served as a sort of substitute parent to the person seeking wisdom from him or her. Even before the Exodus, Joseph was made by God a "father" to Pharaoh (Gen. 45:8), and later the prophetess Deborah is called a "mother" in Israel (Judg. 5:7). Thus often in the book of Proverbs we see the wise teacher addressing his or her pupil as "my child" ("my son" is not the best translation). Parents sent their children to be educated in wisdom attitudes and lifestyles from such wisdom teachers, and these teachers taught their pupils as they would their own children.

Wisdom in the Home

Wisdom has always been taught more at home, however, than in any other setting. Modern parents teach their children all sorts of wisdom, virtually every day, often without realizing it, as they try to help them make the right choices in life. Whenever a parent gives a child rules to live by, from "Don't play in the street" to "Try to choose nice friends" to "Be sure to dress warmly enough," the parent is actually teaching wisdom. Any parent wants his or her children to be happy, self-sufficient, and of benefit to others. A good parent spends time shaping the behavior of his or her children in this direction, talking to them regularly about how to behave. In Proverbs, especially, this same sort of practical advice is given. But

Proverbs subordinates all its advice to God's wisdom, just as a Christian parent should try to do. The advice may be strongly practical and concerned with secular issues, but it should never fail to acknowledge that the highest good a person can achieve is to do God's will.

Wisdom Among Colleagues

One way people refine their ability to make the right choices in life is by discussion and argument. This sort of wisdom is arrived at sometimes by lengthy discourse, either in a monologue intended for others to read and reflect upon (e.g., Ecclesiastes) or in a dialogue among various persons seeking to inform each other's opinions on truth and life (e.g., Job). The kind of wisdom that predominates in the book of Proverbs is called proverbial wisdom, whereas the kind found in Ecclesiastes and Job is usually called speculative wisdom. The kind found in the Song of Songs may be called lyric wisdom. We will discuss these in more detail below. For now, just remember that even so-called speculative wisdom is highly practical and empirical (centered in experience) rather than merely theoretical.

Wisdom Expressed Through Poetry

Students and teachers alike in Old Testament times used a variety of literary techniques as aids to remembering their wisdom. God inspired the wisdom portions of the Bible according to such techniques, so that they might be learnable and memorizable. As noted in the two preceding chapters poetry has the careful wordings, cadences, and stylistic qualities that make it easier to commit to memory than prose, and thus poetry also became the medium of Old Testament wisdom. Proverbs, Ecclesiastes, Job, and Song of Songs, as well as the wisdom psalms and other bits of wisdom in the Old Testament are composed therefore mostly in poetry. Among the particular techniques used are parallelisms, whether synonymous (e.g., Prov. 7:4), antithetical (Prov. 10:1), or "formal" (Prov. 21:16), acrostics (Prov. 31:10–31), alliteration (Eccl. 3:1–8), numerical sequences (Prov. 30:15–31), and countless comparisons (such as similes and metaphors, e.g., Job 32:19; Song 4:1 6). Formal parables, allegories, riddles, and other poetic techniques are also found in wisdom material.

The Limits of Wisdom

It is important to remember that not all wisdom in the ancient world was godly or orthodox. Throughout the ancient Near East there was a class of wise teachers and scribes who were supported, often by royalty, in the task of collecting, composing, and refining wisdom proverbs and discourses. Much of this wisdom resembles the Old Testament wisdom writings, though it lacks the firm emphasis upon the Lord as the origin of wisdom (Prov. 2:5–6) and the purpose of wisdom as to please him (Prov. 3:7). Moreover, wisdom does not cover all of life. Intensely practical, it tends not to touch upon the theological or historical issues so important elsewhere in the Bible. And skill at wisdom does not guarantee that it will be properly used. Jonadab's wise advice to Amnon (2 Sam. 13:3) was rendered in an evil cause; Solomon's great wisdom (1 Kings 3:12; 4:29–34) helped him gain wealth and power but could not keep him from turning away from faithfulness to the Lord in his later years (1 Kings 11:4). Only when wisdom as a skill is subordinated to obedience to God does it achieve its proper ends in the sense the Old Testament means.

Ecclesiastes: Cynical Wisdom

Ecclesiastes is a wisdom monologue that often puzzles Christians especially if they read it carefully. Those who do not read it carefully may simply conclude that it contains ideas too deep to mine for instant value. Such persons usually drop Ecclesiastes and move on to parts of the Bible more likely in their judgment to produce quicker spiritual benefits. Even those who study the book intently may be baffled by Ecclesiastes; it does not, after all, seem to contain very much that is positive and encouraging to a life of faithfulness to God. Rather, most of the book seems to advise in the words of the "Teacher" that life is ultimately meaningless and that one should therefore choose to enjoy one's life in whatever way possible, since death will obliterate everything anyway. The message of cynicism and ultimate meaninglessness comes through in Ecclesiastes in passage like these:

> "Meaningless! Meaningless!"
> says the Teacher.

> "Utterly meaningless!
> Everything is meaningless" (1:2).

I have seen all the things that are done under the sun;
all of them are meaningless, a chasing after the wind (1:14).

> Then I though in my heart,
> "The fate of the fool will overtake me also.
> What then do I gain by being wise?"
> I said in my heart,
> "This, too, is meaningless" (2:15).

Man's fate is like that of the animals . . . man has no advantage
over the animal. Everything is meaningless (3:19).

> As a person comes, so he departs,
> and what does he gain,
> since he toils for the wind? (5:16).

There is something else meaningless that occurs on earth:
righteous people who get what the wicked deserve and wicked
people who get what the righteous deserve. This, too, I say is
meaningless (8:14).

Enjoy life with your wife . . . all the days of this meaningless
life. . . . Whatever your hand finds to do, do it with all your
might, for in the grave, where you are going, there is neither
working nor planning nor knowledge nor wisdom (9:9–10).

> However many years a person may live,
> let him enjoy them all.
> But let him remember the days of darkness,
> For they will be many.
> Everything to come is meaningless (11:8).

Ecclesiastes does contain portions that are not nearly so cynical
or negative about the value of life. But its consistent message (until
the very last verses) is that the reality and finality of death mean that
life has no *ultimate* value. After all, if we are all going to die anyway,
and pass and be forgotten like all the rest, what difference does it
make if we lived a generous, productive, godly life, or a selfish,
wicked, miserable life? Death, the great leveler, makes all lives end
the same! This is almost precisely the philosophy espoused by
modern existentialism, and the Teacher's advice is existential in
character: Enjoy life as much as you can while you are alive (8:15;
11:8–10; et al.) because that is all that God has provided for you—

there is nothing else. Live as well as you can *now*. After this, there is no meaning. The Teacher does give advice on practical living, e.g., on care in speech (5:2–3), or on avoiding harmful greed (5:11–15), or on piety during youth when there is some advantage to it (12:1–8).

But this advice has no eternal value. It is given mainly to help make one's meaningless life somewhat more pleasant and comfortable while one is still young. Ecclesiastes seems to deny an afterlife (2:16; 9:5 et al.), criticize key aspects of the Old Testament faith (e.g., 7:16; 5:1), and generally encourage attitudes very different from the rest of Scripture.

Why, then, you ask, is it in the Bible at all? The answer is that it is there as a foil, i.e., as a contrast to what the rest of the Bible teaches. Ecclesiastes 12:13–14 presents that contrast, and issues to the reader this orthodox warning:

> Fear God and keep his commandments,
>   For this is the whole duty of man,
> For God will bring every deed into judgment,
>   including every hidden thing,
>   whether it is good or evil.

The bulk of the book, everything but these two final verses, represents a brilliant, artful argument for the way one would look at life—*if* God did *not* play a direct, intervening role in life and *if* there were no life after death. So if you want a prescription for living in a deistic world (i.e., a world where there is a God but he does not have contact with people) with no afterlife, Ecclesiastes provides it. The true aim of the book, representing as it does the sort of "wisdom" that Solomon could produce after he had degenerated from orthodoxy (1 Kings 11:1–13), is to show that such a view of life would leave you cold. The view presented ought to leave you unsatisfied, for it is hardly the truth. It is the secular, fatalistic wisdom that a *practical* (not theoretical) atheism produces. When one relegates God to a position way out there away from us, irrelevant to our daily lives, then Ecclesiastes is the result. The book thus serves as a reverse apologetic for cynical wisdom; it drives its readers to look further because the answers that the "Teacher" of Ecclesiastes gives are so discouraging. The advice of 12:13 (keep God's commandments) points away from Ecclesiastes to the rest of

Scripture, especially the Pentateuch (see chap. 9) where these commandments are found.

Wisdom in Job

Ecclesiastes is not the only place in the Old Testament where incorrect advice is found as a foil for God's truth. The book of Job contains all sorts of wrong advice and incorrect conclusions as they come from the lips of Job's well-meaning "comforters," Bildad, Zophar, Eliphaz, and Elihu. As you read through the book you will notice that it takes the form of a highly structured conversation or dialogue. This dialogue has a very important goal: to establish convincingly in the mind of the reader that what happens in life does not always happen because God desires it or because it is fair. In one sense, the book of Job has a purpose almost directly opposite of that of Ecclesiastes. The Teacher in Ecclesiastes wanted to portray God as uninvolved in daily affairs. Job's comforters, on the other hand, represent the viewpoint that God is not simply involved but is constantly meting out his judgment through the events of this life. Ecclesiastes suggests that it does not matter how you choose to live since the final leveler is death. Job's colleagues say to Job that what happens to you in life—good or ill—is a *direct* result of whether you have pleased God or not. They are horrified when Job protests that he did nothing wrong to deserve the sorts of miseries (illness, bereavement, impoverishment, incapacitation) that have struck him. Their message is that when life goes well for a person, that is a sign that he or she has chosen to do what is good, but when things go badly, surely the person has sinned against God and God has responded by imposing affliction. Jesus' disciples were capable of this sort of logic (John 9:1–3), as are many Christians today. It seems so natural to assume that if God is in control of the world, everything that happens must be his doing, according to his will. We must remember, however, that the Scriptures do not teach us this. They teach rather that the world is fallen, corrupted by sin, under the domination of Satan (cf. John 12:31), and that many things happen in life that are not as God wishes them to be. Specifically, suffering is not necessarily the result of sin (cf. Rom. 8:18–23).

Job, a godly man, knew that he had done nothing to deserve the wrath of God. In his frequent speeches (chaps. 3, 6–7, 9–10,

12–14, 16–17, 19, 21, 23–24, 26–31) he asserts his innocence eloquently and also expresses his frustration at the horrors he has had to endure. He cannot understand why such things have happened to him. His colleagues are horrified to hear such talk—to them it is blasphemy. They persist at trying to convince him that he is doubting God by his protestations. One by one they urge him repeatedly to confess his sin, whatever it is, and admit that God administers a fair and just world, in which we get what our choices deserve. Just as tenaciously, and even more eloquently, Job argues that life is unfair, that the world as it is now is not the way it ought to be. Elihu, the final "comforter" to arrive on the scene, defends God's superior knowledge and ways. This is the closest thing to an answer for Job that anyone has yet been able to provide, and it looks as if Job is going to have to settle for Elihu's partly satisfying, partly infuriating answer, when suddenly God himself speaks to Job and the others (chaps. 38–41). God both corrects Job and puts the situation in perspective, but he also vindicates Job over against the "wisdom" of his colleagues (42:7–9). As to the question of whether everything in life is fair or not, Job had prevailed; it is not. As to Job's wondering, "Why me?" God had prevailed; his ways are far above our ways, and his allowing of suffering does not mean that he does not know what he is doing, or that his right to do it should be questioned. His choices are always superior to ours.

This is true wisdom at its finest. The reader of the book of Job learns what is simply the world's wisdom, seemingly logical but actually wrong, and what constitutes God's wisdom and what builds confidence in God's sovereignty and righteousness. Thus the dialogue and the story line combine to make the Old Testament's paramount exemplar of speculative wisdom.

Wisdom in Proverbs

The book of Proverbs is the primary locus of prudential wisdom—that is, rules and regulations people can use to help themselves make responsible, successful choices in life. In contrast to Ecclesiastes, which uses a speculative cynicism as its wisdom foil, and Job, which uses speculative wisdom about the unfairness of life in this world, proverbial wisdom concentrates mostly on *practical attitudes*. As a generalization, it is useful to note that Proverbs teaches what might be called "old fashioned basic values." No parent wants his or her child to grow up unhappy, disappointed, lonely, socially rejected, in trouble with the law, immoral, inept, or broke. It is neither selfish nor unrealistic for a parent to wish a child a reasonable level of success in life—including social acceptance, freedom from want, and moral uprightness. Proverbs provides a collection of pithy advisory statements designed to do just that. There is no guarantee, of course, that a life will always go well for a young person. What Proverbs does say is that, all things being equal, there *are* basic attitudes and patterns of behavior that will help a person grow into responsible adulthood.

Proverbs continually presents a sharp contrast between choosing the life of wisdom and choosing the life of folly. What characterizes the life of folly? Folly is characterized by such things as violent crime (1:10–19; 4:14–19), careless promising or pledging (6:1–5), laziness (6:7–11), malicious dishonesty (6:12–15), and sexual impurity, which is especially odious to God and harmful to an upright life (2:16–19; 5:3–20; 6:23–35; 7:4–27; 9:13–18; 23:26–28). In addition, Proverbs urges such things as caring for the poor (2:22, 27), respect for governmental leaders (23:1–3; 24:21–22), the importance of disciplining children (23:13–14), moderation in consumption of alcohol (23:19–21, 29–35), and regard for one's parents (23:22–25).

Specifically religious language is seldom used in Proverbs; it is present (cf. 1:7; 3:5–12; 15:3, 8–9, 11; 16:1–9; 22:9, 23; 24:18, 21; et al.) but it does not predominate. Not everything in life has to be strictly *religious* to be *godly*. Indeed, Proverbs can help serve as a corrective to the extremist tendency to spiritualize everything, as if there were something wrong with the basic material, physical world; as if God had said, "It is bad" rather than "It is good" when he first looked on what he had made.

Uses and Abuses of Proverbs

A good thing to remember about the Proverbs is that in Hebrew they are called *meshallim* ("figures of speech," "parables" or "specially contrived sayings"). A proverb is a *brief, particular* expression of a truth. The briefer a statement is, the less likely it is to be totally precise and universally applicable. We know that long, highly qualified, elaborate, detailed statements of fact are not only often difficult to understand but virtually impossible for most people to memorize. So the proverbs are phrased in a catchy way, so as to be learnable by anyone. Indeed, in Hebrew many of the proverbs have some sort of rhythm, sound repetition, or vocabulary qualities that make them particularly easy to learn. Consider the English proverbs "Look before you leap" and "A stitch in time saves nine." The repetition of single-syllable words beginning with the letter *l* in the first case, and the rhythm and rhyme of single-syllable words in the second case are the elements that give these proverbs a certain catchiness. They are not as easy to forget as would be the following statements: "In advance of committing yourself to a course of action, consider your circumstances and options"; "There are certain corrective measures for minor problems that, when taken early on in a course of action, forestall major problems from arising." These latter formulations are more precise but lack the punch and effectiveness of the two well-known wordings, not to mention the fact that they are much harder to remember. "Look before you leap" is a pithy, inexact statement; it can easily be misunderstood, or thought to apply only to jumping. It does not say where or how to look, what to look for, how soon to leap after looking, and it is not even intended to apply literally to jumping!

So it is with Hebrew proverbs. They must be understood reasonably and taken on their own terms. They do not state everything about a truth but they point *toward* it. They are, taken literally, often technically inexact. But as learnable guidelines for the shaping of selected behavior, they are unsurpassed. Consider Proverbs 6:27–29:

> Can a man scoop fire into his lap
>   without his clothes being burned?
> Can a man walk on hot coals
>   without his feet being scorched?
> So is he who sleeps with another man's wife;
>   no one who touches her will go unpunished.

Someone might think, "Now that last line is unclear. What if the mailman accidentally touches another man's wife while delivering the mail? Will he be punished? And are there not some people who commit adultery and get away with it?" but such interpretations miss the point. Proverbs tend to use *figurative* language and express things *suggestively* rather than in detail. The point you should get from the proverb is that committing adultery is like playing with fire. God will see to it that sooner or later, in this life or the next, the adulterer will be hurt by his actions. The word "touch" in the last line *must* be understood euphemistically (cf. 1 Cor. 7:1; see chap. 2), if the Holy Spirit's inspired message is not to be distorted. Thus a proverb should not be taken too literally or too universally if its message is to be helpful. For example, consider Proverbs 9:13–18:

> The woman Folly is loud;
>> she is undisciplined and without knowledge.
> She sits at the door of her house,
>> on a seat at the highest point of the city,
> calling out to those who pass by,
>> who go straight on their way.
> "Let all who are simple-minded come in here!"
>> she says to those who lack judgment.
> "Stolen water is sweet;
>> food eaten in secret is delicious!"
> But little do they know that the dead are there,
>> that her guests are in the depths of the grave.

This, too, is a pithy proverb for it includes a whole allegory (story pointing to something other than itself by implicit comparisons) in a few verses. Here folly, the opposite of wise living, is personified as a prostitute trying to entice passersby into her house. The fool is characterized by his fascination with forbidden pleasures (v. 17). But the end result of a life of folly is not long life, success, or happiness—it is death. "Stay away from folly!" is the message of this brief allegory. "Don't be taken in! Walk right past those temptations (spelled out in various ways in other proverbs) that folly makes seem attractive!" The wise, godly, moral person will choose a life free from the selfishness of folly. Proverbs like this are somewhat like parables in that they express their truth in a symbolic way.

Another example that will help focus our discussion of Proverbs is Proverbs 16:3:

> Commit to the LORD whatever you do,
>> and your plans will succeed.

This is the sort of proverb that is most often misinterpreted. Not realizing that proverbs tend to be inexact statements pointing to the truth in figurative ways, a person might assume that Proverbs 16:3 is a direct, clear-cut, always applicable promise from God that if one dedicates his or her plans to God, those plans *must* succeed. People who reason that way, of course, can be disappointed. They can dedicate some perfectly selfish or idiotic scheme to God, then if it happens to succeed, even briefly, they can assume that God blessed it. A hasty marriage, a rash business decision, an ill-thought-out vocational decision—all can be dedicated to God but can eventually result in misery. Or, a person might commit a plan to God only to have it fail; then the person would wonder why God did not keep his promise, why he went back on his inspired Word. In either case they have failed to see that the proverb is not a categorical, always applicable, ironclad promise, but a more general truth; it teaches that lives committed to God and lived according to his will succeed *according to God's definition of success*. But according to the world's definition of success, the result may be just the opposite. The story of Job eloquently reminds us of that.

When these proverbs, then, are taken on their own terms, and understood as the special category of *suggestive* truth that they are, they become important and useful adjuncts for living.

Some Hermeneutical Guidelines

We now offer in capsule form some guidelines for understanding proverbial wisdom.

Proverbs Are Not Legal Guarantees From God

Proverbs state a wise way to approach certain selected practical goals but do so in terms that cannot be treated like a divine warranty of success. The particular blessings, rewards, and opportunities mentioned in Proverbs are *likely* to follow if one will choose the wise courses of action outlined in the poetical, figurative language of the book. But nowhere does Proverbs teach *automatic* success. Remember that both Ecclesiastes and Job were included by God in the Scriptures partly to remind us that there is very little that is automatic about the good or bad events that may take place in our lives. Consider these examples (Prov. 22:26–27; 29:12; 15:25).

> Do not be a person who shakes hands in pledge,
>> or puts up security for debts;
> If you lack the means to pay,

> your very bed will be snatched from under you
> (Prov. 22:26–27).

> If a ruler listens to lies,
>   all his officials become wicked (Prov. 29:12).

> The LORD tears down the proud man's house,
>   but he keeps the widow's boundaries intact (Prov. 15:25).

If you were to take the extreme step of considering the first of these examples (22:26–27) as an all-encompassing command from God, you might well never buy a house, so as never to incur a mortgage (a secured debt). Or, you might assume that God promises that if you default on something like a credit card debt you will eventually lose all your possessions including your bed(s). Your literalistic, extreme interpretation would lead you to miss the point of the proverb, which states poetically and figuratively that *debts should be taken on cautiously, because foreclosure can be very painful.* The proverb frames this truth in specific, narrow terms (shaking hands, losing a bed, etc.) that are intended to point toward the broader principle rather than to express something technically. In Bible times, righteous people incurred debts without any violation of this proverb, because they understood its real point. They were used to proverbs and knew that this one told them *how* to take on debts, not that they were to avoid debts altogether.

The second example above (29:12) is also not to be misunderstood literalistically. It does not guarantee, for example, that if you are a governmental official, you have no choice but to become wicked if your boss (the governor, president, or whatever) listens to some people who do not tell him the truth. In intends to convey a different message: that a ruler who wants to hear lies instead of the truth will gradually surround himself/herself with people who will say what he or she wants to hear. And the end result can be corrupt government. Thus the ruler who insists on hearing the truth, even though it is painful, helps keep the government honest. The words of the proverb point to this principle in a parabolic way, rather than in a literal, technical sense.

The third example (15:25) is perhaps the most obviously nonliteral in intention. We know both from our own experience and from the witness of the Scriptures that there are indeed proud people whose houses are still standing and that there are widows who have been abused by greedy creditors or by fraud (cf. Mark

12:40; Job 24:2–3; et al.). So what does the proverb mean if it does not intent to convey the impression that the Lord is actually a house smasher or boundary guard? It means that God opposes the proud and is on the side of the needy ("widows," "orphans," and "aliens" are terms that stand for *all* dependent people; cf. Deut 14:29; 16:11; 26:12, 13; et al.). When this proverb is compared with Proverbs 23:10–11 and Luke 1:52–53, its meaning becomes much clearer. It is a miniature parable, designed by the Holy Spirit to point beyond the "house" and the "widow" to the general principle that God will *eventually* right this world's wrongs, abasing the arrogant and compensating those who have righteously suffered (cf. Matt. 5:3–4).

Proverbs Must Be Read as a Collection

Each inspired proverb must be balanced with others and understood in comparison with the rest of Scripture. As the third example above (15:25) illustrates, the more in isolation one reads a proverb, the less clear its interpretation may be. An individual proverb, if misunderstood, may lead you to attitudes or behavior far more inappropriate than would be the case if you read the Proverbs as a whole. Moreover, you must guard against letting their intensely practical concern with material things and this world make you forget the balancing value of other Scriptures that warn against materialism and worldliness. Do not engage in the kind of wisdom Job's friends did, equating worldly success with righteousness in God's eyes. This is an unbalanced reading of selected proverbs. Do not try to find in the Proverbs justification for living a selfish life or for practices that do not comport with what the Scriptures teach otherwise. And remember that the proverbs are often grouped in various ways, so that one jumps from topic to topic in reading through them. All of these considerations mean that one must take care to avoid misinterpretation. Consider also these two proverbs (Prov. 21:22; 22:14):

> A wise man attacks the city of the mighty,
>   and pulls down the stronghold in which they trust.

> The mouth of the adulteress is a deep pit;
>   he who is under the Lord's wrath will fall into it.

If you are wise, do you go out to attack a well-defended city and thereby do something good for God? If you have displeased God, is there a danger that you will suffocate inside the mouth of a (very large) adulteress?

Most people would answer no to these questions, adding "whatever they mean, they can't mean that!" But many of the same people will insist that Proverbs 22:26 is to be taken literally to prohibit borrowing on the part of Christians, or that Proverbs 6:20 means that a person must always obey his or her parents *at any age, no matter how wrong the advice of the parents may be.* By failing to balance proverbs against one another and against the rest of Scripture (let alone common sense) many people do themselves and others great injustice.

In the first proverb above (21:22), the point is that wisdom can be stronger even than military might. This is a hyperbolic statement. In style it is not unlike the modern proverb, "The pen is mightier than the sword." It is not a command. It is a symbolic, figurative portrayal of the power of wisdom. Only when one relates this proverb to the many other proverbs that praise the usefulness and effectiveness of wisdom (e.g., 1:1–6; chaps. 2–3, 8; 22:17–29; et al.) does one get its message. Here *overall context* is crucial in the interpretation.

The other proverb cited above (22:14) likewise needs comparison to its overall context. A large number of proverbs stress the importance of careful thought and speech (e.g., 15:1; 16:10, 21, 23–24, 27–28; 18:4; et al.). What one says, in other words, is usually far more incriminating than what one hears (cf. Matt. 15:11, 15–20). You may not be able to control what you hear, but you can almost always control what you say. This particular proverb can be paraphrased as follows: "The kinds of things an adulteress practices and talks about are as dangerous to you as falling into a deep pit would be. Avoid such things if you wish to avoid God's wrath." An appreciation of the full contexts of the individual proverbs will help keep you from misinterpreting them.

Proverbs Are Worded to Be Memorable, Not to Be Theoretically Accurate

No proverb is a complete statement of truth. No proverb is so perfectly worded that it can stand up to the unreasonable demand that it apply in every situation at every time. The more briefly and parabolically a principle is stated, the more common sense and good judgment are needed to interpret it properly—but the more effective and memorable it is (cf. the example, "Look before you leap" cited above). Proverbs tries to impart knowledge that can be *retained* rather than philosophy that can impress a critic. Thus the proverbs are designed either to stimulate an image in your mind (the mind remembers images better than it remembers abstract data) or to include sounds pleasing to the ear (i.e., repetitions, assonance, acrostics, et al.). As an example of the use of imagery, consider Proverbs 15:19:

> The way of the sluggard is blocked with thorns,
> but the path of the upright is a highway.

Here we read language designed to point not to the types of plants found in certain lazy people's favorite routes, but to point beyond itself to the principle that diligence is better than sloth.

The portrayal of extreme devotion of the good wife described in Proverbs 31:10–31 is the result of an acrostic ordering. Each verse begins with a successive letter of the Hebrew alphabet, memorable and pleasing to the ear in Hebrew, but resulting in what could seem to the callous critic or the literalistic reader to be a pattern of life impossible for any mortal woman to follow. But if one gets the point that such a description as Proverbs 31:22 is purposely designed to emphasize by exaggeration the joy that a good wife brings to her family, the proverbial wisdom does its job admirably well. The words (and images) of the passage tend to stick with the reader, providing useful guidance when needed. That is what proverbs are intended by God to do.

Some Proverbs Need to Be "Translated" to Be Appreciated

A good many proverbs express their truths according to practices and institutions that no longer exist, although they were common to the Old Testament Israelites. Unless you think of these proverbs in terms of their true modern equivalents (i.e., carefully "translate" them into practices and institutions that exist today), their meaning may seem irrelevant or be lost to you altogether (cf. chap. 4). Consider these two examples (Prov. 22:11; 25:24):

> He who loves a pure heart and whose speech is gracious
> will have the king for his friend.

> Better to live on a corner of the roof,
> than to share a house with a quarrelsome wife.

Most of us do not live in societies where there are kings. And we do not have the flat-roof houses of Bible times, where lodging on a roof was not only possible, but common (cf. Josh. 2:6). Does reading these proverbs therefore constitute a waste of time? Not at all, if one can only see the transcultural issues expressed in their culturally-specific language. The essential message of the first example cited above (22:11) is easy to comprehend as long as we recognize that a true modern equivalent for "have the king for his friend" would be something like "make a positive impression on people in leadership positions." The proverb *always* meant that anyway. The "king" stands as a synecdoche (one of a class) for all leaders. The specific parabolic language of the proverb is intended to point beyond itself to the truth that leaders and responsible persons are generally impressed both by honesty and by careful discourse.

The meaning of the second proverb cited (25:24) is also not so difficult to discern if we make the necessary "translation" from that culture to ours. We could even paraphrase: "It's better to live in a garage than in a spacious house with a woman you never should have married." For the advice of most proverbs, remember, is given as if to young persons starting out in life. The proverb is *not* intended to suggest literally what to do if you, a male, find your wife to be quarrelsome. It is intended to advise that people be careful in the selection of a mate. Such a selection is a transcultural decision for which the proverb, correctly understood, provides sound, godly advice (cf. Matt. 19:3–11; 1 Cor. 7:1–14, 25–40). Everyone should recognize that a hasty marriage, based largely on physical attraction, can turn out to be an unhappy marriage.

For convenience, we list below in summary form some rules that will help you make proper use of proverbs and be true to their divinely inspired intent.

1. Proverbs are often parabolic, i.e., figurative, pointing beyond themselves.
2. Proverbs are intensely practical, not theoretically theological.
3. Proverbs are worded to be memorable, not technically precise.

4. Proverbs are not designed to support selfish behavior—just the opposite!

5. Proverbs strongly reflecting ancient culture may need sensible "translation" so as not to lose their meaning.

6. Proverbs are not guarantees from God, but poetic guidelines for good behavior.

7. Proverbs may use highly specific language, exaggeration, or any of a variety of literary techniques to make their point.

8. Proverbs give good advice for wise approaches to certain aspects of life, but are not exhaustive in their coverage.

9. Wrongly used, proverbs might justify a crass, materialistic lifestyle. Rightly used, proverbs will provide practical advice for daily living.

Wisdom in the Song of Songs

The Song of Songs is a lengthy love song. It is an extended ballad about human romance, written in the style of ancient Near Eastern lyric poetry. We may call it lyric wisdom. People in ancient Israel, like people everywhere, were very familiar with love songs (cf. Ezek. 33:32). But how does a love song fit within the category of wisdom? Why did God put eight chapters of love poetry in the Bible? The answer is actually quite simple: Whom to love and how to love, the two issues with which the Song is mainly concerned, are among the most basic choices in life, and the ability to make godly choices with regard to these two crucial decisions is vitally important to every believer.

God has created human beings with a large number of brain cells devoted to love and sex. This is a fact of our humanity, and it is part of his design in creation that he declared "good" (Gen. 1:31). But unfortunately, any good thing can be corrupted by ungodly choices. Any human skill can be used for evil as well as for good, and any human desire can be employed in wrong ways instead of right ones. So it is with love and sex. It, too, has been corrupted by the fall of humanity, so that instead of being at all times a source of joy and blessing in monogamous marriage, as intended by God, it is often a means of selfish personal gratification involving all sorts of lusts and exploitation. Humans really do have a great range of choice when it comes to sex. Can a person choose to follow romance wherever it leads, regardless of the consequences? Absolutely. Can people engage in sex in ways that dishonor God? Certainly. Can sex be perverted and harmful? Of course. Can romance be manipulative and cruel? By all means. Can an emphasis on physical technique wrongly displace the tenderness of romance? Surely. But these things need not be. Sex—including romance—can be employed for God's glory in accordance with his original design, if the right choices are made. That is what the Song of Songs is about.

Now, to be sure, the Song has had a long history of odd interpretation, based on a combination of two common kinds of hermeneutical mistakes: totality transfer and allegorizing. Totality transfer is the tendency to think that all the possible features and meanings of a word or concept come with it whenever it is used. An example of totality transfer would be the assumption that "God so loved the world" includes a romantic aspect ("was in love with") as if the word "love" always includes in its meaning the sense of romance every time it is used. That this just cannot be so is seen in the English expression "I just love peanut butter," a fully meaningful statement in which no romantic overtone could possibly be discerned.

In the case of the Song, the totality transfer was made from other biblical love songs. When people first looked for something in the Bible that was similar to the Song of Songs, the closest parallels they came upon were certain kinds of allegories in the prophetical books. These allegories were cast in the form of love songs, telling the story of God's love for his people Israel and how that love was rejected or abused. In other words, some of the same kind of language and imagery is used to speak of Israel's relation to God in these prophetic allegories as is used throughout the Song of Songs. Examples are found in poetic form in Isaiah 5:1–7 and Hosea 2:2–15 and in longer prose form in Ezekiel 16 and 23. From these prophetic love songs some early interpreters jumped to a conclusion. Practicing totality transfer, they assumed that if love songs in the prophets were allegories about God and his people, a love song like the Song of Songs must be the same sort of thing. In an age in which allegorizing virtually all of Scripture was a common practice (see pp. 135–36 earlier in this book), some of the church fathers, well-intentioned but incorrect, came to the conclusion that Song of Songs could be nothing other than an allegory of God's love for

Israel or Christ's love for the church. This interpretation caught on and prevailed until recent times.

But even on the surface, that just is not what the Song is about. It is not part of a prophetical book like the allegorical love songs, and is not obviously allegorical as they are. It does not contain the various clues pointing to Israel's history that the prophetical allegories do, nor is it laden with national symbolism as they are. Instead, it concentrates directly on love between two individuals, a man and a woman, and their attraction for one another. Moreover, it does so in such a manner and at such length that it is really quite unlike the prophetical songs. Nothing in the prophets reads like this, for example:

> How beautiful you are, my darling!
>   Oh, how beautiful!
> Your eyes behind your veil are doves.
>   Your hair is like a flock of goats descending from Mount
>   Gilead.
> Your teeth are like a flock of sheep just shorn, coming up from
>   the washing.
>   Each has its twin; not one of them is alone.
> Your lips are like a scarlet ribbon; your mouth is lovely.
>   Your temples behind your veil are like the halves of a
>   pomegranate.
> Your neck is like the tower of David, built with elegance;
>   on it hang a thousand shields, all of them shields of warriors
>   (Song 4:1–4).

This is the language of a man's adoration of his loved one, in which he compares features of her appearance to beautiful images in life. He is not talking, of course, about things that are strictly similar in appearance, but things that are similarly impressive visually.

And, as a further example, nothing in the prophetical love song allegories is comparable with the following:

> I slept but my heart was awake.
>   Listen! My lover is knocking:
> "Open to me, my sister, my darling,
>   my dove, my flawless one.
> My head is drenched with dew,
>   my hair with the dampness of the night."
> I have taken off my robe—
>   must I put it on again?

> I have washed my feet—
>   must I soil them again?
> My lover thrust his hand through the latch-opening;
>   my heart began to pound for him.
> I arose to open for my lover,
>   and my hands dripped with myrrh,
> my fingers with flowing myrrh,
>   on the handles of the lock.
> I opened for my lover,
>   but my lover had left; he was gone.
> My heart sank at his departure (Song 5:2–6).

This is part of an account of a dream the woman had about how she was asleep and could not get up and move fast enough to keep from missing the man she loved when he called for her. "I slept but my heart was awake" is a poetic way of saying "I was dreaming." We have all had dreams like this, in which we just cannot move fast enough or cannot reach something that we very much want. In this case, the dream serves to heighten the emphasis on the attraction she feels for the man she loves and how frustrating it is when she misses a chance be with him (cf. also 3:1–5).

There are many other kinds of expressions of love and fondness in the Song in addition to visual comparisons and dream sequences. There are also such components as statements of the ardor of love (e.g., 1:2–4), advice and challenge from observers of the romance (e.g., 1:8; 5:9), romantic invitations from the man to the woman and vice versa (e.g., 7:11–13; 8:13), purposely exaggerated boasts about the greatness of the woman by the man and vice versa (e.g., 2:8–9), the need to resist temptation to be unfaithfully attracted to anyone else (e.g., 6:8–9), and declaration that a lover's attraction can be stronger even than the splendor of so great a king as Solomon himself (e.g., 3:6–11 following on 2:16–3:5; cf. 8:11–12). All these are cast in the form of musical poetry, but they are nevertheless all related logically and rationally to life's choices about love, romance, and sex.

Here, then, are some of the considerations that we think will help you use the Song in the way that Scripture intends:

First, try to appreciate the overall ethical context of the Song of Songs. Monogamous, heterosexual marriage was the proper context for sexual activity, according to God's revelation in the Old Testament, and God-fearing Israelites would regard the Song in that light. The attitude of the Song itself is the very antithesis of unfaithfulness, either before or after marriage. Marriage consummates and continues love between a man and a woman. That is what the Song points toward.

Second, be aware of the genre of the Song. Its closest parallels are indeed the love poetry of the Old Testament and elsewhere in the ancient Near East, the context of which was not just love of any kind, but attraction in marriage. Love songs were probably sung routinely at wedding banquets and had great meaning for those involved. They speak of attraction, fidelity, warding off the temptation to cheat, the preciousness of love, its joys and pleasures, and the dangers of infidelity. There is a solid moral overtone and a focusing and harnessing of love into the right context.

Third, read the Song as suggesting godly choices rather than describing them in a technical manner. This is similar to what we have already said about interpreting Proverbs—they are true as suggestions and generalizations rather than precise statements of universal fact. One of the closest parallels in Scripture to the Song is Proverbs 1–9. There one finds poems about the attractiveness of wisdom and the counter-attractiveness of folly, in a manner that suggests lyrically, rather than propositionally, what our right choices ought to be.

Fourth, be aware that the Song focuses on very different values from those of our modern culture. Today "experts" talk about sex *techniques,* but almost never about virtuous *romance,* the attraction of a man to a woman that leads to lifelong marriage. Such experts may advocate self-indulgence, even as the Song emphasizes just the opposite. Our culture encourages people to fulfill themselves, whatever their sexual tastes, whereas the Song is concerned with how one person can respond faithfully to the attractiveness of and fulfill the needs of another. In most of the modern world, romance is thought of as something that precedes marriage. In the Song, romance is something that should continue throughout and actually characterize marriage. Let it be so.

13

The Revelation: Images of Judgment and Hope

When turning to the book of Revelation from the rest of the New Testament, one feels as if he or she were entering a foreign country. Instead of narratives and letters containing plain statements of fact and imperatives, one comes to a book full of angels, trumpets, earthquakes, beasts, dragons, and bottomless pits.

The hermeneutical problems are intrinsic. The book is in the canon; thus for us it is God's Word, inspired of the Holy Spirit. Yet when we come to it to hear that Word, most of us in the church today hardly know what to make of it. The author sometimes speaks forthrightly: "I, John, your brother and companion in the suffering and kingdom and patient endurance that are ours in Jesus, was on the island of Patmos because of the word of God and the testimony of Jesus" (1:9). He writes to seven known churches in known cities with recognizable first-century conditions.

At the same time, however, there is a rich, diverse symbolism, some of which is manageable (judgment in the form of an earthquake; 6:12–17), while some is obscure (the two witnesses; 11:1–10). Most of the problems stem from the symbols, plus the fact that the book deals with future events, but at the same time is set in a recognizable first-century context.

We do not pretend to be able to resolve all the difficulties, nor do we imagine that all of our readers will be happy with everything we say. It seems necessary to say at the outset that no one should approach the Revelation without a proper degree of humility! There are already too many books on "The Revelation Made Easy." But it is not easy. As with the difficult passages in the Epistles (see pp. 58–59), one should be less than dogmatic here, especially since there are at least five major schools of interpretation, not to mention significant variations within each of the schools.

But we are also bold enough to think we have more than an inkling as to what John was up to. So we will lead you into some hermeneutical suggestions that make sense to us. But exegesis comes first, and in this case exegesis is especially crucial. For this is a book on which a lot of popular books and pamphlets have been written. In almost every case, these popular books do no exegesis at all. They jump immediately to hermeneutics, which usually takes the form of fanciful speculations that John himself could never possibly have intended or understood.

The Nature of the Revelation

As with most of the other biblical genres, the first key to the exegesis of the Revelation is to examine the *kind* of literature it is. In this case, however, we face a different kind of problem, for the Revelation is a unique, finely blended combination of three distinct literary types: apocalypse, prophecy, and letter. Furthermore, the basic type, apocalypse, is a literary form that does not exist in our own day. In previous cases, even if our own examples differ somewhat from the biblical ones, we nonetheless have a basic understanding of what an epistle or a narrative, a psalm or a proverb is. But we simply have nothing quite like this. Thus it is especially important in this case to have a clear picture of the literary type we are dealing with.

The Revelation As Apocalypse

The Revelation is primarily an apocalypse. It is only one— though a very special one, to be sure—of dozens of apocalypses that were well known to Jews and Christians from about 200 B.C. to A.D. 200. These other apocalypses, which of course are not canonical, were of a variety of kinds, yet they all, including the Revelation, have some common characteristics. These common characteristics are as follows:

1. The taproot of apocalyptic is the Old Testament prophetic literature, especially as it is found in Ezekiel, Daniel, Zechariah, and parts of Isaiah. As was the case in some prophetic literature,

apocalyptic was concerned about coming judgment and salvation. But apocalyptic was born either in persecution or in a time of great oppression. Therefore, its great concern was no longer with God's activity *within* history. The apocalyptists looked exclusively forward to the time when God would bring a violent, radical *end* to history, an end that would mean the triumph of right and the final judgment of evil.

2. Unlike most of the prophetic books, apocalypses are literary works from the beginning. The prophets were basically spokespersons for Yahweh, whose spoken oracles were later committed to writing and collected in a book. But an apocalypse is a form of *literature*. It has a particular written structure and form. John, for example, is told to "write what he has seen" (1:19), whereas the prophets were told to speak what they were told or had seen.

3. Most frequently the "stuff" of apocalyptic is presented in the form of visions and dreams, and its language is cryptic (having hidden meanings) and symbolic. Therefore, most of the apocalypses contained literary devices that were intended to give the book a sense of hoary age. The most important of these devices was pseudonymity, that is, they were given the appearance of having been written by ancient worthies (Enoch, Baruch, et al.), who were told to "seal it up" for a later day, the "later day" of course being the age in which the book was now being written.

4. The images of apocalyptic are often forms of fantasy, rather than of reality. By way of contrast, the nonapocalyptic prophets and Jesus also regularly used symbolic language, but most often it involved real images, for example, salt (Matt. 5:13), vultures and carcasses (Luke 17:37), silly doves (Hos. 7:11), half-baked cakes (Hos. 7:8), et al. But most of the images of apocalyptic belong to fantasy, for example, a beast with seven heads and ten horns (Rev. 13:1), a woman clothed with the sun (Rev. 12:1), locusts with scorpions' tails and human heads (Rev. 9:10), et al. The fantasy may not necessarily appear in the items themselves (we understand beasts, heads, and horns) but in their unearthly combination.

5. Because they were literary, most of the apocalypses were very formally stylized. There was a strong tendency to divide time and events into neat packages. There was also a great fondness for the symbolic use of numbers. As a consequence, the final product usually has the visions in carefully arranged, often numbered, sets. Frequently these sets, when put together, express something (e.g.,

judgment) without necessarily trying to suggest that each separate picture follows hard on the heel of the former.

The Revelation of John fits all these characteristics of apocalyptic but one. And that one difference is so important that in some ways it becomes a world of its own. *Revelation is not pseudonymous.* John felt no need to follow the regular formula here. He made himself known to his readers and, through the seven letters (chaps. 2–3), he spoke to known churches of Asia Minor, who were his contemporaries and "companions in suffering." Moreover, he was told *not* to "seal up the words of the prophecy of this book, because the time is near" (22:10).

The Revelation As Prophecy

The major reason John's apocalypse is not pseudonymous is probably related to his own sense of the end as already/not yet (see pp. 131–34). He is not, with his Jewish predecessors, simply anticipating the end. He knows that it had already begun with the coming of Jesus. Crucial to this understanding is the advent of the Spirit. The other apocalyptists wrote in the name of the former prophetic figures because they lived in the age of the "quenched Spirit," awaiting the prophetic promise of the outpoured Spirit in the new aeon. Thus they were in an age when prophecy had ceased. John, on the other hand, belongs to the new aeon. He was "in the Spirit" when he was told to write what he saw (1:10–11). He calls his book "this prophecy" (1:3; 22:18–19), and says that the "testimony of Jesus," for which he and the churches are suffering (1:9; 20:4), "is the spirit of prophecy" (19:10). This probably means that the message of Jesus, attested by him and to which John and the churches bear witness, is the clear evidence that the prophetic Spirit had come.

What makes John's Apocalypse different, therefore, is first of all this combination of apocalyptic and prophetic elements. On the one hand, the book is cast in the apocalyptic mold and has most of the literary characteristics of apocalyptic. It is born in persecution and intends to speak about the end with the triumph of Christ and his church, and it is a carefully constructed piece of literature, using cryptic language and rich symbolism of fantasy and numbers.

On the other hand, John clearly intends this apocalypse to be a prophetic word to the church. His book was not to be sealed for the future. It was a word from God for their present situation. You will recall from chapter 10 that "to prophesy" does not primarily mean to foretell the future but rather to speak forth God's Word in the present, a word that usually had as its content coming judgment or salvation. In the Revelation even the seven letters bear this prophetic imprint. Here, then, is God's prophetic Word to some churches in the latter part of the first century who are undergoing persecution from without and some decay from within.

The Revelation As Epistle

Finally, it must be noted that this combination of apocalyptic and prophetic elements has been cast into the form of a letter. For example, read 1:4–7 and 22:21; you will note that all the characteristics of the letter form are present. Furthermore, John speaks to his readers in the first person/second person formula (I . . . you). Thus in its final form the Revelation is sent by John as a letter to the seven churches of Asia Minor.

The significance of this is that, as with all epistles, there is an *occasional* (see p. 48) aspect to the Revelation. It was occasioned at least in part by the needs of the specific churches to which it is addressed. Therefore, to interpret, we must try to understand its original historical context.

The Necessity of Exegesis

It may seem strange that after twelve chapters in this book, we should still feel constrained to contend for the necessity of exegesis. But it is precisely the *lack* of sound exegetical principles that has caused so much bad, speculative interpretation of the Revelation to take place. What we want to do here, then, is simply to repeat, with the Revelation in mind, some of the basic exegetical principles we have already delineated in this book, beginning with chapter 3.

1. The first task of the exegesis of the Revelation is to seek the author's, and therewith the Holy Spirit's, original intent. As with the Epistles, *the primary meaning of the Revelation is what John intended it to mean, which in turn must also have been something his readers could have understood it to mean.* Indeed, the great advantage they would have had over us is their familiarity with their own historical context (that caused the book to be written in the first place) and their greater familiarity with apocalyptic forms and images.

2. Since the Revelation intends to be prophetic, one must be open to the possibility of a secondary meaning, inspired by the Holy Spirit, but not fully seen by the author or his readers. However, such a second meaning lies *beyond* exegesis in the broader area of hermeneutics. Therefore, the task of exegesis here is to understand what John was intending his original readers to hear and understand.

3. One must be especially careful of overusing the concept of the "analogy of Scripture" in the exegesis of the Revelation. The analogy of Scripture means that Scripture is to be interpreted in the light of other Scripture. We hold this to be self-evident, based on our stance that all of Scripture is God's Word and has God as its ultimate source. However, to interpret Scripture by Scripture must not be tilted in such a way that one *must* make other Scriptures the hermeneutical keys to unlock the Revelation.

Thus, it is one thing to recognize John's new use of images from Daniel or Ezekiel, or to see the analogies in apocalyptic images from other texts. But one may not assume, as some schools of interpretation do, that John's readers had to have read Matthew or 1 and 2 Thessalonians, and that they already knew from their reading of these texts certain keys to understanding what John had written. Therefore, *any keys to interpreting the Revelation must be intrinsic to the text of the Revelation itself or otherwise available to the original recipients from their own historical context.*

4. Because of the apocalyptic/prophetic nature of the book, there are some added difficulties at the exegetical level, especially having to do with the imagery. Here are some suggestions in this regard:

a. One must have a sensitivity to the rich background of ideas that have gone into the composition of the Revelation. The chief source of these ideas and images is the Old Testament, but John also has derived images from apocalyptic and even from ancient mythology. But these images, though deriving from a variety of sources, do not necessarily mean what they meant in their sources. They have been broken and transformed under inspiration and thus blended together into this "new prophecy."

b. Apocalyptic imagery is of several kinds. In some cases the images, like the donkey and elephant in American political cartoons, are constant. The beast out of the sea, for example, seems to be a standard image for a world empire, not for an individual ruler. On the other hand, some images are fluid. The "Lion" of the tribe of Judah turns out in fact to be a "Lamb" (Rev. 5:5–6)—the *only* lion there is in the Revelation. The woman in chapter 12 is clearly a positive image, yet the woman in chapter 17 is evil.

Likewise some of the images clearly refer to specific things. The seven lampstands in 1:12–20 are identified as the seven churches, and the dragon in chapter 12 is Satan. On the other hand, many of the images are probably general. For example, the four horseman of chapter 6 probably do not represent any specific expression of conquest, war, famine, and death, but rather represent this expression of human fallenness as the source of the church's suffering (6:9–11) that in turn will be a cause of God's judgment (6:12–17).

All of this is to say that the images are the most difficult part of the exegetical task. Because of this, two further points are especially important:

c. *When John himself interprets his images, these interpreted images must be held firmly and must serve as a starting point for understanding others.* There are six such interpreted images: The one like a son of man (1:17–18) is Christ, who alone "was dead, and . . . alive for ever and ever!" The golden lampstands (1:20) are the seven churches. The seven stars (1:20) are the seven angels, or messengers, of the churches (unfortunately, this is still unclear because of the use of the term *angel,* which may in itself be yet another image). The great dragon (12:9) is Satan. The seven heads (17:9) are the seven hills on which the woman sits (as well as seven kings, thus becoming a fluid image). The harlot (17:18) is the great city, clearly indicating Rome.

d. *One must see the visions as wholes and not allegorically press all the details.* In this matter the visions are like the parables. The whole vision is trying to say something; the details are either (1) for dramatic effect (6:12–14) or (2) to add to the picture of the whole so that the readers will not mistake the points of reference (9:7–11). Thus the details of the sun turning black like sackcloth and the stars falling like late figs probably do not "mean" anything. They simply make the whole vision of the earthquake more impressive. However, in 9:7–11 the locusts with crowns of gold, human faces, and women's long hair help to fill out the picture in such a way that the original readers could hardly have mistaken what was in view— the barbarian hordes at the outer edges of the Roman Empire.

5. One final note: Apocalypses in general, and the Revelation in particular, seldom intend to give a detailed, chronological account of the future. Their message tends to transcend that kind of concern. John's larger concern is that, despite present appearances, God is in control of history and the church. And even though the church will experience suffering and death, it will be triumphant in Christ, who will judge his enemies and save his people. All of the visions must be seen in terms of this greater concern.

The Historical Context

As with most of the other genres, the place to begin one's exegesis of the Revelation is with a provisional reconstruction of the situation in which it was written. To do this well, you need to do here what we have suggested elsewhere—try to read it all the way through in one sitting. Read for the big picture. Do *not* try to figure out everything. Let your reading itself be a happening, as it were. That is, let the visions roll past you like waves on the shore, one after another, until you have a feel for the book and its message.

Again, as you read, be making some mental or brief written notes about the author and his readers. Then go back a second time and specifically pick up all the references that indicate John's readers are "companions in his suffering" (1:9). These are the crucial historical indicators.

For example, in the seven letters note 2:3, 8–9, 13; 3:10, plus the repeated "to the one who overcomes." The fifth seal (6:9–11), which follows the devastation wrought by the four horsemen, reveals Christian martyrs, who have been slain because of the "word" and the "testimony" (exactly why John is in exile in 1:9). In 7:14 the great multitude, who will never again suffer (7:16), has "come out of the great tribulation." Suffering and death are again linked to bearing "the testimony of Jesus" in 12:11 and 17. And in chapters 13–20 the suffering and death are specifically attributed to the "beast" (13:7; 14:9–13; 16:5–6; 18:20, 24; 19:2).

This motif is the key to understanding the historical context, and fully explains the occasion and purpose of the book. John himself was in exile for his faith. Others were also experiencing suffering—one had even died (2:13)—for "the testimony of Jesus." While John was "in the Spirit," he came to realize that their present suffering was only the beginning of woes for those who would refuse "to worship the beast." At the same time he was not altogether sure that all the church was ready for what was ahead of them. So he wrote this "prophecy."

The main themes are abundantly clear: the church and the state are on a collision course; and initial victory will appear to belong to the state. Thus he warns the church that suffering and death lie ahead; indeed, it will get far worse before it gets better (6:9–11). He is greatly concerned that they do not capitulate in times of duress (14:11–12; 21:7–8). But this prophetic word is also one of encouragement; for God is in control of all things. Christ holds the keys to history, and he holds the churches in his hands (1:17–20). Thus the church triumphs even through death (12:11). God will finally pour out his wrath upon those who caused that suffering and death and bring eternal rest to those who remain faithful. In that context, of course, Rome was the enemy that would be judged.

It should be noted here that one of the keys for interpreting the Revelation is the distinction John makes between two crucial words or ideas —*tribulation* and *wrath*. To confuse these and make them refer to the same thing will cause one to become hopelessly muddled as to what is being said.

Tribulation (suffering and death) is clearly a part of what the church was enduring and was yet to endure. God's wrath, on the other hand, is his judgment that is to be poured upon those who have afflicted God's people. It is clear from every kind of context in the Revelation that God's people will *not* have to endure God's awful wrath when it is poured out upon their enemies, but it is equally clear that they will indeed suffer from the hands of their enemies. This distinction, it should be noted, is precisely in keeping with the rest of the New Testament. See, for example, 2 Thessalonians 1:3–10, where Paul "boasts" of the Thessalonians' "persecutions and trials" (the same Greek word as "tribulation"), but he also notes that God will eventually judge those "who trouble you" (the verb form of "tribulation").

You should note also how the opening of seals 5 and 6 (6:9–17) raises the two crucial questions in the book. In seal 5 the Christian martyrs cry out, "How long, Sovereign Lord, . . . until you judge the inhabitants of the earth and avenge our blood?" The answer is twofold: (1) They must "wait a little longer," because there are to be many more martyrs; (2) judgment is nonetheless absolutely certain, as the sixth seal indicates.

In seal 6, when God's judgment comes, the judged cry out, "Who can stand?" The answer is given in chapter 7: those whom God has sealed, who "have washed their robes and made them white in the blood of the Lamb."

The Literary Context

To understand any one of the specific visions in the Revelation it is especially important not only to wrestle with the background and meaning of the images (the *content* questions) but also to ask how this particular vision *functions* in the book as a whole. In this regard the Revelation is much more like the Epistles than the Prophets. The latter are collections of individual oracles, not always with a clear functional purpose in relation to one another. In the Epistles, as you will recall, one must "think paragraphs," because every paragraph is a building block for the whole argument. So also with the Revelation. The book is a creatively structured whole, and each vision is an integral part of that whole.

Since the Revelation is the only one of its kind in the New Testament, we will try to guide you all the way through it, rather than simply offer a model or two. It should be noted, of course, that the basic structure is clear and not an object of debate; differences come in how one interprets the structure.

The book unfolds like a great drama, in which the earliest scenes set the stage and the cast of characters, and the later scenes need all the earlier scenes for us to be able to follow the plot.

Chapters 1–3 set the stage and introduce us to most of the significant "characters." First, there is John himself (1:1–11), who will be the narrator throughout. He was exiled for his faith in Christ, and he had the prophetic insight to see that the present persecution was only a forerunner of what was to be.

Second, there is Christ (1:12–20), whom John describes in magnificent images derived partly from Daniel 10 as the Lord of history and the Lord of the church. God has not lost control, despite present persecution, for Christ alone holds the keys of death and Hades.

Third, there is the church (2:1–3:22). In letters to seven real, but also representative, churches, John encourages and warns the church. Persecution is already present; the church is promised more.

But there are many internal disorders that also threaten its well-being. Those who overcome are given the promises of final glory.

Chapters 4–5 also help to set the stage. With breathtaking visions, set to worship and praise, the church is told that God reigns in sovereign majesty (chap. 4). To believers who may be wondering whether God is really there, acting in their behalf, John reminds them that God's "Lion" is a "Lamb," who himself redeemed humankind through suffering (chap. 5).

Chapters 6–7 begin the unfolding of the actual drama itself. Three times throughout the book visions are presented in carefully structured sets of seven (chaps. 6–7, 8–11, 15–16). In each case the first four items go together to form one picture; in 6–7 and 8–11 the next two items also go together to present two sides of another reality. These are then interrupted by an interlude of two visions, before the seventh item is revealed. In chapters 15–16 the final three group together without the interlude. Note how this works out in chapters 6–7:

1. White horseman = Conquest
2. Red horseman = War
3. Black horseman = Famine
4. Pale horseman = Death

5. The martyrs question: "How long?"
6. The earthquake (God's judgment): "Who can stand?"
   a. 144,000 sealed
   b. A great multitude

7. God's wrath: the seven trumpets of chapters 8–11

Chapters 8–11 reveal the content of God's judgment. The first four trumpets indicate that part of that judgment will involve great disorders in nature; trumpets five and six indicate that it will also come from the barbarian hordes and a great war. After the interlude, which expresses God's own exaltation of his "witnesses" even though they die, the seventh trumpet sounds the conclusion: "The Kingdom of the world has become the Kingdom of our Lord and of his Christ."

Thus we have been brought through the suffering of the church and the judgment of God upon the church's enemies to the final triumph of God. But the visions are not finished. In chapters 8–11 we have been given the big picture; chapters 12–22 offer details of that judgment and triumph. What has happened is something like looking at Michelangelo's Sistine Chapel; at first, one is simply awestruck at the sight of the whole of the chapel. Only later one can inspect the parts and see the magnificence that has gone into every detail.

Chapter 12 is the theological key to the book. In two visions we are told of Satan's attempt to destroy Christ and of his own defeat instead. Thus, within the recurring New Testament framework of the already/not yet, Satan is revealed as a defeated foe (already), whose final end has not yet come. Therefore, there is rejoicing because "salvation has come," yet there is woe to the church because Satan knows his time is limited and he is taking his vengeance out on God's people.

Chapters 13–14 then show how for John's church that vengeance took the form of the Roman Empire with its emperors who were demanding religious allegiance. But the Empire and the emperors are doomed (chaps. 15–16). The book concludes as a "tale of two cities" (chaps. 17–22). The city of earth (Rome) is condemned for its part in the persecution of God's people. That is followed by the city of God where God's people dwell eternally.

Within this overall structure several of the visions present considerable difficulties, both as to the meaning of their content and function in context. For these questions you will often want to consult one of the better commentaries (e.g., Beasley-Murray or Mounce; see the appendix).

The Hermeneutical Questions

The hermeneutical difficulties with the Revelation are much like those of the prophetic books surveyed above in chapter 10. As with all other genres, God's Word to us is to be found first of all in his Word to them. But in contrast to the other genres, the Prophets and the Revelation often speak about things that for them were yet to be.

Often what was "yet to be" had a temporal immediacy to it, which from our historical vantage point has now already taken place. Thus Judah *did* go into captivity, and they were restored, just as Jeremiah prophesied; and the Roman Empire *did* in fact come under temporal judgment, partly though the barbarian hordes, just as John saw.

For such realities the hermeneutical problems are not too great. We can still hear as God's Word the reasons for the judgments. As we may properly assume that God will always judge those "who trample the needy for a pair of sandals," we may rightly assume that God's judgment will be poured out on those nations who have murdered Christians, just as it was on Rome.

Furthermore, we can still hear as God's Word—indeed, *must* hear—that discipleship goes the way of the Cross, that God has not promised us freedom *from* suffering and death, but triumph *through* it. As Luther rightly said it: "The prince of darkness grim, We tremble not for him; . . . the body they may kill, God's truth abideth still—His kingdom is forever."

Thus the Revelation is God's Word of comfort and encouragement to Christians who suffer whether in Red China, Kampuchea, Uganda, or anywhere else. God is in control. He has seen the travail of his Son, and he shall be satisfied.

All of this is a Word that needs to be heard again and again in the church—in every clime and in every age. And to miss that Word is to miss the book altogether.

But our hermeneutical difficulties do not lie in hearing this Word, the word of warning and comfort that is the point of the book. Our difficulties lie with that other phenomenon of prophecy, namely that the "temporal" word is often so closely tied to the final eschatological realities (see p. 182). This is especially true in the Revelation. The fall of Rome in chapter 18 seems to appear as the first chapter in the final wrap-up, and many of the pictures of "temporal" judgment are interlaced with words or ideas that also imply the final end as a part of the picture. There seems to be no way one can deny the reality of this. The question is, what do we do with it? We have already spoken to this question in chapter 10. Here we simply offer a few suggestions.

1. We need to learn that pictures of the future are just that—pictures. The pictures express a reality but they are not themselves to be confused with the reality, nor are the details of every picture necessarily to be "fulfilled" in some specific way. Thus when the first four trumpets proclaim calamities on nature as a part of God's judgment, we must not necessarily expect a literal fulfillment of those pictures.

2. Some of the pictures that were intended primarily to express the *certainty* of God's judgment must not also be interpreted to

mean *"soon-ness,"* at least "soon-ness" from our limited perspective. Thus when Satan is defeated at Christ's death and Resurrection and is "cast down to earth" to wreak havoc on the church, he knows his time is "short." But "short" does not necessarily mean "very soon," but something much more like "limited." There will in fact come a time when he will be "bound" forever, but of that day and hour no one knows.

3. The pictures where the "temporal" is closely tied to the "eschatological" should not be viewed as simultaneous—even though the original readers themselves may have understood them in that way (cf. p. 182). The "eschatological" dimension of the judgments and of the salvation should alert us to the *possibility* of a "not-yet" dimension to many of the pictures. On the other hand, there seem to be no fixed rules as to how we are to extract or to understand that yet future element. What we must be careful *not* to do is to spend too much time speculating as to how any of our own contemporary events might be fitted into the pictures of the Revelation. The book was *not* intended to prophesy the existence of Red China, for example, nor to give us literal details of the conclusion of history.

4. Although there are probably many instances where there is a second, yet to be fulfilled, dimension to the pictures, we have been given no keys as to how we are to pin these down. In this regard the New Testament itself exhibits a certain amount of ambiguity. The antichrist figure, for example, is a particularly difficult one. In Paul's writings (2 Thess. 2:3–4) he is a definite figure; in Revelation 13–14 he comes in the form of the Roman emperor. In both cases, his appearance seems to be eschatological. Yet in 1 John, all of this is reinterpreted in a generalized way to refer to the so-called gnostics who were invading the church. How, then are *we* to understand this figure with regard to our own future?

Historically, the church has seen (in a certain sense properly so) a variety of world rulers as an expression of antichrist. Hitler surely fit the picture, as did Idi Amin for a generation of Ugandans. In this sense many antichrists continue to come (1 John 2:18). But what of a specific worldwide figure who will accompany the final events of the end? Does Revelation 13–14 tell us that such is to be? Our own reply is, not necessarily; however, we are open to the possibility. It is the ambiguity of the New Testament texts themselves that leads to our caution and lack of dogmatic certainty.

5. The pictures that were intended to be *totally* eschatological are still to be taken so. Thus the pictures of 11:15–19 and 19:1–22:21 are entirely eschatological in their presentation. This we should affirm as God's Word yet to be fulfilled. But even these are *pictures*; the fulfillment will be in God's own time, in his own way—and will undoubtedly be infinitely greater than even these marvelous pictures.

Just as the opening word of Scripture speaks of God and creation, so the concluding word speaks of God and consummation. If there are some ambiguities for us as to *how* all the details are to work out, there is no ambiguity as to the certainty that God *will* work it all out—in his time and in his way. Such certainty should serve for us as for them to warn and to encourage.

Until he comes, we live out the future in the already, and we do so by hearing and obeying his Word. But there comes a day when such books as this will no longer be needed, for, "No longer will a man teach his neighbor, . . . because they will all know me" (Jer. 31:33). And with John, and the Spirit and the bride, we say, "Amen, Come, Lord Jesus."

Appendix

The Evaluation and Use of Commentaries

Throughout this book we have regularly suggested that there are times when you will want to consult a good commentary. We do not apologize for this. A good commentary is every bit as much a gift to the church as is a good sermon, good lectures on tapes, or a good counselor.

Our purpose in this chapter is simple. After some words on how you may go about evaluating a commentary as to its exegetical value, we will list the one or two better commentaries for each of the biblical books. There is an inherent problem in such a list, of course, in that excellent commentaries are regularly appearing. We are listing what is available as of our writing. As new commentaries come out, you can evaluate them according to the procedures given here.

The Evaluation of Commentaries

If you are a serious Bible student, you will eventually want to secure, or have access to, a good commentary for each book of the Bible. There really is no completely satisfactory one-volume commentary. One-volume commentaries are usually designed to do the very work we have tried to teach you to do on your own throughout this book. They briefly give the historical context and then trace the meaning of the text in terms of its literary context. This indeed has its value, but much of this you can find in *Eerdmans's Bible Handbook,* for example. What you want a commentary for is basically to supply three things: (1) helps on sources and information about the historical context, (2) answers to those manifold content questions, and (3) thorough discussions of

246

difficult texts as to the possibilities of meaning with supporting arguments.

How, then, does one evaluate a commentary? First, you do *not* evaluate on the basis of your agreement with the author. If the commentary is really a good one, and if you have done your own exegesis well, more often than not you and the better commentaries will be in agreement. But agreement is *not* the basic criterion.

Moreover, you do *not* evaluate on the basis of its "turning you on." The point of a commentary is *exegesis*. what the text *means;* not homiletics, preaching the text in our day. You may make good use of books of this kind in trying to discover how to use a text in the present scene. As preachers we ourselves confess to the usefulness of such books to get one's mind to thinking about the present age. *But these are not commentaries* even if they are excellent models for how to apply the Bible in the here and now. Our concern here is not with these books but with exegetical commentaries alone.

There are at least seven criteria you should used in judging a commentary. Not all of these are of the same kind, nor are all of them of equal importance. But all of these combine to help at the one crucial point--does this commentary help you understand what the biblical text actually said?

The first two criteria are basically points of information that you will want to know about the commentary.

1. Is the commentary exegetical, homiletical, or a combination of both? This simply reiterates what we have just said above. Remember, what you *really* want in a commentary is exegesis. If it also has hermeneutical suggestions, you may find this helpful, but what you want are answers to your content questions, and content questions are primarily exegetical.

2. Is it based on the Greek or Hebrew text or an English translation? It is not a bad thing for a commentary to be based on a translation, *as long as the author knows the text in the original language—and uses this knowledge as the real source of his or her comments*. NOTE WELL—You can use most commentaries based on the Greek or Hebrew text. Sometimes you will have to "read around" the Greek or Hebrew, but you can usually do this with a minimal loss.

The next criterion is THE MOST IMPORTANT, and is the real place to bring your evaluation.

3. When a text has more than one possible meaning, does the

author discuss *all* the possible meanings, evaluate them, and give reasons for his or her own choice? For example, in chapter 2 we gave an illustration from 1 Corinthians 7:36, for which there are at least three possible meanings. A commentary does not fully inform you unless the author discusses all three possibilities, gives reasons for and against each, then explains his or her own choice.

The next four criteria are important if you are going to get all the help you need.

4. Does the author discuss text-critical problems? You have already learned the importance of this in chapter 2.

5. Does the author discuss the historical background of the idea of the text at important places?

6. Does the author give bibliographic information so that you can do further study if you wish?

7. Does the introduction section in the commentary give you enough information about the historical context to enable you to understand the occasion of the book?

The best way to get at all this is simply to pick one of the really difficult texts in a given biblical book and see how helpful a commentary is in giving information and answering questions, and especially how well it discusses all possible meanings. One can initially evaluate the worth of a commentary on 1 Corinthians, for example, by seeing how the author discusses 11:10 or 7:36. For the Pastoral Epistles check it out at 1 Timothy 2:15. For Genesis, 2:17 would constitute a "check point." For Isaiah, it might be 7:14–17. And so on.

The final judgment, of course, is how well the author puts his or her information together in understanding the text in its context. Some commentaries that are mines of historical and bibliographical data are unfortunately not always adept at explaining the biblical writer's meaning in context.

Before we give our lists, let us repeat. You do not begin your Bible study with a commentary! You go to the commentary after you have done your own work; the reason you eventually consult a commentary is to find answers to the content questions that have arisen in your own study. At the same time, of course, the commentary will alert you to questions you failed to ask, but perhaps should have.

Please be warned that the commentaries we list here do not always represent theological viewpoints with which we agree. We are not recommending their *conclusions,* but rather their alertness to the kinds of issues we have mentioned above. Use them with care and caution. We have recommended evangelical commentaries only when in our opinion they were clearly the most exegetically useful for you.

Old Testament Commentaries

At the present time, the only complete up-to-date commentary series that meets the criteria we have described and is also evangelical in theological outlook is *The Expositor's Bible commentary* (*EBC,* 12 vols.). Two such series are underway: *The New International Commentary (NICOT)* and *The Tyndale Old Testament Commentaries (TOTC).* The *Word Biblical Commentary (WBC),* another series also under way, contains among its volumes a mixture of evangelical and nonevangelical commentaries, and each must therefore be evaluated on its own merits. As individual volumes in these series are published, look them over. When any of the series becomes complete, consider buying it. For the time being, the century-old Keil and Delitzsch commentary on the Old Testament is probably still one of the best complete series you can purchase. *The Tyndale Old Testament Commentaries,* now virtually complete, represent perhaps the best starter set of commentaries anyone could purchase. We also think that certain of the one-volume commentaries on the Bible, such as the New Bible Commentary Revised (1970), the International Bible Commentary (1979), and the Evangelical Commentary on the Bible (1989) are excellent additions to anyone's library.

Genesis: Gordon Wenham. *Genesis 1–15* (WBC). Dallas: Word Books, 1987. Joyce Baldwin. *The Message of Genesis 12–50* (The Bible Speaks Today). Downers Grove, Ill.: InterVarsity Press, 1988.

Exodus: Walter Kaiser, Jr. *Exodus* (EBC). Grand Rapids: Zondervan, 1979.

Leviticus: Gordon Wenham. *The Book of Leviticus.* (NICOT). Grand Rapids: Eerdmans, 1979.

Numbers: Gordon Wenham. *Numbers* (TOTC). Downers Grove, Ill.: InterVarsity Press, 1982.

Deuteronomy: Peter C. Craigie. *The Book of Deuteronomy* (NICOT). Grand Rapids: Eerdmans, 1976.

Joshua: Marten Woudstra. *The Book of Joshua* (NICOT). Grand Rapids: Eerdmans, 1981.

Judges: Arthur Cundall and Leon Morris. *Judges and Ruth* (TOTC). Grand Rapids, Eerdmans, 1968.

Ruth: Robert L. Hubbard, Jr. *The Book of Ruth* (NICOT). Grand Rapids: Eerdmans, 1990.

1 and 2 Samuel: Joyce Baldwin. *1 and 2 Samuel* (TOTC). Downers Grove, Ill.: InterVarsity Press, 1988.

1 and 2 Kings: Carl F. Keil. *Biblical Commentary on the Books of the Kings*. Edinburgh: T & T Clark, 1876; reprint, Grand Rapids: Eerdmans, 1970.

1 Chronicles: J. Barton Payne. *1 and 2 Chronicles* (EBC). Grand Rapids: Zondervan, 1988.

2 Chronicles: Raymond Dillard. *2 Chronicles* (WBC). Dallas: Word Books, 1987.

Ezra and Nehemiah: Edwin Yamauchi. *Ezra and Nehemiah* (EBC). Grand Rapids: Zondervan, 1988.

Esther: Joyce Baldwin. *Esther* (TOTC). Downers Grove, Ill.: InterVarsity Press, 1984.

Job: Elmer Smick. *Job* (EBC). Grand Rapids: Zondervan, 1988.

Psalms: Peter Craigie. *Psalms 1–50* (WBC). Dallas: Word Books, 1983. Derek Kidner. *Psalms 1–72; Psalms 73–150* (TOTC). Downers Grove, Ill.: InterVarsity Press, 1973, 1975.

Proverbs: Derek Kidner. *The Proverbs* (TOTC). Downers Grove, Ill.: InterVarsity Press, 1964.

Ecclesiastes: Derek Kidner. *The Message of Ecclesiastes* (The Bible Speaks Today). Downers Grove, Ill.: InterVarsity Press, 1988.

Song of Songs: G. Lloyd Carr. *The Song of Solomon* (TOTC). Downers Grove, Ill.: InterVarsity Press, 1984.

Isaiah: John Oswalt, *The Book of Isaiah, Chapters 1–39* (NICOT). Grand Rapids: Eerdmans, 1981. E. J. Young. *The Book of Isaiah.* 3 vols. (NICOT). Grand Rapids: Eerdmans, 1965–72.

Jeremiah: John A. Thompson. *The Book of Jeremiah* (NICOT). Grand Rapids: Eerdmans, 1980.

Lamentations: Delbert R. Hillers. *Lamentations* (Anchor Bible). New York: Doubleday, 1972.

Ezekiel: Douglas Stuart. *Ezekiel* (Communicator's Commentary). Dallas: Word Books, 1989.

Daniel: Joyce G. Baldwin. *Daniel: An Introduction and Commentary* (TOTC). Downers Grove, Ill.: InterVarsity Press, 1978.

Hosea and Joel: Douglas Stuart. *Hosea–Jonah* (WBC). Dallas: Word Books, 1987.

Amos: Jeffrey Niehaus. *Amos* (The Minor Prophets). Grand Rapids: Baker, 1992. Gary Smith: *Amos: A Commentary.* Grand Rapids: Zondervan, 1989.

Obadiah: John D. W. Watts. *Obadiah: A Critical, Exegetical Commentary.* Grand Rapids: Eerdmans, 1969.

Jonah: Douglas Stuart. *Hosea–Jonah* (WBC). Dallas: Word Books, 1987.

Micah: Delbert Hillers. *Micah* (Hermeneia). Philadelphia: Fortress, 1983.

Nahum: Walter A. Maier. *The Book of Nahum.* St. Louis: Concordia, 1959; repr. Grand Rapids: Baker, 1980.

Habakkuk: Carl Amerding. *Habakkuk* (EBC). Grand Rapids: Zondervan, 1985.

Zephaniah: David Baker. *Nahum, Habakkuk, Zephaniah* (TOTC). Downers Grove, Ill.: InterVarsity Press, 1989.

Haggai and Zechariah: Joyce G. Baldwin. *Haggai, Zechariah, Malachi: An Introduction and Commentary* (TOTC). Downers Grove, Ill.: InterVarsity Press, 1972.

Malachi: Pieter Verhoef. *The Books of Haggai and Malachi* (NICOT). Grand Rapids: Eerdmans, 1987.

New Testament Commentaries

Most people will find a lot of help in reading William Barclay's *Daily Study Bible,* which covers the whole New Testament in seventeen volumes. Barclay is a good scholar—and eminently readable. But for a detailed, specific study we recommend the following (asterisks indicate commentaries that are particularly outstanding):

Matthew: for the general reader: D. A. Carson, *Matthew* (EBC). Grand Rapids: Zondervan, 1984; for the advanced student: W. D. Davies and Dale C. Allison, *The Gospel According to Saint Matthew* (International Critical Commentary), 3 vols. Edinburgh: T & T Clark, 1988–.

Mark: Robert A Guelich, *Mark 1–8:26* (WBC). Dallas: Word Books, 1989; William L. Lane. *The Gospel According to Mark* (New International Commentary). Grand Rapids: Eerdmans, 1974.

Luke: for the general reader: Craig A. Evans, *Luke* (New International Biblical Commentary). Peabody, Mass.: Hendrickson, 1990; for the advanced student: *I. Howard Marshall, *The Gospel of Luke: A Commentary on the Greek Text* (New International Greek Testament Commentary). Grand Rapids: Eerdmans, 1978.

John: for the general reader: D. A. Carson, *The Gospel According to John* (Pillar Commentaries). Grand Rapids: Eerdmans, 1990; for the advanced student: *Raymond E. Brown, *The Gospel According to John* (Anchor Bible), 2 vols. New York: Doubleday, 1966, 1970.

Acts: I. Howard Marshall, *The Acts of the Apostles* (Tyndale New Testament Commentaries). Grand Rapids: Eerdmans, 1980.

Romans: for the general reader: Douglas Moo (New International Commentary). Grand Rapids: Eerdmans, 1993; for the advanced student: *C. E. B. Cranfield, *Romans: A Critical and Exegetical Commentary on the Epistle to the Romans* (International Critical Commentary), 2 vols. Edinburgh: T & T Clark, 1975; *James D. G. Dunn (WBC), 2 vols. Dallas: Word Books, 1988.

1 Corinthians: Gordon D. Fee. *The First Epistle to the Corinthians* (New International Commentary). Grand Rapids: Eerdmans, 1987.

2 Corinthians: Victor P. Furnish. *II Corinthians* (Anchor Bible). Garden City, N.Y.: Doubleday, 1984.

Galatians: for the general reader: Ronald Y. K. Fung. *The Epistle to the Galatians* (New International Commentary). Grand Rapids: Eerdmans, 1988; for the advanced student: *Richard N. Longenecker (WBC). Dallas: Word Books, 1990.

Ephesians: for the general reader: F. F. Bruce, *The Epistles to the Colossians, to Philemon, and to the Ephesians* (New International Commentary). Grand Rapids: Eerdmans, 1984; for the advanced student: Andrew T. Lincoln, *Ephesians* (WBC). Dallas: Word Books, 1990.

Philippians: for the general reader: Moisés Silva, *Philippians*. Chicago: Moody Press, 1988; for the advanced student: *Peter T. O'Brien, *Commentary on Philippians* (New International Greek Testament Commentary). Grand Rapids: Eerdmans, 1991.

Colossians: for the general reader: F. F. Bruce, *The Epistles to the Colossians, to Philemon, and to the Ephesians* (New International Commentary). Grand Rapids: Eerdmans, 1984; for the advanced student: *Peter T. O'Brien, *Colossians, Philemon* (WBC). Dallas: Word Books, 1982.

Thessalonians: I. Howard Marshall *1 and 2 Thessalonians* (New Century Bible). Grand Rapids: Eerdmans, 1983.

Timothy, Titus: for the general reader: Gordon D. Fee. *1 and 2 Timothy, Titus* (New International Biblical Commentary). Peabody, Mass.: Hendrickson, 1988.

Hebrews: for the general reader: F. F. Bruce, *The Epistle to the Hebrews* (New International Commentary). Grand Rapids: Eerdmans, 1990; for the advanced student: William L. Lane, *Hebrews* (WBC), 2 vols. Dallas: Word Books, 1991.

James: for the general reader: Peter H. Davids, *James* (New International Biblical Commentary). Peabody, Mass.: Hendrickson, 1989; for the advanced student: Ralph P. Martin, *James* (WBC). Dallas: Word Books, 1988.

1 Peter: for the general reader: *Peter H. Davids, *The First Epistle of Peter* (Grand Rapids: Eerdmans, 1990; for the advanced student: J. Ramsey Michaels, *1 Peter* (WBC). Dallas: Word Books, 1988.

2 Peter: for the general reader: J. N. D. Kelly, *A Commentary on the Epistles of Peter and of Jude* (Harper's New Testament Commentaries). New York: Harper & Row, 1969; for the advanced reader: *Richard J. Bauckham, *Jude, 2 Peter* (WBC). Dallas: Word Books, 1983.

1, 2, 3 John: for the general reader, *I. Howard Marshall, *The Epistles of John* (New International Commentary). Grand Rapids: Eerdmans, 1978; for the advanced student: Stephen S. Smalley, *1, 2, 3 John* (WBC). Dallas: Word Books, 1984.

Jude: see under 2 Peter.

Revelation: G. R. Beasley-Murray. *The Book of Revelation* (New Century Bible). London: Oliphants, 1974. Robert H. Mounce. *The Book of Revelation* (New International Commentary). Grand Rapids: Eerdmans, 1977.

Index of Names

Scripture Index